FROM ELSEWHERE

FROM ELSEWHERE

BEING E.T. IN AMERICA

Scott Mandelker, Ph.D.

A Birch Lane Press Book
Published by Carol Publishing Group

A BIRCH LANE PRESS BOOK
Published by Carol Publishing Group
Birch Lane Press is a registered trademark of Carol Communications, Inc.
Editorial Offices: 600 Madison Avenue, New York, N.Y. 10022
Sales and Distribution Offices: 120 Enterprise Avenue, Secaucus,
    N.J. 07094
In Canada: Canadian Manda Group, One Atlantic Avenue, Suite 105,
    Toronto, Ontario M6K 3E7
Queries regarding rights and permissions should be addressed to
Carol Publishing Group, 600 Madison Avenue, New York, N.Y. 10022

Carol Publishing Books are available at special discounts for
bulk purchases, sales promotion, fund-raising, or educational
purposes. Special editions can be created to specifications. For
details, contact: Special Sales Department, Carol Publishing
Group, 120 Enterprise Avenue, Secaucus, N.J. 07094.

MANUFACTURED IN THE UNITED STATES OF AMERICA
10 9 8 7 6 5 4 3 2 1

Library of Congress Cataloging-in-Publication Data
Mandelker, Scott.
    From Elsewhere : being E.T. in America
/ Scott Mendelker.
        p. cm.
    "A Birch Lane Press book."
    Includes bibliographical references.
    ISBN 1-55972-304-1 (hc)
    1. Spiritual life–New Age movement.   2. Occultism.
3. Unidentified flying objects—Miscellanea.   I. Title.
BP605.N48M46   1995
001.9—dc20   95-19233
                                            CIP

*This book is Dedicated to all of the Courageous who
left their Bliss at Home—
Now Wrapped in Clay, Wandering in the Valley of the
Shadows of Death
Serving the Dance in the Garden of Samsara*

And, of course—

To the RA Group,
To the Councils of Saturn and Andromeda
To the Vast Assembly of the Confederation of Planets
in Service to the Infinite Creator

OM MANI PADME HUM

CONTENTS

Acknowledgments / ix
Introduction / xi

1. ORIGINS
To the Sleeping Wanderers / 1

2. AWAKENING
Wanderers, Walk-ins, Earth Humans / 11

3. SUBJECTIVE KNOWING: THE PROOF OF E.T. IDENTITY
Who Am I? Who Are We? / 35

4. SHRINKING THE UNIVERSE
On the Psychology of Being E.T. / 54

5. LOVE AND INTIMACY
What We Do When . . .We Are Not Alone / 78

6. THE SOCIAL IMPACT
The Human Side of the Far Side / 104

7. THE WHOLE (OTHER) WORLD IS WATCHING
E.T.s View the Media Viewing E.T.s / 127

8. MISSION
So, Why Are We Here? / 151

9. DEATH
From Elsewhere to Eternity / 175

10. VISION
Coming Attractions of the World to Come / 189

CONTENTS

Appendix 1: A Brief Quiz for Sleeping Wanderers / 207
Appendix 2: Wandering Journey: My Personal Path / 211
Appendix 3: *The RA Material* / 233
List of Informants / 238
Glossary of Terms / 242
References / 248
Index / 253

ACKNOWLEDGMENTS

First and foremost, I would like to give special thanks to Mr. Ross Klavan, who was instrumental in the conception and writing of this book; and to my agent, Stephany Evans, whose committment to the material made publication a reality.

Second, I would like to thank my parents, grandmother, and uncle whose love is unceasing and unconditional, and my closest friends, whose sharing keeps sharp the edge of my growth.

And finally, I want to offer deep gratitude to those Buddhist, Hindu, and Taoist root-teachers who burn brilliant above my Way:

Lin Chi I Hsuan—Sri Tilopa—Yun-Men Chan-Shih
Sri Nityananda—Lao Tzu—Chuang Tzu
Siddhartha Gautama, Chakravartin

INTRODUCTION

I began meeting extraterrestrials in 1965. Such encounters led to the creation of my Star People research in 1967 and the distribution of the questionnaire that has by now, in 1995, produced documentation of thousands of aliens living undetected on Earth.

I find it ironic that for the past forty years or more, some of our finest scientific minds have made a concerted effort to discover conclusive evidence of extraterrestrial life. The quest for alien intelligence has fired the imagination of every thinking person on planet Earth. Thousands of dedicated men and women have devoted their lives and their collective energies in an effort to answer that haunting question: "Is humankind alone in the universe?'

Thirty years ago I discovered to my satisfaction that alien intelligences do exist, and they have been living right here among us on Earth.

Right now, all over the world, thousands of men and women are responding to some remarkable internal stimulus and remembering what appear to be their own past lives on other worlds. It is as if some internal triggering mechanism is going off inside their psyches, thus producing profound memories that remind them that their true ancestral home is a very distant, a very alien, "somewhere else."

In addition to past-life memories of alien worlds, these people are also convinced that they came to Earth in their present life experience to perform a specific mission; and they seem often vibrant with an all-consuming conviction that they must do something to help humankind through the very difficult times that lie ahead for all the citizens of this planet. Some have received visions of terrible cataclysms, vulcanisms, geological changes, the collapse of social structures, the toppling of political establishments, perhaps even the reversal of the planet's electromagnetic field or the shifting of its magnetic poles.

I should at this point stress that the vast majority of the "aliens" whom I have met have been professionals who work in the "helping" vocations of our society. They have been registered nurses, medical doctors, psychologists, social workers, college professors, law enforcement officers, school teachers, psychic counselors, military personnel, chiropractors, and both male and female members of the clergy.

Dr. Scott Mandelker has written this marvelously in-depth examination of these individuals who claim to have come from "elsewhere"—and he quotes speculation that there may be as many as 100 million of these "sleeping" aliens among us, yet to be awakened to their cosmic heritage. If there truly are such numbers of "Wanderers" and "Walk-ins"—the two groups of extraterrestrials on whom he focuses—then he is correct to name them a "subculture" in our contemporary society.

Academically trained, Dr. Mandelker puts aside long-held intellectual prejudices and open-mindly conducts interviews with these men and women of extraterrestrial consciousness and finds them to be sincere, mild, well-spoken, and tolerant—not at all flaky and wild-eyed. His interviewees generally hope to serve as catalysts for a global renaissance of spiritual values and greater awareness. In short, these strangers in a strange land are here to help.

Scattered throughout the remarkable case histories in this book you will discover many speculations and theories. You will not find any final answers that will explain this global phenomenon, for, as Dr. Mandelker advises, it is up to us to make our own conclusions. There is no absolute proof of these claims, one way or the other.

If, however, you make a sincere effort to approach this remarkable subject matter with the same tolerance and open-mindedness that Dr. Mandelker has exhibited, I can promise a most fascinating exploration of the farthest reaches of the human psyche. After such a fair appraisal, you are free to conclude along with a friend of one of his interviewees, "I know you're not lying, but I don't necessarily believe you."

On the other hand, perhaps you, too, will recognize that *you* are really "From Elsewhere."

BRAD STEIGER

1

ORIGINS

TO THE SLEEPING WANDERERS

You are about to meet a group of people who hold one of the most radical beliefs in America today.

Their lives are founded on what is, to say the least, a very unusual claim, an idea that is literally worlds away from mainstream society.

Even with the mainstream becoming more progressive, this is still an obscure underground movement that is buried inside or, perhaps, on the fringe of New Age culture. It's vaguely popularized, sometimes glamorized, but, in fact, this is a real and vibrant subculture of those who believe themselves to be of non-Earthly origins:

They are extraterrestrials.

There may be as many as 100 million extraterrestrials (E.T.s) currently living on Earth. Most of them are what could be called Sleeping Wanderers.

Please understand that I'm not talking about people who claim UFO abductions or other forms of contact with strange beings from someplace beyond our planet. Our story here is a close encounter with individuals who go about their day-to-day Earthly lives centered on the claim that *they are the Visitors.*

I use the term *Wanderers* to describe those E.T. souls who have been extraterrestrial since birth, but who've forgotten who they are and live under a kind of veil of their true being, and then slowly—if they're fortunate—begin to awaken.

As for the number of Sleeping Wanderers, that was arrived at like this: On January 28, 1981, in the twelfth session of channeled information from an E.T. group known as RA, it was stated that there were approximately 65 million Wanderers on Earth (A lot more information on the RA contact is given in Appendix 3). If we calculate further, we can assume the number is much higher today, almost fifteen years later, amidst an ongoing influx of souls coming to help the transition into the New Age. If we estimate, the figure can be revised to a current population of about 100 million—probably one of the strangest secrets of the universe.

More strange, it is a very human story.

It may seem odd to you that there could be a kind of human level for these individuals, but it's undeniably true that they experience ordinary emotions of joy, sorrow, hope, and discouragement . . . just like other human beings. The vast majority of these people—not the children, but the adults—have no idea of their own origins and probably only recognize some of the consequences of being "a stranger in a strange land." Those I interviewed for this book, those who've traveled from confused alienation to self-conscious E.T. identity, represent only a tiny fraction of the E.T. population.

Most of these veiled E.T. Wanderers never connect their deep sense of being different with the fact of being From Elsewhere, so I call them Sleeping Wanderers . . . and to a large extent, this book is written for them. Not "in their memory" but "for their memory"—to jog, jostle, and jar loose those dim recollections of an extraterrestrial past.

Some of these Sleeping Wanderers—those who've been asleep the longest—are *actually the most skeptical and disbelieving about extraterrestrial existence.* After centuries of disillusionment, adrift in the confusion of materialistic human life, they're often bitter and mistrustful of utopian or idealistic pronouncements, so the idea that compassionate E.T. souls might arrive on Earth From Elsewhere to aid in time of crisis seems completely ridiculous. If you find yourself fascinated with UFO/E.T. life, yet intensely skeptical, perhaps you are also one of these "doubting wanderers."

Well, then . . . how can we recognize these "hidden E.T.s"? How do we begin to understand those who take human form to assist the planet but forget who they are and how they came to be here?

During that January 1981 channeling session, when Don Elkins asked RA about the kinds of problems these Wanderers usually face, RA responded that they have

> as a general rule some form of handicap, difficulty or feeling of alienation which is severe, the most common of these difficulties are *alienation*; the reaction against the planetary vibration by personality disorders, as you would call them; and body complex ailments indicating difficulty in adjustment to the planetary vibrations. [italics added]

The implications, I think, are tremendous. This is not to assume that every mental patient, every person in long-term therapy, or anyone with hay fever is actually an E.T.—but I do believe that some of them are. I believe that rather than viewing a sense of being From Elsewhere as a sign of mental disorder, it's possible that in some cases the disorder itself is brought on by the terrible effort of an E.T. trying to adjust to the vibrations and patterns of Earth. I will say this: I firmly believe that some of the so-called insane, and some of the chronic "mentally ill," are actually From Elsewhere and that they are battling a world in which their very presence is denied, derided, and labeled as just plain crazy.

How many people feel an intense alienation that doesn't go away? How many people feel different throughout their lives and never really fit in? How many people go through life with chronic problems of allergies or other ailments of maladjustment to the physical environment? There must be millions. *Maybe 100 million . . .*

Before coming to any conclusions, I want to make it clear that I am not saying everyone is an extraterrestrial. What I am saying is that conventional medical theories, with their pronouncements that alienation is purely a psychological problem or a personality disorder due to childhood trauma, are just one perspective—an Earth-based view. There is another way to look at these problems, and I believe that for some people, that way will go much farther as an explanation.

For some, it may turn their lives around.

Psychology, of course, is a useful tool that can definitely help people understand themselves and learn to release negative emotional patterns. I tremendously value the communication skills I learned along the way to a master's degree in counseling—they are something I could not have picked up in the Buddhist monasteries where I've also spent some time. Therapy, for humans or E.T.s, can be a potent force for change and healthy growth; for individuals, couples, and families. But modern psychology does not explain everything.

The problems come about when psychologists or psychiatrists begin to believe that their model of the mind—a very Western one— is the only true model. They believe that the human self stretches from head to toes, that life and death are opposites, that genetics and social conditioning are the greatest forces shaping personality. Unfortunately, this model of how the mind works labors under the same limitations that cripple their model of the universe. It's why so many clinical therapists spend so much time trying to understand how UFO crop circles, E.T. sightings, alien abductions, ESP, telepathy, and out-of-body experiences are all "psychological events."

The lengths to which therapists go in explaining such paranormal experiences as psychological are often absurd. Some of their expert opinions include: that bodily scars and apparent radiation

4

nausea from claimed alien abductions are just "leakage from the collective unconscious," that the dozens of geometrically precise crop circles (in dozens of nations) were all created by "localized wind storms" or pranksters, and that out-of-body experiences are really just the vivid hallucinations of those born with "fantasy-prone personalities." The literature of this school of thought brings up subjects like "anomalous trauma syndrome" or sleep paralysis, both of which have been given some attention recently in the press. We'll certainly talk about these things in a later chapter, but, for now, it's much more helpful to keep in mind that psychological definitions, no matter how exact, are only one way of seeing it. They are not the only perspective.

Human denial and fear of the unknown are immense and often hide behind the mask of authority. It might be interesting one day to read a psychological study of those "psychologizers," those researchers, who've arrived at such presentable, Westernized conclusions. . . .

Because there is much that does not compute in the rational, materialist worldview, which is the basis of our Western civilization and, now, our global culture, how can we be surprised when the experts scramble for psychological explanations of everything mystical and nonordinary?

Lest you think that E.T. souls are always on the margins of society, bear in mind that several channeling contacts have identified Benjamin Franklin and Thomas Jefferson as Wanderers who incarnated for the purpose of guiding the newborn United States. I believe that—whether or not they understand their veiled personality— many E.T.s are in positions of power around the world, and that some of them are seeking to foster international peace, justice, economic parity, and environmental protection. Many work in the medical professions—a natural venue for serving others—as well as in the fields of psychology, education, and citizen advocacy. Wherever there is the potential for uplifting the human condition, there the

E.T.s known as Wanderers will be found, although few of them have really pursued their spiritual aptitudes, and fewer still would even consider the idea of being From Elsewhere.

So, I like to think of this book as a journey of exploration. The territory that we'll explore isn't on land or sea or even in outer space. Really, it's more a trip through a very *different way of being*, a much more *universal way of being*. . . .

And the best method of transportation is the willingness to keep an open mind. If our minds and hearts are open, all sorts of insights can come to us.

The presence of E.T.s has rarely been given any real analysis or serious research. The experience of E.T. identity has rarely been addressed and often gets lost in a medley of strange and fascinating tales. The personal conflicts, the struggles and accomplishments of those with non-Earthly origins, their transition from confusion to confidence—all of that has been given far too little attention by academics or the mainstream public.

But that's what we'll do here through case studies and the stories of those who are actually living this radical identity. We'll take a look at the experience of being E.T. in America.

And I think things are changing.

Recently I met a Los Angeles video producer who confided in me that he'd had a powerful UFO experience several years back and could definitely accept the idea that some people are E.T.s. He even once had a girlfriend who said she was an extraterrestrial. I'm friendly with a mild-mannered limousine driver who also had UFO experiences in his youth and has no problem with the idea that he is from another world. Like many of those I interviewed for this book, he didn't see his off-planet origins as anything particularly strange. I also met the assistant of a famous Parisian clothing designer who, upon hearing my ideas about E.T.s and Wanderers, rushed out to buy *The RA Material*—RA's channeled statements—in the middle of a San Francisco business trip. He, too, had had

6

UFO experiences and feels very different from his Earthly associates in the glamorous world of high fashion.

I'm trained as an academic and, in conducting my research, have relied on the methods and techniques of cultural anthropology. In the words of the famous anthropologist Bronislaw Malinowski, I've tried to "grasp the native's point of view, his relation to life, to realize his vision of his world." (Please do realize that I also mean her vision of her world.)

We're going to take the phrase "vision of his world" literally here, which means we'll include other planets, as well. We'll try not to cling to a particular nation or a particular culture. The key to our process of understanding has to be a solid respect for the "differentness" of these "natives"—and I've always tried to honor this differentness. Otherwise, how can we really know these people if we don't, at least for a little while, surrender our fixed ideas and preconceptions, our "globocentric" Earth human views?

Most important, this book is not an attempt to prove or disprove anyone's experience.

The question of proof—is it fact or is it fantasy—might well be the bottom line of this entire discussion, but it's imperative to keep in mind that there's no conclusive, final evidence available on either side.

None.

So, at the very heart of our story, we're really discussing this: how the recognition of being E.T. has influenced and determined the quality of these particular lives.

In the case of our E.T.s: What has led them to "recognize" that they are From Elsewhere? Exactly what happens after the realization that one is extraterrestrial? What is the meaning of this sense of identity? And what about all of the people who are also From Elsewhere but don't know it?

In this book I've allowed the E.T.s to speak for themselves.

My field research lasted several years and took me to both the east and west coasts as well as to the southwestern part of the United States. It involved more than twenty-five subjects. A wide range, some lived fairly standard lives and some conducted themselves in a more unusual manner. There were individuals who held everyday jobs; those who held no jobs at all; and those who ran E.T. support groups, lectured in New Age ideas, and counseled others.

Some, as we've said, regarded themselves as Wanderers, a term that applies to those who are in fact E.T. souls from birth and only gradually come to realize their identity. Others defined themselves as Walk-ins and had lived through a dramatic, sudden, "soul-exchange" at some point later in life.

I enjoyed interviewing and getting to know these people. Far from being flaky, naive faddists, the majority of them were serious, reasonable in thought and speech, and not particularly bedazzled by beliefs of being From Elsewhere. They were anything but fanatics.

They were generally mild and well spoken, gentle and peaceable—far more accepting and tolerant than many leaders and followers of conventional religious groups. Only a very few seemed to want converts to their ideas, and fewer still thought they were "glorious heralds of the New Age" or some type of superior being deigning to serve poor, miserable Earth worms.

Having made peace with an unorthodox identity and having then faced the consequences, most of them no longer craved acceptance from the social mainstream. They only wished to go their own way unmolested and take care of their worldly work as necessary. And their worldly work was invariably service to the planet and the people around them.

My research was originally carried out to earn a doctorate in East-West psychology at the California Institute of Integral Studies in San Francisco. I already had a Master's in counseling psychology, had several years of private practice under my belt, and had done a good bit of lecturing on a variety of spiritual topics.

Since I am, myself, not a newcomer to New Age beliefs, a final word about my own personal views and my personal experience would not be inappropriate here:

I personally believe that such a phenomenon as individual souls originating on other planets or in other dimensions and incarnating on Earth for particular purposes is *ontologically* possible—possible as a fact, in other words, rather than valid only for believers. I deeply believe that our universe *does* work this way.

I have always believed that some people can be clearly aware of this for themselves, though they may not be able to either prove it to anyone else or even convincingly argue its metaphysics. Being a poor arguer doesn't mean the phenomenon one believes cannot be true.

I also recognize that others—making the exact same claims— might be speaking from a mixture of imagination and hope, memories of reading and of film. Some may even be suffering a psychotic disorganization, although I have found this to be quite unusual.

Only a rare person, I think, will have an undistorted perception and recognition of his or her specific other-planetary origins— or specific mission here on Earth. Clearly, to retrieve this type of detailed information requires unusual intellectual and extrasensory ability. But I believe that all of these "strange ideas" can indeed be verified by one whose awareness is clear, mature, and spiritually attuned. This, also, may not be proven to others.

You, now reading these words, may yourself believe that accounts of very transformative types of benevolent E.T. contacts are really something of an interdimensional wake-up call for Wanderers. This means that if you've had a UFO or out-of-body experience yourself, one that "changed your life forever," giving you renewed hope, vision, faith, and meaning (or at least increased your spiritual seeking), *then you may very well be a Wanderer.*

There is no way to be sure. In the end, it is up to you to realize what "feels right"—not according to your changing moods and emotions (the usual mode of feeling) but, instead, according to a deep, inner knowing that takes time to gel and may well create conflicts and challenges to your current lifestyle. In this way, the realization of being From Elsewhere may "feel right" but not necessarily make you feel happy, and certainly not put an end to all of your problems.

I do know that E.T. souls are found in every walk of life. Some are successful and effective in Earth's terms while others make do with the ordinary mixture of joy and sorrow. There are still others who are truly "on the fringe," severely handicapped in their interpersonal relations, and even some who are institutionalized.

And one more thing . . .

I, too, have had many of the same experiences as the so-called Wanderers in my study.

During a period of almost two decades, I have traveled much the same route as they, going ever deeper into the question of identity. For me, it's been a journey with many stops along the way: mainstream psychotherapy; serious involvement with Buddhism, Zen Buddhism, and Taoism; five years of intensive meditation in monasteries in the United States, India, and Thailand; training as an academic; studies in Theosophy, the tarot, palmistry, the I Ching, New Age counseling, channeling; and experiences with "hemispheric synchronization," a high-tech method of synchronizing the vibratory modes of the two brain hemispheres that is meant to lead directly to "higher consciousness." So you see, I, too, have been around the block (and maybe around the Universe!).

Finally, through the careful piecing together of "leads and pointers" I, too, have arrived at the conclusion that I am From Elsewhere. And I've spent many years dealing with the ramifications and consequences of that discovery. . . .

2

AWAKENING

WANDERERS, WALK-INS, EARTH HUMANS

All your life you've felt different from every one around you.

Sometimes you thought you were special; then again, sometimes you worried you were weird, certainly out of place. You really didn't fit in.

Even with your family, or your closest friends, you were never completely at home. There were troubling moments when you dared to imagine that you weren't actually the child of your parents. Maybe you felt isolated, walled-off in a loneliness that didn't make sense. And whether you spent most of your time by yourself or you were the most popular person around, there was always this insistent feeling: *Somehow, in some strange way, I'm not like anyone else I know. ...*

Of course, all this might be perfectly "normal." That's what a lot of people said. "Everybody feels this way, don't worry about it." Or, they offered you an acceptable, rational, "normal" explanation. "It's just part of growing up," is what they said.

Probably you pretended to believe them.

But even after you agreed and dutifully said yes to one of those "normal" explanations—whether framed as psychology, conservative religion, or plain common sense—you secretly knew their "answers" really answered nothing. Too many pieces of your personal puzzle still hadn't yet been found. Your life was a painful, confusing mystery that just didn't make any sense.

So, without telling anyone, you pushed ahead. It became an intense, profound search—the struggle to answer the question of who you are. And even if you didn't know the object of your quest, you were definitely a seeker.

There was no shortage of mysteries. Why did certain sights—say, something like the illustration of a futuristic crystal city in a children's book—suddenly set off strange feelings of inner knowing and the sharp pain of homesickness?

Or, seemingly without reason, why did you become altogether perplexed by human anatomy? What had you believing for a moment that something about the people around you was just totally wrong? What was it? *What was this all about?*

Vague memories kept floating beneath the surface of your mind, which, incredibly, seemed to recall your life, but in another kind of civilization. *Was that really* my *life?*

Then, sometimes your sleep was filled with striking, vivid dreams in which you witnessed magnificent visions, heard voices offering instruction, traveled through time and space, or felt flooded with feelings of love and assurance. It felt familiar. It felt wonderful.

Finally, *something happened.*

Gradually, or with shocking swiftness, an answer was presented. Maybe it seemed startling, ridiculous, or even unbelievable. Or maybe you were well-prepared, and you weren't even surprised when everything "clicked." But with all that you had, every sinew, you were certain it was the only solution you could accept.

SOREN'S STORY

The most common E.T. experience usually begins with exactly this kind of intensive yearning, a dramatic search for meaning and personal identity. In my many interviews with those who recognized themselves as being From Elsewhere, these feelings were the most common starting point.

It was because of a sense of profound, inexplicable *differentness* that most people were driven to find the truth of who they really were.

There were some notable exceptions, of course. But the following story—the story of Soren—is an excellent example of how someone lived through "a long, dark night of the soul" before accepting a non-Earthly persona and thus becoming completely transformed.

When I first met Soren, I could have been easily convinced that he was a Southern California surfer . . . which, in fact, he actually had been. A tall bearded blond man in his mid-thirties with piercing blue eyes, he sometimes gets mistaken for the actor Patrick Swayze—and nobody would mistake him for a strange little green being from outer space.

But Soren was a San Francisco hospital technician who, after what he terms a "turbulent path of awakening," finally became "completely clear" that he did not come from Earth, that he was actually an extraterrestrial.

As a child, Soren told me, he was always troubled by terribly profound feelings of "being different." In school, he had almost no close friendships and, instead, spent much of his time scribbling notes to "the Martians" while, in class, he incessantly drew spaceships.

But it wasn't his own artwork that gave Soren that first shock of recognition, it was an imaginative rendering done by somebody else.

Soren was in the second grade. He was paging through a school reader, when he came upon an illustration of a crystal city. Staring down at the book, unable to turn away, Soren remembers being seized by an achingly painful sensation of homesickness. He almost burst into tears. He was far too young to understand his own reactions, but in the days that followed, Soren felt compelled to include crude, childlike copies of this crystal city as the backdrop to each of his pictures of spaceships.

In school Soren suffered under the classic regime for developing psychological repression and self-rejection. As the sci-fi drawings began to cover every piece of paper in his possession, he was harshly reprimanded by his teacher, who told him never to make such drawings again. Nip the "eccentric obsession" in the bud, was her idea. She never wondered *why* this child was so obsessed.

Soren's parents, however, saw nothing wrong with his behavior. They found it very down to Earth; maybe the result of a short attention span mixed with the vibrant imagination of childhood. They were kind to their son and supported his experience. Despite their concern, however, nothing changed—the boy was still alone with his feelings of isolation.

Soren almost never spoke to his parents about being different, and he neglected to mention something else that was going on: regular, nightly "travels" with people he called "my friends"; travels in which Soren seemed to leave his body, board some kind of transport craft, and fly off to visit people on Earth "or elsewhere." Finding little comfort even with his good-natured parents, Soren told me that he was left with only one listener for these stories: his stuffed puppy.

Soren was a lonely child and grew into a detached and alienated teenager.

Adolescence was a particularly bad time for Soren. In his teenage years he found it impossible to believe that life had any value at all. He felt misunderstood and split off from everyone around him. And it was as a teenager, he told me, that his serious quest for his "true self" began, one which stretched through shelves of books on philosophy, psychology, and the fiction of those who were searchers like himself.

Soren was, he says, "disillusioned and in a flat, colorless, two-dimensional world." He was deeply dissatisfied with what the world offered him.

Between the ages of eighteen and twenty Soren's dislocation became so bitter and painful that he began the heavy use of drugs. Finally, he attempted suicide by overdose. When that failed the first time, he tried again. Then, he OD'd once more. What he had was really a death wish fueled by the desire to escape intense psychic suffering.

Soren was hospitalized. And one night, while he was in a psychiatric ward recovering from his third attempt to take his own life, Soren lived through what he describes as a series of vivid out-of-body experiences (OBEs).

These are not at all unusual for those who finally recognize themselves as E.T.s.

For Soren, this was the turning point. And the most striking of the experiences was this one:

He floated away until he was able to see an omniscient vision of the entire Earth from space. But he was not by himself. Suspended and drifting away from the globe, Soren felt he was with a group of nonphysical "beings" and that strangely, he felt an un-Earthly camaraderie with them. He knew himself to be a part of this group.

And in his mind he heard the phrase:

We are gathering. . . .

With a flash of intuitive knowledge, Soren knew this was a reflection of the true communion between all extraterrestrials on Earth and that the purpose of E.T. visitation was to serve this planet during a time of transition. He understood he was an integral part of this gathering group.

But this experience, so lucid and affirming, was only one step in a gradual awakening.

It didn't immediately transport Soren to the conclusion that he was From Elsewhere, but the reality was so strongly felt and so convincing that he was driven to collect more information. It was as if he was determined to make sense of this puzzling experience. Sometimes I refer to these kinds of events as "dropped seeds of mystery," because in many of those I interviewed, they frequently inspired an intense spiritual search.

Soren began reading. Ruth Montgomery, the books of Brad Steiger—everything and anything that dealt with UFOs, E.T.s, and out-of-body experience. Finally, Soren picked up *The RA Material* (See Appendix 3) and experienced a sudden *snap* when everything finally made sense.

Soren arrived at this conclusion: It was possible, he believed, to come from an actual civilization outside of Earth; not simply a vague metaphysical realm, as he had previously imagined. Life beyond Earth did not mean a "formless floating in the ethers" as he had thought before.

Soren began to look for others who claimed a similar experience. This became his path. . . .

The question that immediately presents itself here is obvious: Could Soren have taken a more conventional, Earthly approach? Could he have sought out orthodox counseling to help explain his "ordinary feelings"?

Of course. In fact, to hear him speak, Soren seems quite psychologically sophisticated, more so than most people I've met. Aside from extensive personal therapy, he was enrolled for several years in a master's program in counseling and psychology. He really did seek a "second opinion." He felt terribly guilty for what sometimes seemed like a personal failure—he couldn't follow conventional ways and he couldn't fit in.

Still, Earthbound descriptions sounded to him like music being played off-key, tinny and unconvincing. Soren constantly felt a certain under-the-surface uneasiness that comes from trying to fit yourself into the wrong place.

Pushed on by what he told me was *a sense of deeply knowing something that he couldn't articulate but had to express*, slowly, over a period of years, Soren was able to make the jagged pieces of his life blend together smoothly like the colors of a well-composed painting. Of course, it took him many years to integrate all the implications of being an E.T. on Earth. And this work continues today.

The study of New Age material, he cautions, "only helped clear the fog, but the core feeling of who I was, was always present and unchanged." His outer study only confirmed what he knew deep inside, but had lacked the framework to explain.

Being an E.T., Soren says, is now "more real than the body around me."

WANDERERS AND WALK-INS

Soren is what is known as a Wanderer.

Briefly, in E.T. literature, there are two main types of extraterrestrials: Wanderers and Walk-ins.

These are not the kind of E.T.s who come walking down the ramp of a Hollywood-style UFO. They are, instead, extraterrestrials who incarnate on Earth.

Wanderers are E.T.s right from the beginning, although they're born of human parents, just like the rest of us.

Their awakening almost always comes gradually and follows a long period of loneliness and severe alienation. And, although this transformation dawns slowly, afterward any deep desperation is lifted and it seems like the final link in a long chain has finally appeared. Wanderers often feel as though they're discovering something they've actually always known—*a new vision of a very old truth.* ...

Some of the Wanderers describe the process in terms of an "unveiling" as they learn to accept the identity of a person living on Earth who has nonhuman origins. As you might guess, this can be very difficult.

The term *Wanderer* appears in a number of popular books on the subject. *The RA Material* (See Appendix 3)—one of the more sophisticated authorities on E.T.-related spiritual matters—speaks of

Wanderers at length. A Wanderer is defined as any E.T. who, while coming from another world, is as ordinary as anyone else in mind and body after birth. Only with extensive spiritual effort can they realize their true identity—that they are E.T. souls.

Most important: A Wanderer is an E.T. who volunteers to incarnate on a planet with the desire to help those who are evolving there.

Because of this unusual privilege, to incarnate directly on a planet in which "service" is eagerly needed (a planet which needs a lot of help!) the Wanderer agrees to forget his or her E.T. identity and renounce what might be thought of as the "magical powers' that were enjoyed "back home." Therefore, it's very common for Wanderers to get ensnared in Earthly ways. In fact, it is quite difficult for them *not* to get entangled since there are oh-so-many snares, and part of their hope is "just to fit in" (for purposes of both service and their own peace of mind).

In most cases, the amnesia lasts a lifetime (or *many* lifetimes!). For some, however, there's a germ of discontent and bit by bit they work back toward an understanding of their origins. This is considered "piercing the veil." These are the people I interviewed.

The journey they embark upon can alleviate a great deal of personal pain and fill the void of meaninglessness that they often feel. The search for self-understanding brings order to their lives and resolves the mystery of their "chronic differentness." Soren's story epitomizes this process.

Acute crisis, however, is almost always the experience of the other type of E.T., the Walk-in.

Actually, Walk-in is a very accurate term. It indicates that an entity (E.T. or otherwise, although in my study I only interviewed E.T. souls) has done just that: "walked-in" to a person's body and mind with shocking suddenness. Or, as some describe it, it's as though one experiences a wrenching and unexpected *soul-exchange* or *soul transfer*. Please bear in mind this has nothing to do with spirit possession or obsessing entities. It is considered a completely voluntary process.

The term Walk-in was introduced to the general public by Ruth Montgomery in her 1979 book *Strangers Among Us*. She defined a Walk-in as:

> a high-minded entity who is permitted to take over the body of another human being who wishes to depart. . . . The motivation for a walk-in is humanitarian. . . . [He or She] first completes the tasks of the body's previous owner, and then goes on to do what he must do on his own projects. . . .

For Walk-ins, there is a "new birth," and indeed, I found that their stories were filled with images of death and rebirth. Their awakening is almost always abrupt, tinged with trauma, and, understandably, their metamorphosis is usually felt as some kind of catastrophic life event. What could be more disruptive than exchanging your very soul for another? And what could be more confusing than feeling yourself a fresh, vibrant soul that must labor with negative psychological habits?

The story of Bob's awakening is a case in point.

BOB'S STORY

Bob's story provides a good illustration of the Walk-in phenomenon because Bob is a man who started out with no interest in anything spiritual, metaphysical, or psychological; couldn't have cared less about E.T.s; and, in fact, told me that *Hustler* magazine had been his prime idea of solid reading.

Today, in his late-thirties, Bob is still an ungainly, overweight man with unkempt dark hair. On the day I saw him, he needed a shave. For years he's drifted from job to job, and when I spoke to him he was unemployed.

At thirteen, Bob says, he began using narcotics, and by the time he was in his twenties he was using "not by the day but by the moment . . . from the moment I awoke in the morning to the moment I went to bed at night."

Bob describes himself at the time as "a real rager" who was

often violent and abusive and enjoyed cruelly manipulating other people. Put simply: He was *not* a nice guy!

Yet that all changed over a period of several months when Bob was thirty-seven years old.

At the time, he was a regular at Narcotics Anonymous. One night, returning from a meeting, in what Bob thinks of as a *telepathic impulse*, he heard himself being told to go to the nearby library and begin reading metaphysical literature.

And so he did. There followed, in fact, many visits to the library. And after one of these trips, while he was with a friend, Bob went through the cataclysmic paranormal experience that changed his life. The details of the event are humble enough, but the impact it had was profound.

It happened at a table in a local coffee shop when Bob was talking with a buddy. Bob had brought along a book he'd just taken from the library and placed it in his friend's shoulder bag. During lunch, when he reached to get it, bizarrely, the book had simply disappeared. There was no human explanation for how it had vanished.

Bob says that when he realized the book was gone, and that he knew beyond a doubt he'd placed it there only a few moments before, he shifted into a kind of hallucinogenic haze, started moaning, then "heaving emotionally," and shaking with uncontrolled sobs. Years of pain and torment rushed out of him like the torrent from a huge dam whose walls have split and shattered.

Across a page of his friend's newspaper, there appeared a strange sentence that seemed to float superimposed, as in a waking vision. The sentence read:

YOU HAVE PAID THE TOLL. YOU CAN CROSS THE BRIDGE.

Bob didn't know then that all the suffering of his previous years was finally extinguished—the debt, the "toll," had at last been paid and he was now free to cross over into a much happier life. Which is exactly what happened . . .

For the next four days, Bob says, he experienced feelings, energies, and an intense psychic sensitivity that he'd never known before and certainly never would have believed existed. Remember, this was a man with a near-zero interest in spiritual matters.

During that time, however, Bob felt graced with precognitive and telepathic powers, and he says it was like an "electrical charge" going through his body, a force so powerful that he could survive on two hours of sleep per night. He was filled with energy.

Along with that, Bob was overcome by emotions that had previously seemed reserved for others: intense surges of joy, peace, and tenderness. He also felt "filled with love."

Bob described this to me as a "soul transfer," although he's not completely sure that's what really happened.

He says from that moment, he ended twenty-four years of chronic drug abuse and has not touched any narcotics since—a fact which, alone, was amazing enough for me. As for his current identity, he admits that some of the old patterns are still present but says it's like "Bob is still here, the memory is here, but it doesn't feel like Bob." This is a fundamental confusion that all of the Walk-ins must overcome. His final conclusion provided no great comfort: "I am Bob . . . and I am not Bob."

FAR AWAY FROM CLOSE ENCOUNTERS

Obviously, Bob's tale of awakening didn't require a dramatic UFO abduction, or an encounter with willowy green beings, or the prodigious imagination of Steven Spielberg. Which brings us to some major differences between the E.T.s involved in my study and the other Earth people who say they've made contact with space-faring visitors.

Interestingly enough, the group of people I interviewed did not consider the UFO controversy to be a subject that had any direct bearing on their experience. Most of the Walk-ins and Wanderers I met were uninterested in such debate. They felt no need to prove or argue the reality of UFOs to Earth-bound skeptics and, while they were familiar with stories of government cover-ups, weren't very concerned about that, either.

Instead, they usually spoke of what they were living through in terms of "nonphysical beings, greater awareness, transcendence, spirituality, or information received or channeled from some kind of higher consciousness"—be it Master, spirit guide, or E.T. group.

From time to time, though, I did encounter stories of visitation, but these "meetings" were usually like this one, reported by a thirty-five-year-old architect I'll call Peter.

Peter told me that at a crucial time in his life he was repeatedly visited by an intelligent, sentient "ball of light" that entered his room and eventually led him to what he called "a sense of spiritual fortification."

This odd event followed a period of severe depression in college when Peter was using meditation to heal his psychic pain. Actually, he confessed that he had wanted to "meditate to die," hoping to escape his body and be free of his terrible existential suffering. In this way, he was very much like Soren, who also wanted to end his life. What "saved" Peter, however, were those many visits by a hovering ball of light, which were completely unexpected and almost immediately eased his depression. It was as if a "strong dose of mystery" recharged his will to live and conveyed the fact that he was not really alone.

Even so, there was no sudden personality shift. Peter did not immediately become a more spiritual or integrated person. He still felt detached and on the margins of social life.

Personal integration, as is usually the case, took many years of inner work, and Peter says it was not until he was introduced to the idea of a Walk-in that he was able to finish "piecing together the puzzle." With other "leads and pointers," the information he received about Walk-ins helped him make sense of his experiences. It also explained some of the gradual personality shifts and new ways of thinking that led him to become a more "universal citizen."

"Visitation"—when it occurs—is more likely to happen as a dream experience. That's another major difference between Wanderers and Walk-ins and those who are involved with strictly physical UFO encounters.

For Wanderers and Walk-ins, remember, there is generally no attempt to prove the common everyday, external, physical reality of spacecraft. Other-planetary ships and beings, however, quite often make visits in dreams, and those who claim E.T. identity very openly told me that dreams are a perfectly valid means of E.T. contact and experience. In fact, dreams are considered to be one of the primary ways that benevolent E.T.s awaken sleeping Wanderers to their cosmic heritage.

And this is just what happened to Vicky.

She's a therapist and body worker in her thirties who went through the most gradual, gentle awakening of anyone I interviewed. Vicky very sweetly described how she had felt no doubt, trauma, or confusion about being an E.T. Wanderer, and summed it up neatly: "It was no big deal."

Fifteen years ago, she had a series of extremely lucid dreams involving spaceships, extraterrestrials, and different worlds. And, as is often the case, she was filled with a realization of being at one with the E.T.s, of having a strongly felt common bond. It was not that she was so happy to meet "them," but, rather, she was happy to realize that she, too, was one of them. Their group was, in fact, also her own. It was a feeling of belonging to a single community together.

Being From Elsewhere, she now says, does not necessarily mean coming from any one, static location. So today, Vicky will speak easily about a long personal history of interplanetary travel, reincarnation, and an extensive relationship with a UFO confederation called the Ashtar Command. The name Ashtar refers to the leader of this pan-E.T. group and many New Age books and communiqués are attributed to this "commander."

But again, remember: To understand the experience of Wanderers and Walk-ins, it's important to make certain that our language and theirs share some common meaning—which is more difficult than it appears, given what's being described. Don't forget that concepts can sometimes be as fluid as water.

Also, it helps to move away from those prepackaged images too easily recalled from old Hollywood sci-fi movies or from explanations that are designed only to "discover" *assumed* psychological problems and a failure to socially adjust. The people I interviewed were neither cosmic freaks nor convoluted neurotics. If you spoke with them on nonspiritual matters you'd never know they considered themselves E.T. souls. In many, many ways, they are quite ordinary.

Some E.T.s who speak of the Ashtar Command, for instance, say it's contacted through vivid dreams, psychophysical experiences, and channeled information. Some of them never speak about UFO ships or mystical ideas at all. And the sense of self that might be summed up as "I am an E.T. from another planet" and might give rise to delusions of self-importance, represents only one type of extraterrestrial identity. Some of the Wanderers and Walk-ins I met, like Vicky, consider their cosmic origins with a great deal of humility. Others stay away from any kind of self-definition and, instead, stress a sense of Divine Union.

Rather than featuring UFO landings and high-tech spacemen, most of their awakenings to the idea of being E.T. are deeply emotional, personal experiences that are often paranormal and mystical. Whatever the quality of these events, however, they totally reconstruct a person's way of being and lead to wide, sweeping changes in every aspect of life.

CHRISTIN'S STORY

When trouble entered Christin's life, it came not with a whimper but a bang.

A gay man nearing forty, he was going through a terrible time with his live-in partner who was thinking about leaving him. Then there was trouble in his career as a teacher and administrator. And that was followed by financial problems. Finally, Christin was feeling six of the twelve most common symptoms of HIV infection. His life was taking a nosedive and plummeting fast.

Certain that he was going to die, Christin began to pray every day for relief. When there was none, he started to toy with the idea of suicide.

A therapist friend tried to convince Christin to take control of his life and reminded him of his relation to God, which, Christin says, lifted his depression for brief "bursts of life-passion." He'd go for walks, stroll at night to look at the stars, go mountain climbing.

But the depression would always return like a thick, dark storm cloud.

Without warning, Christin says, he began hearing what he describes as "inner voices." He was given commands. He would be ordered to drive to a particularly beautiful area near his home and contemplate the scenery or told to sit in meditation. None of the demands were weird or scary—all of them were quite uplifting.

Even so, depression weighed on him still.

Finally, while sitting with friends one night in a restaurant, Christin was seized with the strangest of pains and a temporary mental paralysis—"like two or three things were trying to come into me at the same time." He felt like a radio tuned to three stations all at once.

In his mind, piercing through the static, he heard the phrase: *Remember this moment. . . .*

After that, he became terrified, the pain and paralysis became so great that he doubled over, cried out, and was certain he was dying. Friends rushed him to a local hospital, and on the way Christin began to say his goodbyes. He was not surprised about being so close to the end. . . .

It was then that he received yet another inner message. This time, he was simply told to go home: *Just go home now!*

Then and there, in the rushing ambulance, Christin says, he

experienced an out-of-body state that he can only define as an "eternal peace and stillness." For one full minute, he ceased breathing. He felt he was being presented with the choice of whether to live or die. At this point, the voice said to Christin in an almost paternal way:

If you want to live, you have to breathe.

He took the advice. He really *did* want to live.

For several months afterward, Christin told me, he regularly heard in his mind the words: *I have given you a new spirit.* He felt a profound sense of having died and been reborn. And since that time, every aspect of his life has taken root and blossomed.

That was eight years ago. With the help of friends and support groups, reading and meditation, Christin has come to terms with his "nonordinary" identity as a Walk-in. This awakening, he says, has led him to a life of kindness, grace, love, and passion. He feels imbued with "psychophysical energies of a seemingly intelligent design"—energies that have healed him and infused his life with an enviable zest for living.

Today, Christin works in a worldwide service organization and counsels others who have been dealing with similar issues. He has counseled over three hundred people, is a beloved member of his community, and presents a completely successful tale of Walk-in awakening.

I'll return to his unique story later.

WHEN I COUNT TO THREE, YOU WILL REMEMBER EVERYTHING

Betty, at the age of sixty-two, is the oldest person I interviewed. She presents the charming picture of a proper, storybook English lady, with long, curly, gray hair and finishing-school manners.

Born and raised near London, Betty has worked as a nurse, a professional singer, a New Age lecturer, and a teacher of personal development. Her life has been rich and colorful.

She is a good person to know if you want to see someone who's completely at home with her E.T. identity . . . and if you want to hear the story of someone who became convinced of her celestial home not because of trauma, but through a startling moment of recall during hypnotic regression.

When I spoke with Betty, she mentioned to me in the most casual manner that she was "from Antares in the constellation Scorpio." She had arrived at this realization as a child, she said, when she also had the power to speak with nature spirits, read auras, stride great distances rapidly, and regulate her body temperature. Most of those practices, by the way, are a recognized part of Tibetan Buddhist mysticism. This was very interesting to me because I'd long studied Buddhism and spent time in several monasteries. Here was the convergence of Eastern religion and E.T. awareness!

Over the years, Betty says, her paranormal powers have lessened, but not before they so enriched her life that her metaphysical core has continually become much stronger. It wasn't so important that she lost the use of such powers, since their *real* effect was to indelibly impress her with the untapped potential of the human mind. She *knew* the amazing powers latent within all of us.

And Betty, as she'll happily tell you, is a Walk-in. She realized this only later, with the help of a hypnotherapist who helped her regress to the age of six.

During that important year (which Betty relived in the therapist's office), she fell seriously and frighteningly ill with food poisoning that was complicated by mastoiditis, a serious infection of the inner ear. In the 1930s the treatment for this disease was not as sophisticated as it is today, and Betty's parents were told to expect the worst.

Officially, that is exactly what happened. Bedridden and near death, the child Betty was finally pronounced clinically dead. For several minutes, to the attending doctor and fearful family members surrounding her bed, she was thought to have ended her natural life. A mournful silence began to enshroud the room.

"I'm sorry," the doctor said professionally.

"Oh, she's coming back," said Betty's mother, smiling.

The doctor appeared astounded.

"What do you mean?" he asked.

"I can see her," her mother said. "I have a vision of her standing on the other side of a big river and she's talking to a Being all dressed in white. And I know she's going to decide to come back."

The doctor, understandably, was not persuaded.

A few minutes later, however, the body stirred and Betty "came alive" once again. Her mother's prediction had been on the mark.

During one of the hypnotherapy sessions when Betty was in deep regression, many years afterward, she suddenly remembered the exact details of this illness. She started telling her therapist: "And that woman over there is not my mother!"

"Well, what do you mean?" the therapist inquired. "You're speaking about your blood relatives? Were you adopted?"

"No," Betty said.

"Well, what are you saying?"

It was then that Betty recalled her Walk-in, and as a testament to that experience, she exclaimed, "My real mother is Astrid!"

Both Betty and the therapist were shocked.

Who was Astrid? Actually, this was only one piece in the puzzle Betty solved so early in her life. She learned that "Astrid" was her mother in the E.T. society that was her true home.

When I interviewed her, Betty told me she's altogether comfortable with her identity as an extraterrestrial and "regularly visits her homeplanet in sleep," during "dreams" that take her back to the constellation Scorpio. Hers is a life in which the mystical has always been present, so it's not surprising that she is so casual about matters that would astound and confound most other people.

INFORMATION PLEASE

Catastrophic illness was the touchstone for Betty's E.T. experience. And whatever term we use to describe what really happened during that time—hallucination, fantasy, dream, or genuine Walk-in soul transfer—it was a real experience that was incorporated into Betty's life. It changed her forever. A personal event, it eventually led to Betty seeing Betty in a completely different way. And it was something she could never "prove" to anyone but herself. There was no way to "argue its reality." And in any case, she had no interest in proving it.

Christin, Soren, and Bob also experienced their awakenings and transformations after periods of overwhelming, seemingly insurmountable, difficulties. Life and death . . . death and rebirth . . . the end of an old way . . . and the beginning of a new cycle . . .

But that's not what always happens.

For Pauline, life was going smoothly. She'd never been interested in New Age ideas and her E.T. awakening was entirely unexpected.

When I spoke with her, Pauline described the event in language that you'd recognize from any standard psychology textbook. Her transformation, she told me in a furtive but very precise manner, resulted from a subtle interplay between forces conscious and unconscious. Pauline believes she was led by her "inner process," and she was most careful not to label what had happened. That might end up to be misleading. She also felt it wasn't necessary to determine *absolutely* exactly what it was all about. Interestingly, the fact that it had truly happened (and changed her life for the better) was much more important to her than how it had happened. Many of those I interviewed would concur with such priorities.

And in the story of Pauline, the vehicle of transformation didn't seem like a "soul transfer," but more a strange and sudden influx of information—an "information transfer," perhaps, and one that completely altered her life. Only later did she realize it had been part of a larger soul-exchange experience.

Pauline is a thin, attractive woman in her early forties who at the time of her walk-in in 1979 was running a successful jewelry business in California. Without warning, she began having a series of paranormal experiences.

At night, she would experience tremendous surges of energy every time she lay down in bed; but the phenomenon would cease each time she sat up. This went on for several months until one night—as in several previously mentioned cases with other E.T.s—she seemed to actually leave her body. She entered a strange non-physical state of incredible bliss and happiness.

The experience, however, left her terribly confused. And several weeks later something very surprising occurred.

Pauline had never missed a day of work, but on that morning she awoke from a deep sleep, dressed herself in casual clothes, and instead of heading off to her jewelry business as usual, she called in sick. Then, she marched out to her backyard, pulled up a comfortable chair, and proceeded for the next six hours to audiotape an entire two-day seminar on the subject of Inner Focus.

Which was really odd because Pauline wasn't scheduled to give any kind of seminar. In fact, she had no teaching experience at all. She was, in fact, shy and self-conscious about her speaking voice. Also, she knew nothing about the spiritual, esoteric healing ideas that she was including in her talk!

What in the world (or out of the world) was happening?

Not long after that startling morning, Pauline experienced another energy shift. Once again, she lay in bed amazed at what was going on. This time, however, there was something added. Clearly, distinctly, she heard a voice telling her:

You are being healed. . . .

And this was bizarre, too, because not only was Pauline unaccustomed to hearing disembodied voices, she wasn't even aware that she needed any kind of healing. "I felt fine," she told me. Healing for what?

Pauline then began a long period of research and personal reflection and finally sought out a series of spiritual teachers. When I interviewed her, she had at last come to terms with these strange experiences—and the terms were unique and very much characteristic of Pauline.

Reflecting upon these bizarre occurrences of more than a decade ago, Pauline told me she now believes "a presence entered my old personality patterns and changed them." And while she thinks she's a Walk-in, she doesn't pretend to be entirely certain.

Pauline, however, has at last become a spiritual teacher in her own right and says she will go anywhere she feels she's needed to support another person's growth. She's finally come into harmony with the original impulse that guided her to channel and transcribe her seminar on Inner Focus.

Which leads us to a final question in our examination of E.T. awakening.

Having had these experiences—extraordinary dreams, strange voices, energy shifts, paranormal powers, out-of-body travel, visitations—how does one ultimately come to the conclusion of extraterrestrial identity? How does one arrive at this most unusual of statements about oneself?

MY WORLD AND WELCOME TO IT

A writer, therapist, and organizer of New Age seminars, Lucia had still never believed she would have a Walk-in experience herself. She knew what it was all about, but never imagined it had anything to do with her.

In 1989, in her mid-thirties, Lucia, or Charlotte as she was then called, was preparing to host a workshop at her home given by a group of E.T. facilitators from Sedona, Arizona. These teachers, previously of the E.T. Earth Mission group, are somewhat controversial as leaders who guide and assist those claiming non-Earthly identity—in particular, Walk-ins.

Lucia was in the shower that morning when a voice, seemingly "in her head," suddenly told her:

You are going to have a Walk-in experience today. . . .

Then, for hours afterward, she actually kept hearing the phrase, "Today is the first day of the rest of your life." Although, as she told me, it seemed kind of kitschy (an advertising slogan being used to impart spiritual guidance) this was indeed the message she received so clearly.

Then, as suddenly as it began, it ended.

There was a silence. Soon, however, the voice started to give what Lucia described to me as a moment of "inner guidance," instructing her to drive to a nearby field, sit down, and rest. Feeling safe and protected, Lucia did as she was told. While she sat there idly picking at the grass, almost lost in astonishment, she felt "a tremendous overshadowing presence" and the sensation of upheaval, as if all of the energy was leaving her body, making way for new energy to enter.

She felt that there was "a new spirit" entering her. And just as she was getting used to it, the spirit actually announced itself, using her body and her voice, and said:

I am Lucia. . . .

Which was not her given name at the time.

For three weeks after this, Lucia reported, she was graced with a radiantly clear mind, definite telepathic powers, and certainty about her origins as an E.T. and her purpose for being on Earth. Like Bob and Christin, she was in a "state of grace."

But that didn't last.

As with many Walk-ins, these powers faded rapidly, although the experience became a foundation, central and defining. During our interview, Lucia spoke of herself as an E.T. but also said she's "open to the idea that all of my ideas about myself are false."

It's even possible, she went on, that a "delusive negative entity" was toying with her, tempting her with the "glamorous illusion" of being E.T. I was impressed with her open-mindedness. Like Pauline, she was a nondogmatic teacher.

E.T. or not E.T.—that was *not* the question. Nor was it the answer from most of those I interviewed. Recognizing themselves as E.T. souls was only the end of one chapter and the beginning of another.

For the others, as well as for Lucia, identification as an extraterrestrial was known finally in much the same way as any other identity is known: by self-validation. They all came to validate this conclusion on their own.

What was crucial was not the declaration of being From Elsewhere. As with any other declaration of selfhood, the most important factor was the degree of psychological integration. It finally became real when it was an insight that became a part of themselves—and when it had, it improved and enriched the quality of their lives. This is true for every one of them.

Wanderers—E.T.s from birth who come to self-understanding only gradually—were less in need of outside support or validation. There was no need to prove their identity to anyone. They eventually came to a deep, inner knowing of who they were. It confirmed what they had always suspected and wasn't much of a surprise.

Walk-ins—who underwent a transformation suddenly and in the midst of Earthly life—seemed more likely to require some help. It was not unusual for Walk-ins to declare a non-Earthly "soul transfer" while remaining open to some other explanation. The whole experience was often so baffling that a dogmatic conclusion was impossible. The very basis for their sense of self had been shifted and rearranged.

Bob, the E.T. who ended more than two decades of drug addiction when he experienced his Walk-in, will today still comment, "I can feel real neurotic sometimes." And as we've said, he identifies himself as "Bob and not Bob," an identity confusion that is common among Walk-ins who've recently undergone their strange metamorphosis.

Peter, the architect who witnessed "intelligent balls of light," is no longer confused about his E.T. identity but does make a clear distinction between "the old personality and the new personality." I had to smile at Peter's understanding of what transpired because he wondered if maybe he had a "Walk-in without a walk-out." (That last one, by the way, is not a common term.) Apparently Peter feels that his "old human soul" remained alongside his E.T. transfer, but he, unlike Bob, did not talk about himself as feeling "neurotic."

What's also interesting is this: The overwhelming majority of those I interviewed did not stress the importance of their E.T. status and did not generally think of themselves as *aliens*.

Perhaps this was most succinctly stated by a woman I'll call Linda, who lectures internationally on the role of Walk-ins in society. Linda is counselor, author, and leader of a spiritual community in Oklahoma. She's one of the most practical and grounded of those I met.

Linda says she had a walk-in experience several years ago and definitely knows herself to be from Sirius. However, she never stresses this in her presentations. Instead, she says, being From Elsewhere is "just a piece of information."

Linda says "the walk-in experience allows a person to face their own foolishness."

That foolishness, she says, is the imprisoning belief that a time-space identity is so very important after all. She says that what we really are is not the personality; what we really are is an embodiment of the Absolute Divine Totality. This is a lot more freeing than the notion of being either an "Earth human" or an "E.T. alien" and does away with the notion that anyone is more holy than anyone else. We are all Holy.

Whether as Wanderer or Walk-in, Linda says that E.T. identity opens up an experience that's really available to all humanity. It is the experience of being united with the cosmos, of being a brilliant thread in the Universal Tapestry of All.

3

SUBJECTIVE KNOWING:
THE PROOF OF E.T. IDENTITY

WHO AM I? WHO ARE WE?

NEW AGE, OLD VIEW

If we're actually going to come face-to-face with the reality of extraterrestrial beings, we must first open our minds to a new view of reality itself. This is neither easily said, nor easily done.

It might help to start this part of our journey with a quote from the scientist and dolphin researcher John Cunningham Lilly:

> The attempt to define all mystical, transcendental, and ecstatic experiences which do not fit in with the categories of consensus reality as psychotic is conceptually limiting and comes from a timidity which is not seemly for the honest, open-minded explorer.

For our purposes, this kind of openness is even more important because the initial experience of Walk-ins and Wanderers—mystical, transcendental, or ecstatic—leads to a discovery that is worlds away from ordinary thinking. It also leads to questions of verification. One might go along with the reality of a transcendental experience—but to be led by that experience to the conclusion that one is an extraterrestrial soul?

It's understandable that those around you might ask for ID at the door.

Verification of, or "proving," extraterrestrial identity plunges us directly into the heart of a central question of existence—anyone's existence, regardless of which planet they call home. With a discussion of verification, we're headed into a basic philosophical maze—not only into *who we are*, but also into *how we know who we are*. It's an inquiry that, when taken seriously, can upend our trust in common everyday reality as surely as the experience of an E.T. Walk-in.

As the Zen philosopher Alan Watts once wrote: "Trying to define yourself is like trying to bite your own teeth."

I've used the Watts quotation here because it holds a lot of wisdom, but I'd like to offer one slight amendment. We might enrich the kernel of truth in his words by tacking this phrase onto the end of it: *And yet . . .*

This is because, in some ways, this slippery attempt at self-definition, this "biting our own teeth," is exactly what all of us are doing every moment of every day, all the time, whether E.T. or John Doe. Every aspect of our reflexive, unthinking day-to-day living, even down to our most minor actions, is always being lived inside this ebb and flow. It's a tide formed by the question: *Who am I?* And each of us must go on asking—and answering—this inquiry from moment to moment. Even without referring to extraordinary reality, we're forever redefining ourselves. And yet, we almost never stop long enough to consider who it is, or *what* it is, that's the seat of such constant experience. We usually don't pause to look back at the *I* who partakes of all the richness and color of basic experience. . . .

When it comes to verification—proving that *this* is who I really am—a person who claims ordinary, everyday identity will have exactly the same difficulty proving who he or she is as someone who announces he or she's E.T.

Except . . .

Except for our unquestioning reliance on the ideas, narratives, and documents that are commonly accepted as "real" by the powers that be. Namely, the external, social world. Caught naked, without any solid proof of identity, John Smith will be able to prove he's John Smith only as long as he can call for outside help, find the proper documents, or have someone else vouch for him. He's OK up until the moment he steps over a socially agreed upon line. After that, he's in big trouble.

And, what if, one day, the question *Who am I?* suddenly gets answered by a truly radical claim: I'm a Wanderer, or, I'm a Walk-in?

How does one go about proving such a statement, something which, in the everyday world, sounds unstable, illogical, and downright bizarre? And how can one ever be sure?

The only way to gain certainty is through a process called, "subjective knowing."

I use this phrase to introduce an entirely different way of thinking and feeling, one that often makes many people uncomfortable. Subjective knowing is a process that allows us to know something for ourselves and by ourselves—without assurance from the outside world. We validate our own ideas without empirical proof. Subjective knowing connects us to a more personal reality.

This is *not* the same as the statement that "no proof is needed" or "if you think it's so, it is so." It is *not* an invitation for anyone to mockingly assume an outrageous identity with which they've truthfully never connected. In subjective knowing we use ourselves in a manner that's closer to the way of the artist, actor, writer, or musician and farther from that style of thinking that makes us prosecutors at our own trial with our every idea and feeling placed in the dock for judgment.

What Wanderers and Walk-ins offer us is much more than the

statement *We are From Elsewhere*. They hope to be catalysts for a global renaissance of spiritual values and greater awareness. What sets their message apart from traditional religions is their acceptance of the possibility of many roads to Heaven, many paths to spiritual development. As always, the key to such growth is greater attunement to the quiet voice within. Listening to, and then wisely following the dictates of your inner self is the complete opposite of the tendency to follow expert pronouncements and external authorities. Unfortunately, many of us renounce some or all of our personal responsibility and trade our own vision for a moment of security. In that way, we lose our precious powers of inner guidance. The pervasive social game in which we blithely "follow the leader" almost always brings disastrous results. Very few people are even aware they do this, and fewer still recognize the tremendous wisdom of the individual human soul.

Therefore, it becomes necessary to chance a step into another way of viewing reality, a way that often differs from that of parents, teachers, bosses, and what passes for conventional wisdom.

One possible starting place for this broader view is outlined by the Zen philosopher D. T. Suzuki, in his fine compilation *The Essentials of Zen Buddhism*:

> As for reality, it must be taken with naked hands, not with the gloves of language, idealization, abstraction, or conceptualization. . . . Reality can be handled only by Reality. This means we must put away completely all our beautiful structures, philosophical, theological or otherwise, at least for a while. . . . Dressing ourselves is all right, but then we become too conscious of something other than ourselves—I mean our surroundings. No objection is made to social mindedness, but rather to our becoming controlled and enslaved by those exterior things.

The E.T.s I interviewed hope to help us not by proving their reality (i.e., not by petitioning their UFO brethren to "land on the White House lawn") but by offering their ideas. By this perspective:

The process is the purpose. The journey of our lives is the point of our lives. *The journey itself is the point*—the orientation of mind that seeks to learn from our every experience.

By the friction of daily interaction, by the veil that shrouds certainty, by the insistent human drive to understand, we're led onward to greater awareness. And in this process, the vehicle is as it has always been: subjective knowing. This is the great work of "turning within," the central point of all esoteric traditions. It is no less than our lifeline to immortality and the meaning of our lives. It is also the central boulevard to the worlds of Walk-ins and Wanderers.

When you've read or heard something and, through a mysterious inner process, come to "know it for yourself," this is an example of subjective knowing in action. All of us use this process to a great extent, no matter how rational we think we are. Indeed, one definition of mental illness is the inability to validate anything within ourselves, which leaves us in the dark field of confusion.

But, what if one day you ask yourself the question *Who Am I?* and it's answered in an unexpected manner: *I'm extraterrestrial.* The first time someone encounters this kind of other-worldly, extraordinary, or even outlandish idea, the most common reaction is to pull back and stay safely away from serious investigation.

If that's how we've responded to questions of E.T. identity, then our reaction to this answer will be amusement, perhaps, or even contempt, at the other end of the spectrum. We might allow the accused to get away with a light sentence using the insanity defense: Anybody who honestly believes that they're an extraterrestrial is so radically breaking away from mainstream thinking that the person is almost certain to be crazy.

Our judgment of craziness, of course, will be handed down only after we've asked the Wanderer or Walk-in to prove himself by some kind of demeaning magic trick. *If you're really an E.T., then dematerialize! Read my mind! Show me your spaceship!*

It's a common approach, and no more than a form of ridicule and bullying. It's also an outlook that badly mixes up the everyday world with the world of spirit, one that shows just how much we tend to use the wrong tools for the wrong purposes. Does such close-minded taunting really help us? I don't think so. It keeps us protected, happy to be on the outside of the question, and "in control"—where it's only possible to learn about the mundane view that we already hold, and never to venture anywhere new.

The entire question of identity is usually handled in this kind of simple, concrete manner. Identity is seen as a driver's license that never needs renewing, it's assumed to be fixed and unchanging. Our nationality or our job, our race or religion—these are the "normal" ID cards proving who we are. The proof offered here is only what the outside, social world will accept. Sadly, it is the "jury of our peers" that is given final say as to who we are allowed to be. And I wouldn't be surprised if we could trace this behavior back to our ancestors. It's very possibly a holdover from the age of tribes and animal packs, when the individual was merely "a unit of the group" instead of a distinct, individuated whole.

A uniform proves you're a policeman, a diploma proves you're a doctor, and so on. No one needs to recount the number of deadly wars fought throughout history in which the spark that cost millions of lives was ignited by nothing more than a supposed threat to national identity. And we've all heard too many tales of friends who've been thrown into terrible, painful crises that rattled the very roots of their self-worth after they've lost a job or suffered a financial setback. Their identities were bound up in external objects.

Those who believe they are extraterrestrial souls, however, are dealing with a claim so shocking to our deeply held preconceptions that it upsets everything we know about the world. Empirical proof? If one of our E.T.s *did* dematerialize in front of her critics—or suddenly sprout antennae—most of the skeptics would swiftly rationalize and just continue on with their doubting! Empirical proof is impossible because it would never be accepted. Such is the hold that comfortable, everyday reality has on us; it affords a protection we feel we can hardly do without.

The E.T.s say we can do better than that.

Along our path, we'll go much farther when we jettison this one common mistake: *We think we already know the nature of reality.*

We'll learn a lot more if we stop pretending to have a superior vantage point or a final answer. The experience of identity is too rich to be discussed within the narrow borders of coldly linear thought, simple logic, or with the secret, unspoken agenda that merely supports our own disbelief. Perhaps the best place to start is with the understanding that . . . *we really don't know how the Universe works!*

Yet, we can get to the inside in the way an actor or writer creates a character, we can feel our way into the hearts and minds of those who claim a more cosmic experience, and do our best to understand the implications of what they are saying; not just their words, but rather the meaning they hold for our lives. All it requires is that we employ the amazing resources of the imagination. In that way, even the most committed skeptic might walk away with his rejection still safe and sound, but having learned something nonetheless.

The E.T.s themselves counsel just such an approach. They also recognize the very intimate nature of self-validation and the fact that it is only by subjective knowing that each of us can arrive at a more integrated, comprehensive view of reality. For the benevolent ones, who seek to aid our personal growth, they confine themselves to offering us "catalyst": grist for the mill, bits and pieces of mystery, like crop circles, that inspire our deepest aspirations. As one of the "Confederation" members stated during a channeling session:

> We offer them (Earth people) no concrete proof, as they have a way of expressing it. We offer them Truth. This is an important function of our mission—to offer Truth without proof. In this way, the motivation will, in each and every case, come from within the individual. In this way, the individual vibratory rate will be increased. *An offering of proof or an impressing of this Truth upon an individual in such a way that he would be forced to accept it,*

would have no usable effect upon his vibratory rate. This, then, my friends, is the mystery of our way of approaching your peoples. [italics added]

Which is to say: The benevolent E.T.s treat us as adults. Without forcing upon us a set of new paradigms, they appear in ways that simply catch our curiosity. And for those ready to uncover hidden truth, the tools are provided to turn over every boulder in our path.

I KNOW I DON'T KNOW

Now that we realize our journey must be traveled alone, perhaps we can more closely examine some of the scenery through which we find ourselves wandering.

We're dealing here with people who've undergone an extraordinary experience of awakening after a "death" of their old identity. All of them have come to espouse some concepts that had been altogether "alien" to them before their new sense of self took hold. The psychologist Stanislav Grof spoke in detail about a similar process during a conversation with physicist Fritjof Capra that Capra includes in his book, *Uncommon Wisdom*:

> The complete death-rebirth process always represents a spiritual opening. People who go through that experience invariably appreciate the spiritual dimension of existence as being extremely important, if not fundamental. And at the same time their image of the physical universe changes. People lose their feeling of separateness; they stop thinking of solid matter and begin to think of energy patterns.

And Grof goes on to say that consciousness can be seen as something

> primordial, which cannot be explained on the basis of anything else; something that is just there and which, ultimately, is the only

reality; something that is manifest in you and me and in everything around us.

Subjective knowing is the only way to validate such awareness. Paradoxically, sometimes this process leads to subjective *unknowing* or a greater uncertainty as to what really is and is not. In speaking about her current Walk-in awareness, which came to her first as an internal voice while she was showering, Lucia told me, "It's a constant experience. It feels like I'm on the wrong planet at the wrong time. It's a constant inner voice."

Like most of the E.T.s I interviewed, Lucia said there was no one, single moment when she was suddenly and irrevocably certain that she was an extraterrestrial. The final identity shift took place gradually, over time, and was accompanied by a "feeling of inner knowing."

"But it was such a huge awakening to myself," she went on, "that it felt like a different life-stream."

No absolute certainty about who she is, maybe, but what I found most interesting when I spoke with Lucia was something else I'd heard from a number of those who claim to be From Elsewhere: *There seemed to be very little need for such absolute certainty.* In fact, as I put on my professional role as "the impartial researcher," I think I sounded more concerned about it than they did! After I'd asked Lucia several times about how she could be certain, she finally said, "In something so subjective, I would never say I'm 100 percent sure. But I wouldn't say that I'm 100 percent sure of anything."

I said to her, "Well, as someone who does therapy and counseling with people claiming to be From Elsewhere, don't you have to eventually ask them: *Are you sure?*"

It's different than that, Lucia said, it's more subtle. Her advice to anyone on the verge of claiming E.T. identity wasn't *you better prove it now.* Instead she counseled others to: *look deeply into yourself and determine your motives.* How strongly do you really feel this new identity? Can you live like this? And, if so, how is it going to feel to live your life on Earth with this radically misunderstood sense of self? (Misunderstood by society, that is.)

I heard the same kind of subjective unknowing when I spoke with Bob. He, too, stressed the importance of "process"—the process of continually coming to grips with radical conceptions of self that at a very deep level feel right.

Bob told me that his own personal acceptance of being From Elsewhere took place over several years, and that "nothing clinched it" for him; even now, he said, "I'm still growing." I had to smile when he finished by confessing, "Actually, I consider myself to be normal . . . or as normal as you can be in this society!"

But, for the purposes of the interview I acted as though I knew very little about what he meant, and so I put to Bob the same question that I asked Lucia. I kept returning to it, pressing for an answer, because it's certainly an interesting point—how could he have had this extraordinary series of experiences without anything coming along to validate it for him, to "clinch it," as he said.

I asked, "Hasn't that been difficult?"

"Not at all," Bob answered with the nonchalance I'd heard so often from E.T.s. "The issue of being an E.T. soul or not isn't such a big deal."

At first, he said, right after the Walk-in, some kind of definite "closure" had been important, "but through time, as I got more balanced, I got comfortable with a lack of closure. Now? Identity is just an ongoing process. It's a way of exploring life."

"I've reached a point," Bob concluded, "where I'm all right with whatever it is. I'm comfortable with the way I am, no matter what." Which could be taken as a statement of psychological maturity whether or not the person believes in E.T.s or distant home planets.

I put some of these same questions to Una. She's a visual artist, a very childlike woman in her mid-fifties who paints, draws, and lives a kind of idyllic country life with what she calls a "special connection to plants and animals."

When I asked her what it was, exactly, that pinned down her identity for her, she answered, "Hey, it's not like a big Boom! or anything, it's a series of things. Change in perception is one of them. I view the world very differently now. But there was a lot of doubt for a long time and that only cleared up gradually. There wasn't any one moment where I woke up and said, *Yeah! This is it!*"

Eventually, Una said, she talked about her feelings with a coworker who had been through a similar experience and that, at least, gave her the feeling that she wasn't crazy, that there was a framework in which to understand what she was going through.

But ultimately, Una said, despite any help From Elsewhere or anywhere, it's self-validation—the willingness to trust and live with your own experience regardless of who else agrees or disagrees—that becomes the key to anyone's identity. And although many of us in the United States enjoy our share of blood, sweat, and tears when we set about the grim task of self-development, it may be that *self-validation* is just an academic way to talk about a process that's completely natural and happening all the time. It might be a process that we can hamper by trying too hard, a process of letting go, being with yourself, accepting yourself, or in the old Taoist formula, *the effortless work of non-doing.* Self-validation is simply opening the door when you yourself are knocking.

As Una told me: "People grow in spiritual awareness so it's natural that more and more of their insight becomes affirmed. All beings become more inner directed. Self-validation is going on even if you don't know about it or don't know how to talk about it."

And through this fundamental means, we become more and more conscious. . . .

YOU'RE NOT LYING—I JUST DON'T BELIEVE YOU

Then, there's the case of Vicky.

"What do you do when people say you're crazy?" I asked her.

"I just laugh," she said, laughing. "It doesn't disturb me at all because I know what I know. I'm very comfortable with my ideas. Also, I can laugh at myself and I can tease *them*. If you can laugh at yourself, then you're not that crazy . . . usually."

Vicky, you may remember, breezed through one of the most peaceful, uneventful Awakenings I've ever heard about. She's an extremely attractive woman in her late thirties. Small and thin, with dark features and a teasing, sly manner, Vicky keeps herself in excellent physical condition. She is from North Carolina and runs her own business specializing in about 20 different kinds of body work and body therapy as well as in color and sound therapies. Of all the people I spoke with who claim to be From Elsewhere, Vicky was the most visibly at ease with her E.T. roots; at times, she was positively vivacious about it.

"Most people, once you talk with them," she said, "are fascinated. They may not agree, but they feel a certain power, a certain sureness, a certain energy that pulls them in. So, a lot of people have told me: I know you're not lying but I don't necessarily believe you."

But Vicky's self-confidence combined with her sense of service means that getting people to agree with her isn't of the utmost importance.

"If I have any goal in my life with people, it's to help them remove the blinders from themselves. They don't have to agree with me. But if they push their boundaries and minds and hearts out a little bit, then I believe I've done them a service. So I have a little bit of a rebellious side that way. I'm kind of an extraterrestrial brat."

It's important, Vicky said, not to camouflage yourself . . . especially from your own "inner vision." And she feels that she never has: "Although I have plenty of things to work on, as we all do, I try to speak the truth, regardless of what happens." For Vicky, it's never a matter of truth *or* consequences, it's a matter of truth *and* consequences.

It's worthwhile, I think, to go into some detail with Vicky's story because her self-assured attitude toward nontraditional identity is so full of light and cheer and encompasses so many positive ways of seeing, that I feel she serves as a good example. And as Vicky herself said to me, "That's the best way to teach, by example."

From one angle, what I understood Vicky to be saying all through our interview was that there's really no need for big, traumatic scenes or dramatic claims when we're dealing with universal ideas.

"There's a big difference between true feeling and sentiment or dramatic emotion," she said. "I'm pretty good at balancing the head and heart."

And, of course, there's a lot of exaggeration in spiritual affairs; I've heard quite a bit of it myself. But Vicky seemed to be saying that much of the sci-fi drama created around E.T. identity is really only a false front, constructed by people who hope to gain glamour or popularity. You have to be careful not to succumb to the temptation of glamour, she said, because it can drown out what's truly important. There are pivotal events, wonderings, and questions in our lives that hold the key to a new phase of learning and self-expression. What's crucial, Vicky believes, is learning to listen to what she terms "the triggers in yourself" and then continuing the journey on your own.

In Vicky's life, continuing this "journey on her own" eventually meant moving into realms of serious study, working to master new ways of helping people. She became acquainted with a variety of body therapies; began voraciously reading spiritual, metaphysical, and esoteric literature (she bought and read two books a week, she said, until she'd built up quite a library); and, finally, she started speaking with those who had firsthand knowledge of cosmic truths.

Vicky was so accepting of her Wanderer origins that her self-study became like an incredibly exciting journey. She described it as a path to regaining her extraterrestrial vision, the native powers and wisdom that she'd lost by incarnating on Earth. These were very focused efforts, backed up by concentrated work, and the process allowed Vicky to move beyond boundaries she would have never thought possible. Increasingly, she was comfortable "traveling between worlds."

In fact, Vicky said, fifteen years before, when she first started paying attention to the "inner triggers" that whispered From Elsewhere, she hadn't done any reading on E.T.s or UFOs and wasn't even a big fan of science fiction. And, as is often the case, one of the most vivid triggers was a dream. Before that night, Vicky had always slept soundly, hardly ever remembering her dreams! Yet, that evening, and on the next two nights, she had exactly the same dream and it always ended in exactly the same place.

Vicky called these "lucid dreams" because she believes them to be objective experiences that took place in a different psychic reality. They were not, she cautioned, happening in the ordinary physical universe that we know, like the claims made for UFO abductions. She considered their "locale" to be spiritual, a more subtle plane of the Earth itself, yet "used" as symbolic communication from her Higher Self.

The dream took place in the house in which Vicky was raised. She was alone in front of a huge picture window when suddenly, the ground began rumbling and shaking and she called out, addressing a question to the Earth itself: *What is going on?*

The Earth replied: *Be prepared for the visit.*

Vicky didn't understand. She didn't have much time to think about it, though, because a strange, whirring sound started and through the picture window she saw a spaceship land right on the lawn of her front yard. Concerned, but not frightened, Vicky grabbed her car keys and bolted for the front door; but when she got outside she saw that her car had been dematerialized.

After that, she ran for a hill near her house and began climbing. At the top, where she could peer over, she spotted another house and two beings she calls "female humanoids" wearing one-piece suits walking toward her. One of these beings was carrying a bag of something, some kind of seedlike material that she kept tossing around in the grass as if gardening.

Vicky again asked the Earth: *What is she doing?*

The Earth replied: *An experiment.*

And at that, Vicky says, she became very indignant, thinking: *How dare she!*

At which point, the humanoids spied Vicky.

They approached her. They came up the other side of the hill and stood before her. Then, Vicky says, something remarkable happened.

She suddenly understood what it was like to be inside three bodies simultaneously: her physical body, which she knew to be "frozen;" her mental body, which was warning her that the humanoids were trying to hypnotize her; and her spiritual body, which raised her physical hand and intoned, *In the name of the One: You can do me no harm because I am of the light!*

With that declaration, says Vicky, bolts of illumination shot out of her hands and flashed into the head of the humanoid, who was completely dazed.

Vicky then took charge. Telepathically, she said to her visitors: *Now that that's out of the way, how is it I can serve you and what is it that you want?*

The answer was: *You have just changed my reason for coming. There are things that I may now show you that you may share with your people.*

Hearing this pronouncement, Vicky felt her sentiments shift and became very protective, concerned that the humanoids would be discovered. The Earthlings, she feared, would react with such shock and terror that they'd attack the humanoids, injure or kill them. She ushered both of the Visitors into her house.

They began trying to share their information.

However . . . as they did so, Vicky began to run wildly around the room shouting: *You can't talk with me until I find a tape recorder!*

And at that moment, she was awakened ... each time, on all three consecutive nights ... in that very same place.

Not only that, but on the first morning, Vicky was rocked awake by her clock radio going off and a DJ's voice raucously laughing about "how people must have been partying last night because we've had three reports of UFOs!"

On the second morning, she awakened a half hour earlier, again to the clock-radio alarm, and this time she heard a talk show discussing government censorship of UFO documents.

On the third morning she woke up because of a phone call from a girlfriend in Hawaii, which came, as always, at the very same point in the dream narrative. The friend told her how an acquaintance had been taken aboard a spacecraft. That event, said her girlfriend, had given her "a sudden urge to call" Vicky.

As I listened to Vicky relate her story, I couldn't help thinking that this was quite a tale, and I told her exactly that. In Jungian terms, we could say she'd had a "big dream," meaning a definite message from the Self. Indeed, it was Jung who described doing therapy as joining with a patient to "address the two-million-year-old man" who is in everyone; it was Jung who believed that our greatest difficulties come from losing contact with our own ancient knowledge.

This is not so different from the way Vicky understood the "message" she was being given in her dream.

"It was the trigger, and I paid attention to it. The funny thing is," she said with a smile, "that I don't really care very much about the actual physical phenomenon of UFOs. But I do have a kind of knowingness about things. I'm almost never surprised, because when things like this happen to me it feels like I somehow already knew about them. They already exist in my worldview."

When Vicky told her family—her birth family—about what had happened and her take on it, she said everyone was very supportive. She described her family as "very tight and very honest," saying that she never felt forced to hide anything and that "there were never any secrets" about her burgeoning interests, or what she does for a living, or how she identifies herself.

"Both my stepfather and my real father think I'm a little out there," she laughed, "but they don't mind. And my mother is incredibly psychic, so she's right out there with me."

No Regrets

The teenager who grew up to be Vicky definitely did not have her eyes on the stars or her head in the clouds. And she probably never considered that her adulthood might be so out-of-the-ordinary, "dedicated to Universal service," as Vicky says. But now that she's here among us, has she realized exactly where she's from? Does she call Earth her home?

"It's one of thousands of galaxies I've called home," Vicky said. "And I hope no one takes that as a statement of simple, physical reality."

In other words, she went on, it's possible to talk about "incarnated souls" or "E.T. souls" that aren't coming from "other planets" but arrive instead from "other *tendencies*," an entirely different type or level of reality. For instance, Vicky told me, she's long had a love for the idea of the Ashtar Command, a federation of extraplanetary civilizations under the supreme jurisdiction of Ashtar. Here, for the purposes of my survey, I let myself listen to Vicky like an outsider. When I asked her to go into her ideas in a little more detail, to explain more about the reality of Ashtar, our talk became as complicated as a discussion of the theological concept of God; not reality, not fantasy, maybe somewhere in between (if you feel it's necessary to measure its objectivity) . . . and probably indescribable.

"So how are you going to be sure about that?" Vicky laughed. "Eventually, you begin to discern what you can be fairly sure of and what's forever going to be open. And I think one of the greatest sources of pain on this planet is people's lack of ability to discern."

Finally, Vicky gave me one of the simplest conclusions I could imagine for a discussion of validating a person's E.T. identity, or any identity—and it was a statement that I was later to hear several times from several of the people I interviewed. It brought us right back to our original question: How do you *really* know?

"Ultimately," Vicky said, "it doesn't matter whether someone is E.T. or not-E.T. It just doesn't matter. They're still here, and they're still doing what they feel they've been put on Earth to do. Declaring yourself to be an E.T. might give somebody comfort, it might give you greater understanding, but it's also not absolutely necessary, it doesn't affect the *nowness.*"

"Well, then," I asked her. "What do you think *is* important?"

"To follow your heart," she answered. "Moving in balance. Perfecting discernment. Speaking for yourself. And being brave."

It was also important, she felt, to mention something else related to the question of validating E.T. identity. When people are skeptical of those who say they're From Elsewhere, even when they themselves have had some deep experience, they're usually basing that doubt on very little information . . . if any at all. What most people know about being From Elsewhere doesn't come from serious questioning, study, or self-discovery. It comes from popular movies, prime-time TV, and the very fertile imaginations of novelists and screenwriters.

Of course, the question could also be turned around. It's just as logical to ask: *How do you know, really know, that you're not E.T.?*

Vicky told me that if people go inside themselves and examine their hearts and then find they *know, truly know* that it is not so, that they are not E.T., "well then, more power to them. Then it is not so for them, that's all." But to discuss an extraordinary possibility on flimsy evidence—namely the doubting Thomases of our sometimes too-rational culture—is not only illogical, it's probably self-deceptive.

Remember, the Wanderer usually has a smoother path when it

comes to being certain of extraordinary identity; the Walk-in often gets thrown for a loop, not knowing *am I From Elsewhere or am I insane? What am I doing in this body?* And sometimes, *Who is this husband? Who are these children?* And quite often: *THIS IS NOT REAL AT ALL!*

But as I said before, even for someone who basically identifies herself as a Wanderer, Vicky showed an amazing degree of confidence in her beliefs and in her extraterrestrial identity. She exuded a powerful feeling that the exact nature of her identity ultimately didn't matter, and that came through in both her statements and her actions. You could tell she was speaking the truth by the definite look in her eyes. She felt that way and she acted that way, which takes an impressive effort of self-awareness and self-recognition.

And with that, I'll give Vicky the last word, because the point of it all, E.T. or not, is to live in joy and fulfillment:

"I feel firmly that I've agreed to it all," she said with a clear sense of recognition. "It's total free will and I haven't regretted any of it. And that comes along with something else. The greatest attribute I now have is joy. Actually, I've always had an incredible feeling of the joy of life."

4

SHRINKING THE UNIVERSE

ON THE PSYCHOLOGY OF BEING E.T.

I really knew when I first talked with them, that this was something that I could not explain psychiatrically. It didn't sound like it behaved like anything that had a psychiatric origin. It behaved like a trauma.[1]
—JOHN MACK, M.D.

THE OFFICIAL WORD

Strange to say, but coming from another planet can actually solve more problems than it creates—unless, of course, we peer at the world through the narrow lens of the conventional view. Then, the mere announcement of E.T. identity is seen, in itself, as evidence of psychological difficulty and emotional distress—to say the least.

It's something like: *I'm OK, you're E.T.*

[1]quoted in the *New York Times Magazine*, March 20, 1994, on why he believes that the stories told to him by several UFO abductees are neither hallucinations nor delusions.

The claim *I'm an extraterrestrial,* stated with a straight face, is usually taken to be so far-out, wild, and beyond the bounds of "reality" that it's obviously the declaration of a disturbed mind. Again, that's the outlook of the dominant culture.

For that reason, the surprising announcement by Dr. John Mack, quoted above, was almost immediately treated by conventional institutions as outlandish and shocking. In its wake, a scornful uproar was heard from the screens of media to the halls of academe—attacking not only the content, but the source, as well.

A Pulitzer-Prize-winning biographer, John Mack is a Harvard psychiatrist and a trained Freudian psychoanalyst—in other words, a highly accomplished and respected member of the mainstream academy. He's a valued participant in the established social sciences, which is the segment of our culture most often asked to make worldly, the otherworldly phenomena of UFO experiences—or, for our purposes, claims of extraterrestrial identity. In short, Mack isn't someone who's supposed to believe that extraterrestrials are actually abducting citizens.

So, it's with this mainstream viewpoint that I'd like to begin our discussion of E.T. psychology.

As Dr. Mack prepared to publish his book *Abduction*—in which he states his belief that some UFO abduction experiences have actually taken place—the powers that be were already reacting with a "generous" spectrum of opinion. Any critique was welcome . . . just so long as it didn't venture too far from patronizing concern, ridicule, or outrage. Quoted by writer Stephen Rae in the same *New York Times Magazine* article mentioned above, the acting chairwoman of the Harvard psychiatry department, Mack's boss, responded, "Nobody believes it. I wish he were doing something else. This is so off-base."

Out of respect for the freedom of inquiry, the university did not halt Mack's research, but the *Times Magazine* article humorously depicted Mack's superior as someone who would rather swallow broken glass than talk publicly about a colleague who believes that UFOs and E.T.s actually exist.

All of which is understandable, perhaps.

In that same article, noted scientist Carl Sagan offered the view that vivid UFO and E.T. experiences might possibly be attributed to hallucinations, scientifically explainable actions of the human mind. Both in the *Times Magazine* and in *Parade Magazine,* Sagan was quoted as suggesting that, "Hallucinations are common and may occur to perfectly normal people under ordinary circumstances." These visions, he wrote, are sometimes the result of a rare condition called sleep paralysis, which affects about 8 percent of the population.

Sleep paralysis, in fact, is one of the most often cited possible "causes" for E.T. and UFO experiences . . . at least, by the mainstream academic and scientific community.

For the 8 percent who suffer from sleep paralysis, the hypnagogic state, that hazy, floating period between sleep and wakefulness, can bring on a terrifying break from everyday life. The victim may lie in bed literally unable to move while the brain struggles to operate on a depleted oxygen supply. Frightening hallucinations may follow along with a feeling of sexual stimulation or the sense that some odd, supernatural presence is hovering nearby.

Some of these hallucinations, for some people, involve seeming experiences of UFO abduction. These can include delusions of medical experimentation, with E.T.s implanting some type of technological device in the human's body or, in some cases, visions that sound closer to religious revelations.

Many mainstream authorities cite sleep paralysis as the real generator of all UFO experience, while others add such possibilities as psychotic episodes, experiences induced by the use of hallucinogenic drugs, the occurrence of drug "flashbacks," ordinary dreams, nightmares, and other happenings that take place in everyday reality. Total that up, and you're left with an impressive list of believable explanations. All of these can also be, and have been, utilized as "explanations" for what's *actually* going on, not only when someone encounters a UFO, but when someone claims to be one of *Them*, taking E.T. identity for himself.

So, at this fairly simple edge of psychology, E.T. contact or identity gets pinned on something akin to a spontaneous biochemical hallucination or delusion, or a fantasy caused by use of an external agent—drugs being the usual culprit. But we don't want to leave it there. I think we should venture a little farther into this conventional, acceptable world and talk a little more about the deeper psychological explanations for E.T. experience. The best place to begin would be with the views expressed by C. G. Jung.

Jung, the great Swiss psychologist, believed that visions of "flying saucers" (in the quaint terms of the late 1940s) were a projection of the collective unconscious. He wrote about them as a symbol of wholeness. Images of UFOs, Jung believed, could be traced back to an attempt by the collective psyche to heal the split that is so prevalent in our shattered times. Some creative UFO researchers have even reasoned that the physical scarring common to abductees is really a product of "leakage" from the collective unconscious. The line between imagination, symbolism, and physical fact becomes most blurry here. . . .

So, on to the Freudian view. . .

This includes the belief by some mainstream psychologists that E.T. or UFO experience is a comforting balm, a way for the mind to cope with certain devastating psychological wounds. Here, we often find mention of childhood incest trauma, and the thinking that E.T. identity or UFO abduction may be the way these victims of sexual abuse psychologically defend the mind against pain. Abductees, then, would be incest victims revisiting earlier trauma through fantastic and possibly ego-gratifying hallucinations. They create a "fantasy" that both expresses the crime and defends from the assault. The crime is communicated in a veiled form (using something like false "memories" of E.T. sexual probes, etc.) while the images of extraterrestrials might also represent feelings of rage—

and possibly, desire—that are too painful to be admitted to consciousness. Not only that, but the E.T. images would be "impossible" stand-ins for the real perpetrators, most likely the mother or father. These images are then projected outward, placed about as far away from the sufferer as possible—in outer space.

Here's another example of mainstream psychological opinion, this one found in a nicely reasoned 1983 article from the *Psychoanalytic Review* (volume 70, number 2) entitled, "*E.T.*: An Odyssey of Loss." This piece, written by Jeffrey L. Dezner, a UCLA psychiatrist, views the Spielberg film *E.T.* through the lens of fairly straightforward psychoanalytic thought, describing it as a "dramatic metaphor about the loss of a parent by a latency-age child."

Remember, though, our study here is not so much concerned with Earthlings who have contact with E.T.s, but with humans who, themselves, believe *they are E.T.s*. There's a big difference, obviously, but the article does shed light on some mainstream thinking; in Dr. Dezner's description of what the E.T. character represents, for instance.

The film version of *E.T.*, Dezner writes, is the story of a young boy, the main character, Elliot, who's struggling to cope with his father's abandonment and absence. He does this through the process symbolized by the character E.T.: a cinematic vision of the "inner child," of fantasized omnipotence, magical thinking, and imagined magical powers. If we choose to see the film in the manner Dr. Dezner suggests, then the character E.T. becomes, as Dezner writes, an image that shows "we all have within us things we felt were lost and given up for dead." E.T. identity might then be considered a healing cover-up for the painful loss of a significant other—be it parent or spouse—and helps the person overcome disappointment and regain a sense of self-importance.

That's why, in one of the final scenes of the film, as E.T. gets set to depart, he points to Elliot's forehead and assures him he will always be there (in the mind)—an action that grants Elliot permission to hold onto the vivid, fluid imagination of childhood without denying the tragedies of the real world.

Standard psychoanalytic thought also includes many ideas concerning a male child's unconscious envy of his father, and a resulting unconscious death wish against the male parent as the child contests for the mother. Here, the abandonment, or death, of the father might stir up all kinds of troubling, or actually unbearable, reactions in the child: a guilty, ecstatic happiness; sadistic glee; feelings of omnipotence. These murderous feelings—imagined to be successful in this case—would be quite terrifying for a child. To deal with them, he would create an alternate identity—becoming an E.T., perhaps—and so be able to deny what was deepest in his heart.

Still in the vast area of mainstream psychology, we could explain E.T. phenomena by saying it represents a "denial of death"; that the insistence on past lives and future soul transfer speaks to the fundamental human desire to remain vertical to the Earth. This "death terror" is considered by some to be universally present in all humanity. There are several authors who've explained every aspect of human culture in these terms.

And there is yet another view: religious conversion. In my own research, I've noticed many similarities between a person's awakening to off-planet origins and to what I would call "the phenomenology of religious conversion." Both experiences can suddenly explode the safety of a comfortable everyday life, they can forever change the way you view the world. In the aftermath, the personality has to be completely rebuilt. There are some striking similarities in the step-by-step process, but a major difference, I think, is that the E.T. awakening is nondenominational and usually brings the new or unveiled E.T. soul toward some form of service, dedicated to the evolution of the planet. And unlike many religious converts, our Wanderers and Walk-ins generally didn't ask for permission to be of service; most of them shunned worldly clerical authority, official institutions, and were not interested in marching

59

to a standard set of beliefs. Also remember, that there are major differences in the awakenings of Wanderers and Walk-ins.

Finally, I want to mention the view of those in the sciences who believe that extraterrestrial life is a reality, but still deny that E.T.s are here on Earth among us, right now. I'll summarize this outlook with remarks made by Frank Drake, a professor of astronomy and astrophysics at the University of California, Santa Cruz. Quoted in *USA Today* (December 16, 1993) Drake said that

> The evidence supports the idea that there are almost countless systems of living things in the universe. There are perhaps tens of thousands of civilizations in our galaxy and even more abodes of more primitive life.

He went on to say,

> Everything we know about the formation and the evolution of the solar system, planets, and of life on Earth, says that the whole sequence of events was the result of completely normal and, in fact, inevitable processes. So what happened in our solar system and on Earth should have happened in many, many places.

So, it sounds reasonable. But E.T. life here on Earth? Doubtful, says Drake, who expands upon this skeptical view by saying that other civilizations would have to be thousands of light years away from us. He takes this to mean that deliberate travel between worlds would be highly implausible. He assumes no other means of transport than those currently understood by our human scientists on Earth.

But among these "countless systems of living things" or in one of these "tens of thousands of civilizations," isn't it more plausible that there would be modes of intergalactic travel that we haven't begun to dream about? It seems naive for us to assume that planetary races far in advance of our own don't have technologies that are equally advanced. A quick peek at planet Earth would be enough to convince anyone that we're probably not the most evolved race in the universe. It could be, for instance, that what we on Earth call "powers of mind" and toss away in the heap marked "occult" might have been developed over *millions of years* by more advanced civilizations. Their abilities would be tremendous. And, of course, keep in mind that our understanding of the laws of physics might not be the zenith of all possible knowledge. ...

Well, if you've come this far with me, you've been on a quick and easy tour of some of the more conventional opinions heard from mainstream experts to explain why someone would say: *I'm an extraterrestrial.* I wanted to put these views forward in a respectful way because I believe it's best to consider all perspectives, get as much information as possible, and then draw conclusions. Possibly, you're satisfied with one particular school of thought explaining how non-E.T.s see this strange phenomenon. If so, you might want to read on so you can find out more about how the other side thinks.

And then again, you might not be satisfied. You might even find you agree with one or more of the conventional explanations, but still feel a nagging doubt, as if you know there's something more. Maybe the expert opinions don't fit your own experience.

In which case, you may be approaching that other reality ... and you may be edging toward understanding something more about what it's like to hail From Elsewhere.

In the Beginning

Now, after examining a selection of the standard psychological explanations for E.T. identity, let's pose a question: What if they're wrong?

Or, better yet: What if they're right, but they don't go far enough? What if the opinions of conventional science are fine, and sometimes hit the mark, but they're limited by the very point at which they start out: the idea that our universe—perceived physically, through the senses—is the only reality there is?

And it's also important to remember this: All experience that can be called nonordinary is beyond the constrictions of either/or. This includes claims of being an E.T. soul. The possibilities of a metaphysical reality are not necessarily destroyed just because you get a good fit with a psychological explanation. In many cases we can see that both worlds exist simultaneously. Even if those who say they are E.T. souls have suffered emotional scars here on Earth, that doesn't eliminate their potential reality, a reality that Earth has yet to understand. The emotional, the intellectual, and the metaphysical are simply different frequencies of human experience—at the level of "soul" or "spirit." Because something is a fact at one level doesn't negate the existence at other levels. Once an E.T. soul becomes incarnated here on Earth, he or she participates in the life of the planet, and confusion or trauma is a common result . . . for E.T.s and Earthlings, alike.

Let's take an example from mainstream psychology: the analysis that describes E.T. identity as a child's way of dealing with the loss of a parent.

With compassion, we can say that this kind of healing fantasy is one of the saving graces of the human mind, but we might also remind ourselves that the extraordinary claim of being a Walk-in or a Wanderer is not found in all adults who've suffered such a tragedy as children.

It's not too wild to say that for some children, Earthly loss stirs up a deeply buried memory of a more distant, perhaps more painful separation. Following this line of reasoning, a particular event— sad and troubling on planet Earth—might function something like a "screen memory," or a "false" recollection that protects the mind from another, more frightening and deeply hidden emotion. If that is what's happening, then the loss of a parent on Earth would be painful not only because of its ordinary, here-and-now implications, but because it would pack an additional charge: It would stir up the terrible pain of losing the off-planet family and the original home-planet group. This kind of "reverse psychologizing" should not be too readily dismissed.

These are certainly possibilities to consider as we listen to the words of the E.T.s in our study. And keep in mind that conventional explanations are not the end of the journey, but possibly the very start. As explained here in an excerpt from *The UFO-nauts*, by Hans Holzer:

> For we must never forget that we are neither at the pinnacle of scientific discovery, nor at the end of the road leading toward a better understanding of the universe—for all we know, we may be at the very beginning, certainly no further along the way than the middle, at best. It is one of the fallacies of modern science to think of itself as having reached great heights beyond which lies little that is new. The opposite is true, and in the course of future discoveries many previously held ideas concerning the nature of the universe will have to fall by the wayside.

Again, the realization of E.T. identity doesn't necessarily cancel out any mainstream position. I'll be the first to acknowledge that there are E.T.s who, as human beings living on Earth, have Earthly psychological problems. There are also frauds, flakes, and crack-pots who claim to be extraterrestrial and fit quite nicely into the categories of conventional psychopathology.

And beyond the reality of psychological confusion, there are numerous groups making all kinds of unorthodox claims. We can find people speaking the deranged ramblings of drunks and drug addicts—with flying pink elephants, crawling spiders, and remote invisible spy cameras. We can read about the religious visions of mystics from all cultures—visions of legions of angels, radiant Buddhas, and dancing fairies. And closer to home, we have the garden variety TV preachers, Sunday school teachers, and aged respected rabbis telling us in all sincerity of the parting of the Red Sea, the evil doings of Satan's hordes, and the miraculous virgin birth of

Lord Jesus, the only Son of God. Some of these "radical" claims are even considered indisputable facts.

Maybe it seems strange, but all these beliefs can be traced back to a similar psychology and an underlying assumption—which we've referred to as subjective knowing (discussed at length in chapter 3). Every one of these beliefs takes subjective knowing as a valid means of understanding our experience. It will not comfort rabbis, priests, and gurus to be told that they share so much with drunks, drug addicts, or the Walk-ins and Wanderers who are none too far away. . . .

Many people will argue that there's no comparison between the idea, say, of Jesus' miraculous birth (which is written in the Bible, our most revered book) and the weird hallucinations induced by drugs. But in terms of being verified, there's no difference at all. Both visions and ideas are accepted through faith and proven by self-confirmation. Some hard-boiled scientists refuse to accept *any* cultural beliefs that aren't proven by empirical, demonstrable, hypothesis-testing experiments. Yet, most of what humans believe to be true comes from nothing more than a blend of objective experience, personal psychology, and psychospiritual factors—through the process, again, of subjective knowing. Once we level the playing field in this way, we can be a bit more broad-minded when we think about those who say they're E.T.s.

What I found in my research was this: The recognition and integration of E.T. identity brought on a positive psychological change in almost every person I interviewed.

Let me give you some examples.

The E.T. I've called Peter—he's the professional architect who found relief from years of depression after witnessing a "ball of light," and who, for a long time, had suffered from other serious mental trauma. After a series of UFO visitations, Peter told me that his personality was so much better developed that today he is "articulate and smooth," comfortable with people, committed to self-improvement, and doesn't waste time: "I don't do things if I'm not going to learn something."

Another example comes from a woman named Erika. She's now "more cooperative and less bossy, learning to listen and to help others listen." Bob, who suffered so with his drug problem, found he has an easier time "being truthful" and understanding others. Finally, there's Lisanne, who has conducted workshops for dozens of emerging E.T.s. She says: "Many [Wanderers and Walk-ins] are more successful in business and in their professional lives [after awakening] as they realize their information-accessing potentials"— the inner guidance we've spoken about elsewhere under the label subjective knowing. Ironically, it's the belief in being From Elsewhere that seems to make these people of greater use to the society that spurns them, and gives them much greater skill to engage with others in constructive, cooperative ways.

BEING DIFFERENT

Do E.T.s ever lose that core sense of feeling like strangers?

For Wanderers—who've worked through the pains of a lifetime of feeling different—despair often turns to strength with the realization that their deep feelings of alienation have a very logical cause: *They are aliens.*

Once this off-planet, transcendental personality is well integrated, Wanderers usually sense that many of their difficulties have been explained and they actually do become more balanced.

For Walk-ins, though, the journey can be a little more difficult. Surprise is important here. Walk-ins are almost always stunned by the abrupt psychological changes they experience, as well as by shocking events of obvious spirituality. Ultimately, they come to understand this as the first influx of a new E.T. soul or an aspect of Higher Self—and they make their lives over, framing those lives with interplanetary knowledge.

What leads up to the recognition of E.T. soul is also different for Wanderers and Walk-ins. A chronic loneliness from childhood on—that is the story most often told by Wanderers. They weren't necessarily involved in obviously troubled relationships, while for Walk-ins it was just the opposite. Walk-ins were almost always in the thick of dysfunctional families, poor relationships, or some severe psychological conflict before they accepted themselves as E.T. souls ... and then, this extraordinary event revolutionized their lives. Their emotional struggles settled, and generally they showed new health, vigor, and self-esteem. That was true even though their identities were a little less stable than those of Wanderers.

When this new E.T. identity was integrated—which was no easy task—almost all of the E.T.s I interviewed then moved on to the question of meaning. They had to redefine their lives. This was usually worked out in terms of world service, giving themselves socially, but with a global understanding. I heard many, many stories of the cycle, which ran from the pains of psychological struggle to spiritual transformation to a complete readjustment and, finally, to what seemed, literally, a "new burst of life."

Still, there always seemed to remain a shadow of alienation, a belief that, as E.T.s, they were essentially different from all others. There is profound differentness at the core of their being, I think, and it marks off Wanderers and Walk-ins as unique, even from any other groups pushed to the fringe of mainstream society. All of these groups may feel in some way out of the ordinary, but E.T.s occupy an isolated position even within the New Age population. It's been my experience that they're often misunderstood, and sometimes shunned, by the crystal and pyramid faddists, as well as by many UFO researchers. And E.T.s must eventually face the fact that they stand alone, not only from the New Age, but from any age— excluded also by the more traditional religious groups, even those usually thought of as esoteric or mystical.

So, this sense of differentness, in the E.T. population, blends with some "psychological styles" and beliefs that I think contribute to a truly singular view. Unique to E.T.s:

- a path of development that eventually puts global or universal viewpoints at the center of their lives;

- a deeply held, working vision of all people as metaphysical, spiritual beings;

- a belief in cosmic unity that, ironically, means that while feeling forever different from others around them, they actually don't make much out of the duality *E.T. versus Earthling;*

- ideas and perceptions that are always nestled within the enormous dynamics of cosmic time-space evolution;

- an affinity or identity with beings on other planes and planets, mostly nonphysical, and rarely confined to UFOs;

- and, of course, a feeling that their primary experience of life is existence as a nonphysical soul that originated on another planet or in another realm.

Because they believe themselves to be here on Earth "on assignment," here to fulfill a definite mission, the E.T.s are very much like workers on contract in a foreign culture. *From Elsewhere,* far from home and true community, often lonely and solitary, they are like the homeless wanderers in Asian folktales. This pervades every part of their lives and their psychological style. Within their strange and unique set of beliefs, however, E.T.s manage to experience an abundance of such ordinary feelings as joy, sorrow, discouragement, and hope.

NAIVE TO SELF

Looking at the shape of an individual life often gives us a better sense of this psychological wholeness.

In the story of Vikram we have an example of somebody who

has integrated his extraterrestrial identity and seems comfortable and relaxed in that experience.

Vikram is a man of medium build in his late thirties. He has dark black hair and mature, thoughtful features. He grew up in suburban New York and has worked as a housepainter, advertising salesman, and screenwriter. In 1982 Vikram attended a channeling session, and it was there that he had his first experience of his own extraterrestrial identity. For more than ten years now, he's identified himself, *to himself,* as a Wanderer.

Psychologically, Vikram says, before his recognition of being an E.T. soul, "I was naive to self, I didn't know myself that well."

But that knowledge didn't emerge until many years of misunderstood E.T. experience, especially events that were buried in childhood. It was around the age of twelve, Vikram told me, that something happened to him that was so vivid it later changed his entire life—but only after he was able to make it a part of himself. One summer evening, while playing outside on the sidewalks of his Long Island neighborhood, Vikram, for the first time, saw a UFO.

There he was with a group of friends, all on bicycles, just talking and hanging out on the streetcorner, when suddenly a tremendously bright, white light rose up from the other side of a clump of trees. Everyone in the group saw it. Everyone but Vikram and one other friend shrieked and ran away. The light moved "at a blinding rate of speed, completely silently," he said, and the two preteens on bicycles were no match for the streak of light. It was so brilliant that it was difficult to look at, but Vikram remembered taking a dare and staring into the light so that he could see that it emanated from a fascinating elliptical shape, a UFO. He was elated. Chasing the craft with a feeling of intense excitement, there was no way in this world (or any other) that Vikram and his friend were going to catch it.

Twelve years later, over drinks at a New Year's Eve party, Vikram met a woman who had grown up in the same suburb but on the other side of town. Very openly, she began speaking about the things that honestly interested her: the spiritual, the metaphysical, and the reality of UFOs. Why did she believe that E.T.s were visiting Earth? Because, she went on, about twelve years before, back in their hometown, she had actually seen one—and when she described it, Vikram and this young woman both realized it was the same ship that Vikram had witnessed with his friends, only the woman had spotted the craft from another point of view.

"That meeting was a very validating thing," Vikram said, "and I still get goosebumps remembering it. Something out of the ordinary; and for her, it was a life-changing event also."

But, seeing something zooming around from outer space is very different from thinking *you come from outer space.*

Vikram's later realization of his E.T. identity was the result of several channeling sessions in California that left him comforted and accepting of himself. The feeling, he says, was astonishingly deep. He went to these sessions to help piece together jagged shards of experience that started in childhood, and there was no other way he could complete the puzzle. It was the first channeling event he'd ever gone to, but he described the people who'd brought him to the event, and those who were attending, as "supportive and incredibly loving," and he felt more comfortable than he had in years.

At that first session the entities Ashtar and Hilarion, both considered distinctive teachers, often related to other UFO/E.T. groups, were channeled.

"In short order," Vikram said, "psychological work that I'd done, this sort of gap in me that I'd felt my whole life . . . kind of an empty feeling, a constant feeling of being a loner and outsider . . . it all synthesized in a very remarkable way. I began to have a sense that I really might not have birthed here."

This was in 1982, and Vikram says that for the rest of that decade such feelings grew more powerful and he became more certain of their validity.

"Everything that ensued after that first contact," he told me, "led me to believe that not only was I not from this planet in terms of my soul origin, but that I had extremely strong connections with an intergalactic consciousness which came to me as something known as the Galactic Brotherhood of Light."

Belief in a specific intergalactic group varies with the individual Walk-in or Wanderer—and by no means do all of them claim to have these affiliations. In Vikram's case, the growth of his identity from lone extraterrestrial on Earth to member of a brotherhood, came about after numerous channeling sessions. It was a kind of "knowingness," he said, and continued

> The information that was coming through the channel just made some kind of amazing sense, and as I fell into it, it was almost like a feeling of coming home. Something so intimately familiar about the energy, the lack of ego—amazingly profound! There was no payoff anywhere, not from identifying with a larger group, no large amounts of money were changing hands, nothing like a cult. I was just very clearly comforted by the information from the channel.

Belief that he was part of an intergalactic brotherhood became a main feature of Vikram's view of himself. He told me during our interview that as recently as one week before our meeting he'd had "specific contact with an aspect of myself that I believe to be a lightship commander."

It should be understood, however, that while Vikram is confident his deeper E.T. roots are grounded in this "brotherhood," the explanation of his involvement is somewhat hazy, even to himself. And he'll be the first to admit it.

Vikram says his initial sense of being part of the Ashtar Command was later validated by a channeler who indicated her own feeling that he was, actually, still important to the work of the command, despite his confusion.

Five or six years later, Vikram told me, he became "intimately involved" with another woman who did channeling, and they attended a large formal channeling event at which there was an invocation to a group called, the Council of Twelve. Vikram had no idea what they were talking about—and it didn't matter. During this session, he says, he went into "a very profound altered state," and it was in this other realm of consciousness that he received information saying that he was actually a representative of the Council of Twelve, related directly to the Ashtar Command.

But there was more. Vikram told me that this "profound altered state was like an energy entered my chest and held me back on a couch for about an hour and a half." He called this, "the most incredibly intense experience" of physical energy he'd ever had.

> I had kundalini rising up my spine, and a really profound, expanded state of awareness . . . and a very definite sense of this being not only friendly contact but actually very welcomed reassurance of this long-standing affiliation with the very same entities being channeled. It wasn't some errant energy, *it was as though my family had come to visit as a way of quickening my energy.* [italics added.]

After this experience, he said calmly, "things shifted."

> I basically found myself prone to moving into a consciousness that was new to me. Areas were penetrable that were new to me in the sense of being able to have a cosmic awareness that I'd never ever really personally had any real experience of . . . as though my reality were literally changing. . . . I had conscious contact with vibrations of what I would have to say were very different entities, including my own highest awareness, my own highest self.

There were repeated energy shifts in his body, Vikram said. If you were standing beside him, this is what it would have looked like:

"I would basically snap back, have my head snap back rapidly as though an energy were either entering or exiting with a tremendous amount of force. Sometimes it would be almost painful because it would be so intense."

Nothing like this had ever happened to Vikram before. The channeling sessions, however, had changed all that. They'd brought on the dawning awareness of his extraterrestrial soul. When it was over, he was left with a very new and different way of seeing the world.

And the "weirdest" part of it was that it didn't seem "weird" at all. Vikram told me he wasn't frightened and never had any sense that he was being controlled or violated. It was more like the return of something vaguely familiar, a resurrection; his Total Self was coming back to life.

As he now says: "I believe that there are beneficent as well as negative E.T. influences on this planet." Today his life is built on the belief that his own soul origin is not of Earth. If someone doesn't accept his beliefs, Vikram feels it would be very difficult to enter any kind of close friendship. The other person, he says, would have to be able to set aside his or her own beliefs, at least for the moment, to tolerate Vikram's "far out" ideas.

There are mainstream psychologists who would take the mere fact of these remarks as a sign of emotional distress, but Vikram showed no evidence of such trouble. Indeed, he seemed happy with himself, busy with his own interests, and working at what he believed were important contributions to help people expand their awareness.

THE ELOHIM OF PEACE

I'm not sure exactly how to introduce you to Tomas—close disciple of Christ (Sananda), follower of Maitreya (World Savior), and dubbed by others, he said, the Elohim of Peace.

These would be rather large claims to make even if they were coming from some world-renowned leader with a massive barrel chest and great booming voice. But when, in fact, they come from somebody who's shy, softspoken, and without many friends; who's chosen an extremely hermetic lifestyle with almost no social contact; then we might really ask some questions. And it's his beliefs, Tomas said, that make being with others almost impossible. He feels that no one would truly accept him. Over a period of six years,

Tomas told me, he was in the company of friends only about a dozen times, spoke English to others for only about twenty hours, and was not involved in any intimate relationships.

Maybe some background information is handy here. . . .

Tomas is a short, wiry man in his mid-twenties with dark features and a light foreign lilt to his speech, a souvenir of his native Eastern Europe. He speaks in a voice that often seems to be emanating from some other zone of reality. A university student of literature in his homeland, he was working on a book at the time of our interview, but was making a living doing contracting and repair work.

I've juxtaposed the story of Tomas alongside that of Vikram not because Tomas was showing any overtly psychotic behavior, but because, as opposed to Vikram, his realization of E.T. identity—and much more than that—seems to have driven him psychologically inward to an unusual degree. Some of this, I think, is due to his age: Tomas's E.T. soul has been on Earth a shorter period of time than some of the others I studied. Because of this, and because of his intense spiritual commitment, many of his bridges to "other worlds" are still very strong. He's more dislocated. Obviously, Tomas has more than a few psychological knots to untangle.

Even so, whereas Vikram seemed to be a more mature E.T. soul as well as a more mature man in Earth terms—entering into relationships, holding down a job, taking up some of the guise of a "regular guy"—Tomas still burns with a passion for the Spirit, for enlightenment, for the beatific touch of the Higher Self, for nothing less than sainthood. Monklike, almost ascetic, he's sacrificed one entire part of his life to concentrate on another.

Tomas's story also illustrates one of the main psychological conditions of E.T. life: the fear of rejection. It's not a simple concern. For most of those with E.T. roots, this fear of rejection is made even stronger by fears of never being fully understood. Most Walk-ins and Wanderers keep quiet at first about their metaphysical notions, their spiritual experiences, and their off-planet identities. Then, slowly, and selectively, they learn to share them—Vikram is a good example. At this point, they're able to integrate their extraterrestrial selves and benefit from their new ideas, sometimes helped along by small islands of support. Still, they often feel surrounded by a lack of understanding and continue to face a painful social isolation.

Tomas, of course, was isolated to an enormous degree.

As a Wanderer, he always felt drawn to the cosmos and the universe, topics he found far more interesting than anything else. Astronomy was his great love, but not sci-fi—he emphasized that he was interested only in factual, serious works. This was in Eastern Europe, where his interest in the heavens was so great that by age twelve he'd almost completely stopped seeing people so he'd have more time to study. When I asked Tomas if he'd combined this reading with any religious studies he said he had not. He was given no religious training in a homeland then under Communist rule, and he had been (in his words) "raised up free of that whole nonsense."

All of which later led him to an interest in Asian philosophy and then to the bizarre experience that was to entirely change his view of the world.

One night as a teenager, Tomas awakened from a dream to see a strange golden circle in front of him. Tomas described this not as a vision. He said that when he opened his eyes he was not even in his room any longer, and that the golden light was simply an experience that was more real than any other experience he had ever had, including those of ordinary, waking reality.

"It had a tremendous potential of energy," he said, "and I was shocked. But it was too interesting to turn away."

After a while, the golden circle disappeared and in its wake came a period of total darkness, "just darkness without anything else in it, the ideal darkness." It was then that his sixth *chakra* (at the center of his forehead) "exploded with a bouquet of light beams" that he likened to the sights and sounds of a thunderstorm (Chakras are considered "energy centers" or vortices of non-physical force which are key to the process of spiritual unfoldment. The ancient

Hindus state there are seven such centers in the human body). His entire body filled with beams of light that shined from his fingers and toes, and, amazingly, he could view the inside of his own body as well as the outside.

Then the light faded. Tomas found himself returned to his room feeling that his previous sense of himself—mind, body, emotions, perceptions—had been burned away and he was now as much an infinite void as he was a human being. He was an infinity, a whole universe. He said it was difficult to describe these perceptions because the experience seemed to obliterate all dichotomies like inside-outside and me-not me. The room was filled with the smell of ozone, he said, like the aftermath of a summer thunderstorm.

This went beyond the typical E.T. experience and sounded to me like an actual taste of "cosmic consciousness," what the Hindus call the Supreme Godhead.

But the effect was less than one might expect.

Tomas was not driven to seek psychological or medical help and his day-to-day life remained fairly stable. However, from that night on, he lost interest in his daily, everyday reality because it now seemed so flat. He remained something of a hermit, took up the study of Zen, and soon left Eastern Europe for the United States.

Years later—about a year before our interview—Tomas said he'd had another "strange" experience. This time, it involved an occult group . . . and Maitreya, the future Buddha. The experience started with a dream in which, as he said, "two beggars approached me asking for some change." After a while, he gave them a few coins but when he touched the hand of one beggar, Tomas says the entire scene switched around so that it was nothing but a black screen on which there appeared the words SECOND COMING.

This woke him up. Tomas peered around his bedroom until suddenly he realized that someone was hovering above him, "someone that I seemed to know." Even so, he still felt a strange lack of attachment. That ended when the Being actually entered Tomas's body. It put its hands on the back of Tomas's head, "seemingly working on my brain," he said, using such extreme psychic pressure that he feared he might pass out. The Being seemed to control him. But just as Tomas felt pushed to his limit, the Being took off, disappeared. Tomas was left alone once again.

There were some other, similar experiences after that, and they led Tomas to believe that he was dealing with Maitreya the World Savior. Now, Tomas entered what he called "a very intense seeking" of his identity. He investigated past lives, took part in channeling, talked to spirit guides, participated in readings at the Berkeley (California) Psychic Institute, and spoke with other psychics. During this period, Tomas says, he went through another kind of reality that he could barely describe—like a dream but not a dream—in which he was "healed" by extraterrestrials.

Tomas's final sense of identity was settled in a way that is unnecessary for most other Walk-ins and Wanderers. Specifically, he needed to be "told by others" exactly who he was. He couldn't validate his own identity. And if his ideas seem a little difficult to fathom, Tomas had more to tell me. He said that "while many of my past lives were lived on other planets" his ultimate identity "is even more strange."

At this point in the interview, I was ready for anything.

"This comes not from my own experiences," he explained, "but from what I've been told by other people."

"Okay," I said. "Go on."

Tomas talked about how he'd been given this information by an occult master in Oakland, California. It was there that he was told that he, too, was a master: an Elohim of Peace, on the same level as the Cosmic Christ. This would not be much different than, say, being on the same plane as Buddha, or the Universally Awakened One.

As an Elohim, Tomas said, he was one of the seven logoi of the solar system (the seven central Beings of our system), one of only two or three people who'd ever achieved this level. These few individuals, it's believed, will be the primary ones assisting the Maitreya in the salvation of planet Earth.

"My whole sense of myself can be very strange at times," said Tomas, which I regarded as something of an understatement. "It is as if the Whole is being expressed through me." When I played the role of naive interviewer and asked him to say more about his idea of the Whole, Tomas refused with a firmness I hadn't heard in his voice before. He said we would just have to let it go at that.

This was fine with me, since his beliefs seemed to border on the grandiose, to say the least. Nevertheless, I enjoyed speaking with him. Despite the sometimes odd and grand nature of his claims, Tomas is likeable and friendly. While his ideas may be a bit inflated, his personal experiences were, no doubt, profound if not ecstatic.

And in the area of wider identity, Tomas spoke with great confidence, without doubts, aware that words, names, and labels are a blind guide to the greater realities of the universe.

To those who are skeptical, Tomas said: "Find out who you are."

To those who demanded proof of his, or even their own, identity, he said: "Proof is not the point, there *is* another way of knowing."

And for all the odd imagery of his story and the solitude in which he wraps himself like a cape, Tomas expressed a contentment that I've rarely encountered among the more skeptical Earthbound souls who shun any notion that our world may be different than it seems.

"The universe provides good ways for everything," said my unusual friend toward the end of our interview. "It's just a matter of finding those ways."

It seemed clear to me that Tomas had hit upon at least a few of the more remarkable ways.

5

LOVE AND INTIMACY

WHAT WE DO WHEN . . . WE ARE NOT ALONE . . .

The language of love is the language of the cosmos; and here on Earth, when we want to wax poetic or sing about love and intimacy, we often turn to phrases concerning the heavens, the moon, and the stars.

Even so, this chapter was by far the most difficult one for me to write.

That's because the question of intimacy brings us to the very crux of E.T. alienation, directly to the core of the extraterrestrial dilemma: a loss of love.

We're speaking here not only about love in the Earthly romantic sense, but about the sorrow that's suffered when one is bereft of the all-embracing love and joy of the home planet. The Wanderer or Walk-in here on Earth has actually gone through a double loss— *the break with his or her extraterrestrial group, and the alienation from his or her E.T. self.* We might say that, in this sense, we're talking about *E.T. orphans*. They come From Elsewhere and are never quite able to escape their loneliness or their desire to recapture that sweet feeling of fusion with the group, to return to an absolute sense of completion, or to regain their native spiritual awareness. All this, they believe, is their birthright.

Not only that, but if they attempt to end the heartache by coupling with a partner on Earth, the relationship can reignite these homeplanet memories, causing even more pain.

It's possible, of course, to interpret these feelings in terms of common Earth psychology—and there are many people who would be satisfied with such an explanation. They might even be helped to lead fuller and happier lives.

But we're concerned with the others, the people who aren't comfortable with the "common wisdom," who feel that their own experience isn't mirrored in those psychological terms. Our attention here is reserved for people who feel that, no matter what the Earthbound explanation, *something remains unanswered;* the people who believe they're here to assist in the work of evolution and that evolution is about *increasing love, expressing more openness and understanding.* Perhaps I mean the sleeping Wanderers who wish to awaken. . . .

For anyone who seriously comes to believe they've uncovered an extraterrestrial self or soul—anyone who's living a life based on the belief that he or she is From Elsewhere—sex and intimacy can mean difficulties that are truly from beyond.

During this part of my research I wasn't led to any "typical cases," because the effect of E.T. identity seemed to vary with each individual.

What I did encounter, however, were certain stories that I think might allow us to reach a better understanding of what it's like to have affairs of the heart when much of the world thinks you're out of your mind; stories that can highlight some of the major problems of how it feels to experience closeness here when you know you've come from very far away.

AM I A WALK-IN?

It is one of those sultry early August mornings in Palo Alto, California, when it seems that you're seeing everything for the first time.

The heat makes all color turn a soft pastel and there's still a slight blanket of mist in the air.

A woman I'll call Barbara is driving Route 280 North, heading to her job at one of the nation's most well-respected university hospitals. She's a registered nurse, an administrator with the epidemiology program, and she drives this route every morning in exactly the same way.

But this is not like every other morning, and Barbara is extremely preoccupied.

I'm doing all the right things, she says to herself. I'm married, we have financial security, a house, and two cars. So ... why am I so miserable?

As she watches the traffic, Barbara is thinking about how hard she's been pushing herself, spending long, tedious hours at a job that no longer suits her, where she's "making more and more money and getting less and less satisfaction." When she's not working at the hospital, she's the editor of a professional journal, and, as if that's not enough, she's also been going to school at night.

Added to all that, Barbara has been worrying about her marriage, and, as she drives to work this morning, she's pondering divorce. For some time now, she's been feeling that beneath the surface-level happiness, her relationship is not what it seems; that her husband of nearly twenty years has become a distant man with almost no connection to the heart, mind, or spirit. It seems as though they're doing all the right things, but only because they're sleepwalking.

This time of trouble has brought on some other problems. Barbara is concerned about her appearance and her physical health, and over the past several months her weight has climbed drastically to well over two hundred pounds. She knows she's living "too much in my head," as she puts it, and needs to "reclaim" her body. Recently, she's started seeing a bodyworker and a psychotherapist, and, as she heads for her job, she's thinking about that, too.

Suddenly, the morning's routine drive changes.

Up ahead, near the freeway's Page Mill exit, she sees two cars slam into one another and watches in horror as pieces of metal and a hubcap are tossed spinning high in the air.

The other cars, whipping along the freeway in the rush to get to work, begin slamming on their brakes and the morning quiet is torn apart with the scream of screeching tires, shrieking horns.

Barbara reacts, as well. She steps down hard on the brakes of her car—and almost as though she sees it happening to someone else, she feels the brakes lock.

"I don't know why I wasn't killed," Barbara said to me.

Her car spins out of control. Whirling around and around she finally ends up careening backward through the fast lane until she hits the center divider, which throws her back into traffic again, so that now she's sitting at the wheel face-to-face with oncoming cars.

Miraculously, she isn't hit.

"It was like someone had parted the cars," Barbara says, "and told them: *Make way, she's coming through!*"

She got away without a scratch, she told me, and didn't require a trip to the emergency room.

"A highway patrolman helped me get the car back in the right direction, and, basically, I continued on to work. Later, I learned that my axle was bent. But that was all."

Well, not quite.

When Barbara related this story to me, it was four years after the fact, but it was obvious from the tone of her voice and the frightened expression in her eyes, that the scene was still incredibly alive for her. As she described the accident to me, her face and voice radiated a new intensity—but an intensity without exaggeration. She wasn't trying to impress me. Barbara speaks with a measured confidence that sounds wonderfully connected to the words she's using.

In discussions of esoteric topics, I sometimes hear people who sound as if they lack faith in what they're saying, like they're trying to sell me something. Some of their claims seem patently grandiose, with a hidden need to prove their specialness (you'll hear some of those claims as we go through this book). But Barbara had none of those qualities. I was very comfortable to sit and listen to her unusual tales, and I distinctly felt that her stories were true.

Somehow, after witnessing the morning's crash on the freeway, she was actually able to get through the rest of her workday. Barbara returned home physically unharmed, but somehow she knew that this brush with disaster on a normal weekday morning had completely shattered her life.

For four days afterward, Barbara said, she could do nothing but lock herself in her room alone, sit on her bed and weep until she thought she couldn't weep anymore. After that, she would feel as though she was going numb, slipping into shock.

The close call had cut the last weak strands of her old way of living.

"It was a period of intense grieving," says Barbara. "A psychological death process. The realization that all the dreams, all the things that had led me up until that point in my life, weren't going to carry me into the future. I was just left wide open." She could only wonder: Now what?

There was no fast answer to that question. First there was a necessary period of mourning, and when that was accomplished, Barbara experienced what she describes as "almost a state of grace." Her days alone—grieving and weeping—brought on that calmness that the poet Emily Dickinson described so beautifully with the line, "After great pain, a formal feeling comes." It was a sensation of detachment that was paradoxically mixed with the beginnings of other, possibly higher, emotions: a rising sense of purpose in her life, a desire to be of greater service, a shift in awareness.

"I had absolutely no control over that car. Something greater than my personality was operating there in terms of getting away unscathed." Barbara felt as if she was being protected, invisibly guided to safety. She had never felt this way before. . . .

It's only now, years later, that she's able to explain exactly what happened. With the grieving over, she says, and the state of calm carrying her forward, it was clear to Barbara that her entire world was different. *She* was different, although she wasn't quite sure how. All she knew was that every relationship in her life was going to be altered in some way, and whatever unconscious deals and agreements she'd made with other people, whatever the secret dynamics, all bets were off. Those hidden deals were no longer functioning. It was as if her old, routine, habitual ways had all broken down.

"When I went out and talked with people after the accident or when I talked with my husband, it was very strange. Other people were dealing with me based on a history that I didn't feel I had any connection with any longer."

As if some other power were moving her, Barbara began to build a different life. She left her job. She and her husband began seeing a marriage counselor, and, after seventeen years together—a marriage that was childless because of the scars of Barbara's own difficult upbringing—she decided she wanted to get pregnant. A little more than a year after that terrifying morning on the freeway, Barbara gave birth to her first child, a daughter.

Things seemed to improve along with the many adjustments Barbara made, and she began to "settle down" a bit more.

There was just one problem.

Barbara wasn't Barbara.

She was not the human Barbara that family, friends and co-workers could talk to, say hello to, and identify from everyday life. She no longer felt like the person she had been before the near-death car accident.

It was only later, about a year after her daughter was born, that Barbara finally got an answer to her question: Now what?

One morning she awakened with the odd compulsion to sit down on the edge of her bed and just stare into the bedroom mirror. For a long time she sat there and studied her own reflection, and, as she did, Barbara began talking to herself in a voice that sounded almost like it was coming from some other part of her, a much wiser and more knowing part. She began asking herself over and over the question that had been at the edge of her awareness, but which was expressed in words that she had rarely used:

Am I a Walk-in?

The question shocked her. Barbara was a nurse with experience in bodywork and psychotherapy, and over the years she'd attended a number of classes in New Age, or spiritual, practices. The term *Walk-in* was certainly coming From Elsewhere, but not from nowhere. "This New Age stuff," as she sometimes called it, offered startling ideas for alternative medicine. Techniques to ease pain and to expand consciousness, that's what interested her: dream analysis, acupuncture, accessing, imaging, and meditation. In fact, her wish for a more focused and receptive way of life had led Barbara to begin meditating for ten minutes every morning.

So, although she'd heard the term *Walk-in* before, she'd never seriously considered that it might actually apply to her. She remembered the phrase from a videotape about E.T.s that she'd seen in a workshop, and from time to time it had been mentioned by some of her New Age friends. But, in the past, whenever Barbara was asked if she had a claim to extraterrestrial identity, her reply was a smile and a very definite: "Of course not! You must be joking!"

Now, however, she heard herself saying something quite different. She suddenly felt compelled to ask that strange, otherworldly question: *Am I really a Walk-in?*

Could it be true? The words set off a shock response, says Barbara, and there was an incredible rush of energy "as if some higher consciousness within me were replying." And suddenly, looking into the mirror at the reflection of her own eyes, she knew the answer: *Yes.*

It was as if something had dramatically fused a variety of troubling, unexplained experiences.

Barbara now rushed to consult the leaders of a New Age workshop with whom she'd become acquainted. She urgently needed to hear a more experienced opinion. When she told them of her discovery, they listened patiently and, without condemnation, talked with her . . . and agreed. Barbara was a Walk-in.

This experience, Barbara now believes, turned out to be the first of what were eventually three Walk-ins. But in extraterrestrial concerns as well as Earthly life, the old cliché holds true: The first one is always the hardest.

Leaving the home of her New Age friends, walking down the front path to her car, and now considering herself a Walk-in, Barbara says she had an overwhelming experience of integration: a rush, like all the pieces of her personality were in sync for the first time. This is what might be called a "crystallizing moment," and it's common for newly realized E.T.s.

And it was at that moment, in a wave of joy, that Barbara decided to "share this information" with her husband. She simply wanted to let him in on the most important realization she'd ever had.

From her description of a troubled marriage, I could almost guess what was coming.

Barbara confirmed it: "He totally freaked."

They were in a restaurant, in an intimate atmosphere, with low lighting and candles at every table; a setting Barbara chose carefully so the conversation could be considerate, even gentle. At what she deemed exactly the right point in their conversation, Barbara broke the news to her mate: *I'm an extraterrestrial.*

He couldn't believe what he was hearing.

"If you're an extraterrestrial," her husband said disdainfully after a long pause, "then turn that light on across the room . . . without getting up to walk over there."

Barbara attempted to explain: "It doesn't work that way. That's not what I'm here for."

Trying to make him see how serious she was, Barbara asked him to use her new E.T. name, which at that time was Alisa. His answer: "No way." He was not about to humor this craziness, even if it *was* his wife!

The man reacted, Barbara says, "just like he was afraid of me, very hostile, so full of anger, like when he looked at me he was seeing someone with antennae coming out of her head." She was shocked.

Before the conversation was finished, her husband turned red-faced and furious, stood up, and stormed out of the restaurant.

From that time on, says Barbara, even through the painful process of divorce, not only would her husband refuse to use her E.T. name, but he refused to call her by any name at all. It was his way of getting some small taste of revenge, and it didn't stop there.

On the rare occasions he spoke to Barbara, he wouldn't address her personally. He wrote her letters that arrived without any heading. If he deigned to use her name at all, it was on his child-support checks and there, it was Barbara's legal name; in fact, it's solely in financial matters, Barbara says, that she still allows herself to be addressed by a name that she feels is no longer valid for the person she's become.

Barbara's acceptance of E.T. identity touched off a climactic encounter in another relationship, as well: She decided she would no longer see her mother.

Barbara still carried the emotional scars of a painful, chaotic childhood. Her "birth mother," in Barbara's words, was a woman addicted to Valium, a woman who had attempted suicide several times and blamed Barbara for all these troubles. Barbara's father, who had died some years before, was an alcoholic who buried himself in his drinking and his work. And there is the possibility of incest, she says. Although it's a very painful subject, she's now in therapy to work through those possible traumas. Being a Walk-in, Barbara realizes, does not solve all problems or heal all wounds.

To help her organize these incredible events, Barbara sought out the opinion of a therapist who was familiar with the issues of E.T. identity, and particularly with the problems of Walk-ins. Beginning to untie these knots in therapy, Barbara's newly awakened E.T. self was finally able to decide she had no debt to pay and there was no reason to suffer through a "physical relation" with her mother—a relationship that was still abusive and unhealthy. Barbara could rely on herself to provide the support she had previously hoped to get from her parent.

This maternal relationship was ended with the kind of determination that Barbara had never been capable of before, and afterward Barbara had nothing to do with her mother for several years. (As of this writing, however, Barbara says she's undergone a third Walk-in, part of whose purpose is to heal that relationship. She's therefore reestablished contact with her mother and the two women are trying to come to terms with one another.) In fact, Barbara believes that each of her three Walk-in souls has had a particular role to play, particular issues to "work on and work out." The specific work of the third Walk-in was to heal her old family traumas.

All this brings us to Barbara's relationship with her daughter.

At the time of the divorce, Barbara's daughter was four years old and was soon sent off to live with Barbara's ex-husband. Her new personality still raw, Barbara was just learning to find her own way, and Barbara didn't feel ready to care for anyone but herself. In the swoon of her Walk-in "aliveness," she most definitely stated to her little girl: "You are *not* my daughter," which must have inflicted severe trauma.

That's one danger of realizing E.T. identity: emotional insensitivity. This degree of callousness is rare, I think, but many people I met did show a kind of coolness, the aloofness of those who feel themselves quite different from run-of-the-mill humanity. This may sometimes translate into a "superiority complex," but it's more often a kind of inwardness that goes beyond the mistaken duality of superior-inferior.

Two years later, Barbara's ex demanded that she take the little girl back. Barbara now says she's been forced to face the idea of becoming a caretaker and mother again—this time, alone. Finally, she's accepting it: Mother and daughter are slowly learning to live together and love one another and Barbara sees her nurturing of the child as a very important part of her life.

But most crucial, Barbara says, "is my relationship with myself. A whole different level of intelligence is operating in me now." Intimacy with oneself, of course, is the most challenging kind, as well as the basis for any other kind of relationship.

Barbara has learned to give herself room, although it's slow going, she told me. "I try to keep in mind that it's my life. And I'm still in transition." Most of the Walk-ins I met have become quite familiar with constant change—"mild upheaval at all times," as one of them said! It seems to be part of their nature. But, of course, it makes human intimacy much more difficult.

Barbara's story, though, can show us how one Walk-in devoted a great deal of time and effort to continually modifying her close relationships. As she came to better understand her E.T. identity she was able to work through the sense of being different—*inferior as well as superior!* That also made it possible for her to take better care of herself . . . and her intimate friends and family.

KEEPING COOL

I've gone into Barbara's story at some length, not because she's "typical," but rather because in living through so many extremes she illustrates a variety of E.T. experiences that we can understand more easily.

Still, it's important to remember: Most (but not all) E.T. marriages break up; some (but not all) who claim E.T. identity come from dysfunctional homes; and a few (but not too many) of those From Elsewhere claim to be incest victims. Not all Walk-ins and Wanderers feel it necessary to share and discuss their new identities with others, and very few have claimed to be multiple Walk-in personalities. The great majority that I interviewed seemed to embrace radical ideas within very ordinary lives.

But despite this "cloak of the ordinary," the Wanderers and Walk-ins who spoke with me refused to be pigeonholed into any kind of category; they were wary of that style of thinking in general. Having a cosmic and spiritual approach to the world, one that is enriched by their knowledge of many planets and many lives, the approach of the E.T.s could almost be called a multi-incarnational, or multiplanet, perspective.

So this often means they reject the "neat labels" that are bandied about in our highly psychological society. It's common for these E.T.s to say No to merely putting their intimate relationships on the couch, since their initial E.T. experience has been so real, and its meanings so potent. Everyday explanations, they believe, are far too narrow to really contain what they'd lived through.

Imagine it something along the lines of what would happen if you wrapped planet Earth in a map of the world—maybe it would look the same, you can see the same shapes, but there the likeness would end. That's how the E.T.s see the usual explanations of their most intimate relationships. Dry concepts don't answer the deeper questions or dull the pain.

An everyday approach also blunts the differences between Walk-ins and Wanderers. According to the woman I've called Lisanne, who's been a successful spiritual counselor all over the world and who's authored numerous articles about holistic healing and past-life therapy, the Wanderers tend to be more emotionally detached.

"If they've peeled back their own Earthbound self to come into contact with an original identity, one that's extraterrestrial, then they usually don't have the emotional resources to navigate," she says. "They've been denying too much. In my workshops, they usually come to see that, emotionally, they've missed the boat." These E.T.s often have great difficulty accepting the intensely human emotions they've inherited from the cycle of incarnations here on Earth.

On the other hand, says Lisanne, Walk-ins can also show a degree of emotional detachment in relationships "partly because they feel they have a great deal to learn and do . . . and a great deal to accept within themselves" after the tumultuous Walk-in event. Indeed, emotions are a challenge for even the most human of Earthlings.

Lisanne told me that in her work she isn't surprised to find some basic emotional differences between those who claim E.T. identity and those who do not. But she's not so sure that what's often read as coolness or detachment in E.T.s is not simply "the art of not clinging"—it might not be so different from describing someone as possessing a cool, dispassionate, scientific temperament. Perhaps these E.T.s are simply less emotional, but not necessarily emotionally stuck or inept. And indeed, if your mind is in the stars, it's tough to keep your feet on the ground—and it's difficult to focus on such "mundane" events as family picnics.

"What you hear a lot," Lisanne said, "is an interest in a universal, galactic perspective. That tends to make family life secondary." Maybe like the eccentric inventor who forgets his wife's (or her husband's) birthday . . .

For these people, time is spent in other ways. Reading, meditation, channeling, group membership, personal spiritual exploration . . . these were the activities that I heard mentioned most often. About a third of those I spoke with said they felt closer to nature, even to animal and plant life, than they did to people. And about a third of those who hail From Elsewhere surprised me by stating they simply didn't feel very connected to people at all and didn't think much about it. They enjoy their solitude and have no deep yearning for personal relations.

I found this quite interesting. The sense of being different seems to be an ongoing social thorn that is sometimes best removed by solitude.

When they *did* want to be with others, most of the Wanderers and Walk-ins felt most comfortable with those who'd come out of the closet regarding their E.T. identity—which brings us to another major dilemma faced by people who believe that they're From Elsewhere. . . .

To Tell or Not to Tell

The sad statistics for divorce in America usually give a marriage about a fifty-fifty chance of survival. For those who claim identity From Elsewhere, at least according to those I interviewed, the likelihood of divorce is a bit greater: just over 50 percent. But in a country with such a high marital casualty rate, it's difficult to say whether E.T. identity is the real cause of a breakup.

Usually, the difficulty lies in finding a partner who's sympathetic to what, admittedly, might be heard as an outrageous claim: *I'm an extraterrestrial.*

And as one E.T. told me, "What you believe and feel is important, but mostly, it's whether you share what you believe and feel. That's how you get intimacy." Sharing is always the bridge.

I heard that kind of comment quite often from those who claimed E.T. identity: that when people truly share a worldview, or to be more precise, an out-of-this-world view, they're much more likely to be intimate with their partners. Sometimes the relationship is even better than it was before.

One of the women I interviewed, for instance, first had to realize her E.T. identity before she was capable of enjoying a close and enduring lesbian relationship. She'd been sharing an apartment in San Francisco with a roommate, also gay, who really couldn't stand her. Both women, however, were taking part in past-life therapy and, after some time, they "discovered" they'd come from the same planet "in another life." That led to the acceptance of an E.T. soul, a love affair, and a life of intimacy where before there had been no connection—only anxiety and a lot of missed signals. Their bond turned out to be something they'd previously thought to be just an idiosyncrasy. *Both were From Elsewhere.*

And then there's the unusual relationship revealed by the story of Inid, a small, pretty woman with short brown hair who grew up in New York and now lives in California with a man she says is a husky outdoors type. She told me her husband didn't understand her E.T. ideas and as far as they both were concerned, that was perfectly OK.

"He's interested in other things, like hunting and fishing . . . and in discovering his own truth," she said. "And even though he doesn't really hook into E.T. identity, a lot of his old patterns have been shaken loose. He's supportive and he's very much in tune with his own development." Because he accepts her identity and her path, Inid doesn't need to make a big deal about being From Elsewhere. Their bonds of intimacy are based on other elements of their life together.

Inid believes that she has completely integrated her Walk-in personality and that she's here, on Earth, for service. That's usually the way it is with Wanderers and Walk-ins. In this case—a rare one—her marriage has improved despite their not sharing E.T. roots. But she's rendered personal service to her immediate relationship, and helps her husband in his own personal growth. For that, she says, he's very grateful.

Of course, it's one thing to talk about sharing—it's another thing to actually do it.

Not everyone wants to sit down and have a heart-to-heart talk about being extraterrestrial. Almost everyone I spoke with practically shuddered when I asked the question about whether they'd announced their E.T. reality, and whether they were eager to share their newfound E.T. identity with friends, lovers, and parents. It's a major decision that has to be reached individually—not only for each person who will tell, but taking into consideration each person who will hear, as well. The stress imposed by such a shocking revelation can easily rupture years of companionship. Again, it all depends on the strength of the bond.

SHARED JOY

This process of coming out of the world one used to know almost always gets a predictable response. The "new" extraterrestrial goes through a lot of worry, sweat, and tears over what to do; finally decides to express his or her deeper feelings; does so; and then is faced with contemptuous laughter, ridicule, embarrassment, and sometimes suggestions of mental illness. If they're lucky, they're greeted by curiosity and openness. Unfortunately, a "soft landing" is extremely rare.

Soren, our California surfer who resembles the actor Patrick Swayze, tried to talk about his E.T. identity once or twice with his family, but that was enough. He came away "frustrated, disappointed, and misunderstood."

As a child, he said, his parents thought it was fine that he had imaginary friends (not knowing that, to him, they were very real). They also shrugged off his talk about Martians and spaceships (which, he believed, he was actually visiting). This policy, which I'd call one of "benign avoidance," apparently kept his parents comfortable while they tolerated what they considered a "childish fantasy."

These childhood travels aboard spaceships, Soren said, were "more real than life around me," and actually left him with a beautiful feeling of "shared joy" among those "dream figures" From Elsewhere; a sensation of joy so powerful that he described it as "rushing up my back and exploding in my head." It was an intimacy he deeply wished to share, but which he was never able to find anywhere else.

As an adult, Soren told his parents about his E.T. identity and came away feeling humiliated. These days, he's more careful when he makes such revelations, but he's no longer thrown back into his own pain and confusion, he says. Without wishing in any way to shock or disturb, he told me it's usually the other person, the one he tells, who gets so thrown by his pronouncement that it limits the relationship from that point on.

These limitations, Soren explained, are "other people's preconceptions of what's possible in life. Maybe they believe in only a physical reality or that life exists only here on Earth. Then it's very difficult to share with them. But you're not stopped. You can give.

Just remember, it's intimacy without the specifics." Which means he still feels free to love, nurture, and care without expounding upon the details of his somewhat complex spiritual beliefs.

Even though Soren feels comfortable with his E.T. identity and no longer feels the sharp, driving need to tell people about his extraterrestrial origins, he would prefer something else.

"Unimpeded communion," he says. "Of course!"

But that's not about to happen. Currently, while rarely "compelled or triggered to tell someone" who he really is, Soren trusts his impulses. The best way to put it is: *Follow your hunches and not your fears.* Having followed his feelings, not worrying about what the response will be, Soren says he has encountered less ridicule and a great deal more interest. The more comfortable he's become with himself—as an E.T. and as an ordinary person here on Earth—the more he can wait before sharing one of his deepest, most personal truths.

WE'RE ALL WANDERING

Another solution to the question of to-tell-or-not-to-tell was offered by Matthew, a forty-one-year-old Wanderer from New Jersey who works in the media as a producer and writer. He's a small, slight man with a pale complexion set off by very black hair. Matthew went through the same experience as many of those who claim E.T. identity from birth: early dreams and visions, a childhood of philosophical wondering, a sense that the human body is somehow not quite correctly proportioned, sharp loneliness, a feeling of being From Elsewhere, and an understanding that some supposedly strange landscapes were more home than "home."

Matthew feels he's been living as extraterrestrial all of his life, a Wanderer who woke up quite early to his deeper truth.

He was one of the only people who told me, "I never had any resistance to my identity and I don't understand why anybody should. I never rejected the notion."

Even so, he is not convinced that sharing such information leads to better relationships. That's because, he says, the question of being From Elsewhere should be made as unimportant as possible.

I was surprised to hear him use the word *unimportant.*

"Issues of identity aren't that crucial for intimacy," he explained. "Getting support from other like-creatures is fine. But it might sometimes be more valuable *not to tell*, and to experience that discomfort. To be around people who don't accept your identity and feel that unease, and then *still* try to gradually influence the world and help people . . . " This challenge was most valuable to him.

Matthew sounded so sensible that I decided to push a little bit to make sure he wasn't simply giving answers he thought I might like to hear. I told him that there are some people who claim to be E.T.s who feel they can't be around anybody—literally *anybody*—who doesn't agree with their view of the universe.

"Well," Matthew said, "even E.T.s can have emotional problems." To which we might add: Just like anyone else.

Frequently, he went on, there are those who brag about their E.T. identity because they want to boost their cosmic egos; or they talk about being the "commander of a spaceship" so they can sound exotic and "special." Now, this doesn't mean that they really aren't From Elsewhere, it's only that they use this information to support their personalities, which is worlds away from the real center of extraterrestrial being. Integrate your E.T. self with your humanness, then move on to more important matters—that's the task that faces those From Elsewhere.

"It's like sitting at the feet of a guru," Matthew said. "Nothing could be more intimate and more public at the same time. And you have to put up with a lot of guru-shit to get to the real juice. But that's a good process: to learn to separate out the juice. Because ultimately you find that the juice is in yourself. Then you turn from your teacher and go off on your own."

"And what do you think happens then?" I asked.

Matthew answered by saying, "Then, being a Wanderer becomes a paradigm for all of us."

"The more self-aware you are," he said, "the more you realize that in one way or another, once we wake up, we're all wanderers here!"

Does that mean that every soul on Earth comes From Elsewhere? I don't think so, and neither does Matthew. He's just giving us a reminder that for all of us, Earth is a schoolhouse. We're all here to learn some essential lessons and then move on. All souls travel the universe in the great return to cosmic awareness—those who have always considered Earth their home, as well as those who are "just visiting."

PAULINE'S PERILS

There is also, I believe, something we can call "nontraditional intimacy," an out-of-the-ordinary style of closeness that's on the edge of the New Age or, at the very least, off the beaten path.

Here, there's a kind of warmth and intensity that seems to focus its attention on other areas in life—but without rejecting love or marriage, children or relationships.

The story of Pauline is a good example. She's the woman who had never missed a day of work in her life until the morning she felt compelled to call in sick and afterward experienced a strange and luminous infusion of cosmic information. Before her Walk-in, however, Pauline, in her marriage, was walked-on and walked-over.

"I was a doormat," she admits.

Becoming an E.T., though, was like lifting up that doormat and finding the magic key that had always been hidden beneath.

"It's a question of evolution," Pauline says. "It's a question of living through a meeting of energies—the joining of light and dark. As human beings, I think we have the potential to live in that energy, rather than feeling like we have to suffer this world until we go somewhere else. I don't believe we'll go anyplace else until the consciousness on this planet is changed." And also, she believes, the meeting place of spiritual aspiration and material restrictions might be the best place for learning.

Pauline is so waif-like, so thin and unadorned, that she definitely looks like a visitor to this world, but a visitor who's comfortable with the fact that she's only here on tour. These days, she consciously claims no permanent home but acts as a roving spiritual counselor on a constant journey wherever she's requested. At the time of our interview, she was about to cross the continent again to go help some friends in Washington, D.C. What struck me most, when we were speaking, was the quality she exuded of having total trust in her own experience and her own intuition, moment to moment, whether that experience was good, bad, or completely confusing.

Her Walk-in, Pauline says, actually taught her how to trust and, once she learned to rely on herself, it changed her experience of intimacy. This introduced her to a paradox: she suddenly lost her need to be Number One.

"I arrived at an attitude that I wasn't important and I wasn't not-important," she says. "It just didn't matter."

That sounded to me like true *humility*, a state that can be achieved when the false sense of ego stops demanding a constant seal of approval. It's the transcendence often mentioned by Western mystics and those who espouse Eastern philosophy. But completely on her own, just by listening to her deeper self, Pauline learned that same type of detachment.

"It changed everything for me," she says.

Two years before her Walk-in, Pauline's marriage had ended. In the months that followed, she felt terribly unhinged and drifted through a series of mindless sexual encounters and unhappy relationships, "just the same mistake lived over and over again."

Trying to pull herself together, Pauline accepted an offer to stay for a while with an old friend, a man who owned a beach house on the California coast. And that's when she lived through that intense, inexplicable, and strangely illuminated morning that completely altered her personality. This was the culmination of years of strange Walk-in "energy fusions."

Pauline stopped seeking; she stopped yearning to be in a personal relationship. Instead of stacking up the same old unhealthy patterns, she was overwhelmed by a sense of purpose. She felt driven to devote herself to service and started counseling everyone who wanted her help, traveling anywhere she felt her presence was required. She was what we might call a genuine *wandering Walk-in*, who had come close to achieving "the best of both worlds."

It was her work with "evolution," Pauline told me, that eventually allowed her to meet people who were more "open to the dark and the light." And that's where she was in her life when I talked to her: a woman enjoying many friendships but no steady romance, who liked people much more than she had before, and who had arrived at a "place" in her life that felt much healthier than where she'd been. Hers was an example of ideal psychological development coming from the recognition of E.T. roots.

"The Walk-in made me much more realistic and dispassionate," Pauline said. "I've willingly given up a lot of things. I don't think there's anything wrong with *things*, it just wasn't right for me. I've given up a home with three bedrooms, two cars, all the things you're supposed to want. And when relationships end, I'm now able to recover very quickly and move on."

Pauline has two grown children. She says that since her Walk-in she's let go of a kind of clinging relationship with them, as well, and become somewhat detached.

"I like them, they're nice people, but I stay in touch with them out of a mother's sense of obligation. It's almost like the feeling that a grown child usually has with a parent, but here it's the other way around. They have to live their own lives." She welcomes their independence—just as she honors her own.

When I questioned whether she wasn't simply withdrawing from people, Pauline very calmly explained that, no, it was something else. Being close or being distant, obsessively worrying over your place in every relationship—that isn't what she was talking about, she said. *Profound intimacy wasn't the only sign of maturity or psychological growth.* There are difficulties in human relations; and that is going to be true for those who claim E.T. experience as well as for those who don't.

Then Pauline surprised me by saying something that was strikingly similar to a statement made by Matthew.

What interested her more, she said, was this: the Walk-in experience as a paradigm for the New Age; an integration of many personalities in one, of many realities in one, of bringing spirit into matter in a way that honors both.

Because when it comes to the body, Pauline said, you can't trade it in.

"The first, the real intimacy, is to respect the body you walked into," Pauline says. "And in that sense, we're all similar to Walk-ins. At some point, we all walked into our bodies. So don't discard it. Don't ill-treat it. You have to learn to surrender to yourself that way before you can be comfortable with anyone else. *The body is born with courage, it's the ego that makes you afraid.* If you just start with the inborn courage of the body you're in, you'll have all the courage you need and a good start on any other kind of relationship."

That "the Walk-in experience of union is a paradigm for the New Age," that being "a Wanderer, learning and moving on, is a paradigm for all of us" or simply that the body's innate courage and wisdom are all that's needed . . . these ideas come from knowledge that seems beyond time, wisdom gleaned from the meeting place of the past, present, and future.

Even so, Pauline's statement—of joining spirit and matter in a way that honors both—brings us to one of the most difficult subjects of this New Age or any other. By this I mean the sensual, the sexual, and how the physical body that temporarily houses a conscious E.T. soul gets along in that most earthy of Earth pastimes.

HORNY ALL THE TIME

We'll begin with the story of Bob, the man who recovered from a dissolute life of drug abuse and self-punishment when he experienced what he says was "probably" a Walk-in.

Prior to that event and its personal cataclysm, the then-bearded and burly Bob lived a life, he told me, of "compulsive sex," which he experienced as a "continual physical need," fueled by strip shows and such reading matter as *Hustler* and the cheaper porno mags. His attitude toward women, he told me, was simply "hunt and conquer."

"To put it bluntly," he said, "I was horny all the time."

And afterward?

The answer, which was spoken with a wide-eyed expression and in a straightforward, plain voice, took me off guard. I wasn't sure I'd heard him correctly and so I repeated what I thought was his reply.

"You mean, now you have *no* sex drive?"

"Very little," Bob said. "Maybe 10 percent of what it was before."

Bob's current lack of sexual desire even extended to the visual pleasures of "checking out girls in the street," of which he said, "I can take it or leave it . . . but usually I leave it."

And that quenched desire was currently—and obviously—an issue in his marriage, he acknowledged; a comment that made both of us laugh because it seemed like the E.T. version of a familiar marital complaint. In Bob's words: "To me, sex isn't that important. To her, it is. She'd like to do it more often." As Bob and I spoke, I wondered whether his wife would have ever imagined herself married to a chaste E.T. . . .

For Bob, though, the sexual is now viewed as "an interference with my meditation process. I need a lot of time alone to shut off externals and meditate on my ideas and experiences." This need for solitude and spiritual focus is common—and obviously does not encourage family togetherness or leave much opportunity for a "happy, healthy sex life."

To provide more space for meditation, Bob has started living in a separate room from his wife and claims they've both become used to the arrangement. Whether his Walk-in leads to his wife's walking-out, however, remains to be seen; one wonders how long a marriage can last when sex and intimacy are seen as little more than disruptions to a partner's meditation practice.

While Bob's story is definitely at the far end of the spectrum, the extraordinary experience of E.T. awareness does often seem to mute sexuality.

I usually heard this explained as "energy going to a higher level" in the case of some Walk-ins—or, as I was told, the experience changes your priorities so that you simply have too many other important things to do. In the case of Christin who, as he said, "was gay before and gay after my Walk-in," sex became "less of a driving force. I didn't need to use it to validate myself anymore. I just took it for granted."

There is also the story of Barrie, an East Coast psychic who conducts Star People workshops, who says that claiming E.T. identity had no impact at all on the sexual part of her human being.

Barrie told me she was happily married, had always enjoyed her sex life, and that her husband was in sync with her New Age views. One reason for the lack of drama, Barrie said, might be that she's a Wanderer, and so she's been an E.T. from the start. Barrie has never been uncomfortable with viewing herself as someone from another reality, and when she realized "for sure" she was a Wanderer, it simply confirmed old ideas. Her sex life continued without much change, just like other aspects of her family life.

The acceptance of E.T. identity very rarely seemed to lead to an over-the-moon sexual experience.

One exception was the story we talked about concerning the San Francisco lesbian relationship that blossomed after mutual past-life therapy, but this was one of the few examples of regained, dynamic sexuality following E.T. awakening. For most E.T.s, sex is just not that important.

And then there's Lucia, one of the New Age teacher, writer, and seminar organizers whose Walk-in took place in the middle of a shower. She actually grounds herself in the sensual.

Lucia says, "I can't say with 100 percent certainty that I'm a Walk-in because the whole experience is far too subjective. I'd say I have an E.T. soul. And I definitely know it's in a female body." We both laughed.

As for any changes in her sexual appetites, Lucia told me, "None. I was always happy with that part of my life. Any changes I've been through were just part of getting older. I'm not quite as absorbed."

But I think it's best to conclude this chapter with the comments of Inid, a woman whose full story we'll delve into later. Like Lucia, Inid is also very much willing to include the sensual and sexual in her E.T. experience. She had other ideas that I found more difficult to accept. For instance, she was certain that at one time, she was the sole representative on Earth of a confederation of extraterrestrial races. That's a somewhat grandiose notion, of course, but still, her thoughts about sexuality were most grounded.

The sensual, she said, is one of the best parts of her extraterrestrial existence. Sex is one of the "perks of being on Earth, in a physical body." And while the Walk-in experience had not increased her sexual drive, Inid said it had definitely intensified the experience.

"It's been really wonderful," she said. "I had a strong connection before. Afterward, it was more so."

I was glad to hear that and told her so. I felt that I'd been hearing too much about matter and spirit being split apart, with matter definitely on the losing end.

"Too many asexual E.T.s," I said. "I start to feel a bit disconnected myself."

"Sex for me was heightened," Inid said with a big smile, "and it seemed so new and so fresh. But, you know, it was like that with everything. I remember once, after the Walk-in, I was sitting in my son's car just watching everything go by, observing all the different

things, just sitting there thinking about how incredible, how wonderful it all was. And I remember tasting a hamburger and suddenly
having that sensation of *really* tasting it, having a milk shake, too.
How great that was, like it had never happened before. Almost
like imagining that *every time I did anything it was the first and
the freshest time.* That's how sex was. I just kept thinking . . .
Wow!"

6

THE SOCIAL IMPACT

THE HUMAN SIDE OF THE FAR SIDE

When the E.T.s finally do phone home, who picks up the tab?

And if you seriously believe yourself to be an executive officer with the interplanetary Ashtar Command, does that mean you still have to answer to your boss at work? Do you still have to take out the garbage?

Eventually, worlds collide. Say you've come up with the most stirring, eloquent metaphysical theory—does that spare you from paying the rent? Does it save you from facing the possibility of rejection? For those who pass through the most enlightening galactic revelations—do they still have to worry about getting to the market on time?

Anyone claiming to be From Elsewhere will tell you: *The Awakening process is only the first stage in a transformation that will eventually mean a clash with the world as we know it.* It's an inevitable meeting, and it's destined to shake the individual life down to the very core.

TWO CULTURES

When your world is turned upside down, how do you keep your balance? How do you side with the stars and still make your way in the sand? How do you actually function in the common, concrete realities of Earthlife?

The answer is: by a belief that you're a part of two cultures at once, a *dual-culture member* as it's sometimes termed in the more formal, academic halls of professional anthropology.

By accepting both of these cultures, a Walk-in or Wanderer is able to "swear allegiance" to one group and still take part in the activities of another, all the time seeing him or herself as somewhat on the margin of society. It's not that they've divided their loyalties; the Wanderers and Walk-ins I spoke with who claimed to be From Elsewhere remained solidly on the side of Elsewhere and always identified with "the Beyond." But they were extremely aware that they had to find a middle way if they wanted to make the best of two or three possible worlds.

"It was strange to feel that I'd changed," as one E.T. described it. "I started seeing a slow, subtle difference in all my relationships and I knew I had to deal with it."

Most told me that socially they were making the best of a difficult situation. Almost all of those I met had a tough time in mixed company and made close friends only with other like-minded people; this was true for them in almost every relationship. Sometimes, however, it wasn't a conscious decision.

In the words of Vikram, the screenwriter and housepainter who chased after a UFO on his bicycle as a boy: "I'd say 75 percent of the people I contact closely are Wanderers, but I don't seek them out. *We just get together naturally.*"

Not everyone felt "homesick" for their former planet or their original world—so, regardless of the movies, "phoning home" was not something that E.T.s seemed to worry about a lot. And then again, there was one young woman I interviewed who said that she was certain that her true husband was still living Elsewhere and that he would never travel to planet Earth—that was the reason she was always disappointed in the men she dated. (I joked with her that if feeling like that is a sign of being From Elsewhere, the ranks of female extraterrestrials are going to soar!)

When we begin to investigate the "this world" part of being "out of this world," the answers change a little depending on the person and depending on whether someone is a Wanderer or a Walk-in. But if you wanted to draw an emotional map of the path that's usually followed when an E.T. "confronts" Earth society, it would come out something like this:

First, one goes through feelings of alienation, a sense of what I can only call *chronic differentness*. Then, there's a move into a period of intense conflict; a conflict that finally crystalizes into an awakening of E.T. identity.

With that act of self-awareness "completed," the newly "realized" E.T. quite often finds him or herself imbued with deep feelings of affiliation, connected to people who share a view of this world but who see completely different worlds, as well—sometimes completely different lives, spirits, souls, realities, zones, and vibrations.

After that, understandably, there is a final, definite break from the mainstream. Perhaps psychologically, perhaps physically, or both. If they were isolated, unhappy, lonely, or alienated before the extraterrestrial event, those with E.T. identity eventually find themselves living "on the fringe," sometimes happily and sometimes not. Such deep loneliness often persists, but in some ways I take this to be a "fact of life" here or Elsewhere—an existential loneliness. Accepting one's Wanderer or Walk-in identity doesn't always make that loneliness easier to bear, and I'm not really sure how it can be helped. Many of our E.T.s simply said: Don't expect answers, it's all an ongoing process. And loneliness is part of the equation.

Another part of that equation involves constant work on the

self. Most of those I interviewed thought that their personal work was very similar, if not the same, as working for society.

"What I'm doing right now," said a woman I'll call Julie, "is working on *me*. I'm clearing. That's so I can reach a higher vibration and project the light out of me. I think, basically, there's nothing to do here on Earth but to be all that we are and to keep clearing to open our hearts. It's not about stockpiling information." Gaining knowledge is not as helpful as purifying our intentions.

Clearing, by the way, is a process that Julie now teaches, in which (as she explains) the imprints of past incarnations are cleared away. But that's probably not the kind of talk that you would have heard from the Julie of ten years ago. At that time, she was employed as a corporate recruiter finding high-level executives for banks in the Los Angeles area—definitely *not* bent on self-purification.

Julie's story was one of the most complete cases of individual upheaval that I encountered in all my interviews. I think it can definitely teach us a different way of thinking about E.T. identity, and about how the radical revision of self can make one's social world come tumbling down.

Instead of watching from the outside, feeling astonished that anyone would so completely follow such outlandish beliefs, remember that we'll probably learn more if we view these changes from within. Then we can start to feel what it's like to be an ordinary person seized by the force of a new identity and a powerful sense of purpose, responsibility, and obligation—even if that new enthusiasm seems odd to everyone else.

As Julie came to realize, if you try to grasp enlightenment on the corporate fast track you'll find yourself running far behind the truths you seek. Those truths, it seems, are always moving ahead at the speed of light.

WE ARE THE EXPERIMENT

Now in her late forties, divorced, with two children, Julie is a short, trim blonde whose intense manner becomes even more direct as she punctuates each sentence with jabbing hand gestures like somebody who's used to speaking in public. She impressed me as a woman completely open to different points of view, but who, at the same time, doesn't suffer fools gladly. Julie is not afraid to speak her mind or give you straight answers.

Today she's an administrator and counselor for one of the better known holistic spiritual centers in Santa Fe, New Mexico.

Ten years ago, though, at the time she discovered she was an extraterrestrial Wanderer, there was another Julie. This was a Julie who grew up in a comfortable Beverly Hills home with all the material goods and gifts anyone could ask for; a Julie who did pretty much what was expected of her, day-in day-out.

She traveled in the same circles, with the same friends, from childhood on. And when she ended up married, having two children, and working in corporate Century City, it was cheered by family and friends as the kind of secure, interesting, well-heeled, well-paying, respectable life that any sensible person would envy.

Secretly, however, Julie's heart was in another world.

While she had not yet learned to commit herself fully, Julie had always quietly held the belief that she was psychic and destined for some kind of special task. Over the years, she was slowly becoming more and more interested in metaphysics, spiritual matters, and esoteric subjects.

"I had the belief," she told me, "that I was born on Earth in the normal way, but that my soul was From Elsewhere." This is the precise description of Wanderers.

One night when her husband was away on business, Julie lay awake in bed listening to the sounds of an empty house. She heard the click of the pipes, the ticking of an antique clock, the creaking wood. She was falling asleep, thinking of her husband, her children, and feeling a vague dissatisfaction.

That's when Julie noticed a strange white light streaming from the hall through the doorway of her bedroom. She sat up and flicked her night-table light on and off a few times, but the eerie whiteness in the hall remained. It was no trick of the shadows. In fact, under Julie's disbelieving stare, the mysterious glow now started to thicken so that it became not only a white light but also a whirl of curious smoke whisking up and down, swirling around to form a shape.

Fascinated and terrified, Julie watched. She saw this bizarre smoke-and-light entity wind around in twists and turns to then sculpt itself until it began to look like a seven-foot Being, possibly a man, but one that appeared like a holographic image towering over her as it stood in the doorway.

"I was very fearful," she says. "It was like a white light but I could definitely see a man standing there. And then, suddenly, I somehow knew that this was an entity with the name of Ashtar." (The E.T. ship commander whom many New Age channels say they contact.) She had never heard of Ashtar before that night.

Julie had plenty of time to prove her intuition correct. She told me that this incredible image actually remained standing in place for close to two years! Like a young child with a new toy at home, Julie would rush back from work every evening to see the persistent image. In the evenings it was white; but in the daytime, the form changed to a kind of bright, periwinkle blue. And directly across from this image, projected onto the wall of her hallway, there suddenly appeared a small rainbow that shone with every possible color. It was there even if the day was cloudy; and while not everyone was allowed to view Ashtar, Julie said, the rainbow remained for anyone's enjoyment.

But there was even more to come.

Two days after her vision began, Julie experienced a second visitation. On that evening, her hallway was slowly filled with golden light, and this time, as Julie stared from her bed, she says that an apparition of Jesus suddenly appeared: "There was no mistake about it, he was standing right there.

"He started projecting light beams on me, first one and then two. I have never felt such an incredible feeling of total love in my life," Julie said. "I don't remember what happened after that."

Apparently she lost consciousness. In the morning when she awoke, Julie says, she saw that Jesus was no longer present but that directly underneath the wood of the doorjamb, there still shone a little bit of golden light—and that light, she said, remained there always.

Now, all of these visions and visitations, remember, were happening to a woman employed as a corporate recruiter in the financial industry, usually a very button-down zone. One might expect to see visions of bulls and bears—even hope for them—but not religious revelations. Julie wasn't about to dismiss her experience so easily, however; such a pattern of avoidance was what had put her life off track in the first place. She'd been rejecting her own perceptions, denying her own feelings and deeper thoughts.

Julie headed for L.A.'s Bodhi Tree bookshop. This place is an eye-opener for anyone who's been seeing too straight for too long. It's one of the most famous esoteric bookstores in the country, redolent with incense and filled with thousands of volumes from Ashtar to Zen. There, wandering among the crowded shelves, looking at the Tarot cards, the crystals, the I Ching coins, Julie felt oddly drawn to a book by and about the Ashtar Command.

She bought the book. In a restaurant across the street, she sat down and began reading.

"I just started to sob uncontrollably," she said. "I was in hysterics. I kept reading and I felt so tapped into it, it was incredible. I just vibrated to it. It was like everything in my life just fell into place." The silent puzzle was being solved.

That experience marked her departure. In mind and spirit, Julie had finally broken away from what she had been brought up to believe was the only possible "real world." She began to frequent channelers in Los Angeles, and now, after eight years of channeled material, Julie believes that Ashtar and Sananda (believed by some to be the original name of Jesus) had agreed to appear and awaken her that night so she could, in turn, help awaken others.

Through her own extensive channeling, she also came to believe that what occurred during her evening of visions was actually a form of time travel. It would be more accurate to say she was reliving an experience that had been long forgotten: an initiation ritual, during a past time when she was actually able to clearly see Spirit.

"And I still can," Julie assured me. She didn't want to take that much further and chose not to reveal exactly what else had been channeled during her sessions except to assert that she learned she was an E.T. soul, that her home planet was Sirius, that during many past lives she had appeared on Earth at other key points in history, and that she was tightly connected to power spots around the planet. Julie also said that she was given incredible information about the pyramids and some of the secret combinations of "fire letters" and was told that her name was one of the seventy-six sacred names in the Book of Enoch.

"Do you really need to know more?"

I said I thought that was enough.

What struck me most was that if you seriously viewed your life in this manner, how could you still worry about finding a parking space in Century City every day? Maybe you could, but it would be hard, to say the least.

For Julie, it turned out to be impossible.

"It takes a lot of courage to get rid of all the garbage we have in our bodies so we can transmute," she said. "See, I really believe . . . *we are the experiment*."

"What do you mean?" I asked.

"This has never been done before, humanity. Even if there's life on other planets, we're the center of the experiment now. We're becoming more alive in body and we're actually getting rid of the denseness, the garbage. We're changing our DNA. We're incorporating more and more into this physical body and that's never been done before."

Julie was open about her new outlook, but it took her three years before she could completely break away from the old world that had been her home. She got divorced and began to change friends; she started looking for "a job that would let me do my work." Finally, she felt compelled to drive from Los Angeles to New Mexico, and when she reached the majestic high desert mountains of Santa Fe, she vibrated with a powerful feeling that she had, at last, found her true home on Earth.

"Spirit," she said, "told me everything. It told me what would happen. It even told me not to rent my house but to sell . . . and how much to sell it for! I got three offers the first day."

Remember, however, these were all events taking place in the everyday world. And the reaction of others? From her mother to her closest friends, said Julie, "they all thought I was insane. There was no support at all. The only person who seemed to understand, believe it or not, was my ex-husband and we talked a lot by phone."

I was intrigued that Julie had fallen right into one of the most basic mistakes made by new E.T. souls who are testing their wings; but she also learned something from it. For a while, she said, she became convinced she needed to save *everyone*, whether they wanted to be saved or not, especially her own family. Everyone, she thought, owed it to Julie to listen and profit from her incredible experience. What she learned—and it did take a while—was that she was here on Earth to work, and that work is really a gradual, painstaking process rather than an ego-centered heroic triumph. She explained: "I have many friends who've realized they're E.T. souls, but who've stopped doing the work. They don't have the courage. It's uncomfortable when you're bringing this stuff up, it's terrible. It means a total change. But it feels so good once you've cleared it, you know. You're clearing your emotional body, actually clearing it out cellularly." From increased "purity" comes increased love and wisdom—fruits of "the path."

I told Julie that her story sounded like the tale of someone coming to accept her own amazingly powerful purpose. She had cast off from the mainstream social world because she felt it was not really her own, despite the fact that almost everyone she knew regarded her social position as incredibly responsible and important. She then found her way to another place, one in which Julie, herself, felt a deep, unambiguous sense of belonging and obligation, perhaps a connection that transcended the boundaries of time.

She agreed totally.

"With E.T. identity comes a responsibility of Beingness," she said. "It's a huge responsibility. You have to work on yourself. That's what it's all about. It's not about spouting all this crap and then not being it yourself. The more we open our hearts, the more it becomes an awesome light, just like one candle touching another."

She took a deep breath. "Once you've gotten this, you can't pretend you haven't. You've stepped over a line."

There's no going back.

I'M MY NUMBER ONE GUINEA PIG

As I've said, what happened to Julie differs only in degree from the stories I was told by others who'd realized they were E.T.s.

A change of jobs, a new home, the end of a marriage or close relationship, a troubling confrontation with family or the cutting of ties with old friends—much of this can only be worked through because of an intense feeling of mission and purpose. That's what puts the juice into the engine that allows the neophyte E.T. to buck the strength of social trends and rededicate his or her life.

I also found, not surprisingly, that the rocky ride of this social earthquake can be made a lot smoother if the new E.T. has some background or experience in psychology, metaphysics, or esoterica. Everything helps, everything from mild interest and a little reading to intense study, meditation, and various forms of bodywork and therapy. All of this work gives us greater self-understanding, patience, and insight—a real boost in difficult discussions. But what if your partner knows nothing about this?

Inid, who's been married, divorced, has two children, and now shares a home with an "outdoors type of man," asks, "How can you live with somebody and not tell them who you are?"

She then described her partner as someone who's interested in "fishing, hunting, riding motorcycles, and knowing the truth," but when she showed him something she'd written about E.T. identity he never finished reading it.

"He didn't understand," she says. "He didn't really care one way or the other." You can imagine how isolated she felt.

And when she revealed to a good friend that she'd had an extraterrestrial experience there was another uncomfortable moment. The friend's answer was a wide-eyed, "Gee, I hope they don't come and take you away!" So, it was difficult to find someone who would try to understand the depth of her feelings.

A different example comes from Barrie, the East Coast psychic who conducts Star People workshops. She told me she felt almost no social turmoil because she'd worked as a therapist and most of her friends were already "into metaphysics." She had both the inner skills and outer support to create a smoother transition to her new identity.

And there was Lucia, who has been leading Walk-in support groups for years, and who says that several days before her own Walk-in she spontaneously began shedding friendships and relationships that suddenly felt wrong.

"Eventually, without my consciously thinking about it," she told me, "only those people with deep spiritual ties remained." As she changed, her social network adjusted right along with her.

Interestingly, at the time, Lucia was married to a man I'll call Justinian, who also claimed a pretty solid background in these matters: a psychology degree from a major university; a great deal of esoteric reading; meditation; yoga; and many years of study in Theosophy, the Alice Bailey tradition of ageless wisdom. He was already teaching others about spiritual growth. With all of this preparation, he was well qualified to support his wife during her unusual transformation.

And *his* transformation is an interesting story in itself. It didn't surprise me when Justinian credited all that previous work for his own fairly smooth transition which, as he put it, "allowed me to make the necessary adjustments and bear the increased loneliness."

Unlike many others, he was prepared for his wife's personal transformation, which seemed to have begun before the actual Walk-in event. It was almost as if Justinian was gradually awakening. I thought he made the metamorphosis sound like the most reasonable thing in the world when he explained that his years of study had taught him that, regardless of which spiritual path he chose to follow, *he'd have to make renunciations*. The realization of E.T. identity has no Earthly patent on personal hardship. All paths of transformation are difficult.

"It was like a drama unfolding that was orchestrated by some Higher Self so I could go through the changes," he said. "But I was already oriented to contacting my Higher Self." Long ago, he'd acquired the habit of listening to his inner voice.

Justinian is almost forty now and has strong, piercing dark eyes, short black hair, and a well-trimmed beard. It's sometimes oddly disconcerting to hear him talk about these subjects—he looks so much like the classic image of an old-time magician. Still, I could hear that he'd paid a great deal of attention to ideas about the cosmos and he'd come to a number of interesting conclusions, among them a somewhat different explanation of Walk-ins.

Most Walk-ins, he said, may be something closer to what he termed a "fragment exchange," the result of an infusion of energy from a greater, more spiritualized aspect of the Self. Even so, he believes that his own soul—whether Greater Self or not so great—is definitely of extraterrestrial origin. He also believes that his soul has existed on this planet for a long, long time. In this way, Justinian sees his present life as just one portion of a continuum of lives unfolding in various times on various worlds. A liberating view, indeed.

Justinian lives in California and spends a lot of time developing subtle energy technologies for spiritual growth, every so often lecturing and conducting workshops as a metaphysical teacher or counselor. You'll hear the idea of "double culture" when he talks about his feelings for Earth, a kind of pleasant attachment and a serious nonattachment at the same time. While he stated most profoundly that "home is really the Higher Self, so you don't have to identify with a physical home," Justinian also made me laugh. With great enthusiasm he quickly added: "But Earth is a great place to be! It's full of challenges!" I said that was putting it mildly.

His Walk-in, Justinian continued, happened in 1988, during a time he refers to as "a year of death. Renouncing, renouncing, renouncing, renouncing." He was forced to let go of many cherished attachments that year.

It sounded, on the surface, like a fairly undramatic Walk-in, though, one which was connected to deepening meditation, a New Age workshop, and the many realizations he arrived at after lots of spiritual searching.

While this "fragment exchange" forced him to sever some friendships, it also allowed him to draw closer to other people he already knew, enriching those more spiritual connections. A subtle selection process gained speed.

"So, in a lot of ways," Justinian said, "even with all the renunciation, when it was over, there really wasn't much of a change socially. When I think back on it, I'd already broken with a lot of those people." Again, an example of a smooth transformation.

This was also a case where a new E.T. had the good fortune to find that his Walk-in was a step-up; which was exactly the direction Justinian took on the business ladder.

His company, which was involved in the research and development of subtle energy technologies, showed new energy of its own.

"Business just exploded that year," he says. He got out from under years and years of frustrating experiments, too-careful preparation, stalling and "playing around," and arrived at a time of concentrated, absolute effort as though he'd tapped into some aspect of his Higher Self. He was now solidly behind his own work.

Justinian also had the rare experience, as we've said, of being married to a partner who shared many of his beliefs. As he put it, "the Walk-in enhanced our relationship." Justinian was married to Lucia, the spiritual counselor. And when he told his birth family a little (but not all) of what he was going through, he says, "my mother believed me, she got it, she didn't think it was a joke." And the strong bond they'd always shared was able to carry them through this new wrinkle in the road. They still enjoy a close relationship.

It's possible, I thought, that his mother remembered Justinian as a little boy in the Midwest, the boy who would walk into the fields at night, stare longingly up at the stars and pray for the E.T.s to come and pick him up, "to take me home," as he recalled. "I've had an E.T. orientation all of my life." Perhaps, it's his mother's simple unconditional love for her son that makes his radical beliefs palatable.

"In a way," he says, "I always believed I was From Elsewhere." But this remained a somewhat vague sense until he grew older. In high school and college, he went on, there was the usual clash with society, and society was the winner. Justinian put his E.T. feelings aside and concentrated on growing up. It's very common for adolescents to display this "rejection of differentness."

"The emotional dynamics of being a teenager made the feelings dissipate a little. Now, though, it feels like everything's just right." So, he's come "full circle."

Justinian, I think, showed many of the qualities of what I would describe as a "mature Walk-in," a concept I'll deal with later when we discuss the psychology of E.T. identity. Probably because of his years of training, he was able to work at integrating all aspects of his personality, and when I asked him to generalize about how he now dealt with others, Earthlings in particular, he explained it like this: "I carry these issues with me so I can learn to master them myself and by doing that, I'll be helping others. There's no better way to help others than to work it through yourself. I'm my own number one guinea pig."

He takes full responsibility for his feelings and so "purifies his intentions." His dedication is a beacon for many. . . .

THE SPIRAL PATH

Justinian's attitude of helpfulness and calm isn't unusual for Wanderers and Walk-ins; it's an attitude shared by many of those I interviewed. A paradox, perhaps, and maybe a lesson in itself, but many people who've lived through these extraordinary, nontraditional experiences, who claim a new and remarkable identity, also seem somehow *ordinary*. Most of them could even be described as humble. I think that quality of humility might even help them rediscover a place in society once they've achieved their E.T. Awakening. They almost always downplay the quality of being different, and that tends to put others at ease.

But, again, to be fair, this humility usually grows out of turmoil and revolution; a revolution in consciousness, in personal reality, and in how one gets around in the everyday world. Which brings up another shake-up that allows the new E.T. to reenter society after Awakening and to then grow steadily more comfortable with a new life on "the fringe."

What kind of shake-up do I mean?

Reality itself gets turned upside down.

We've already met Christin, a gay man who is one of the chief executives of a well-known global peace group and who lived through an extremely dramatic Awakening—a Walk-in that seemed to threaten his very survival at its most critical moment.

"I think it was a death in some ways," says Christin, "almost like it was the intervention of God that allowed my physical body to stay alive." He felt as if he were at the edge of his life.

What Christin needed was the vision to see that his own reality was important, that the social world could come second. It wasn't an easy job; it rarely is.

Christin was brought up with a religious background, a suburban Lutheran experience, he says, but it was really an unsatisfying show of religiosity he got at home, not a deep spirituality. Although he was involved in meditation groups in the weeks just before the actual Walk-in, he felt that here, too, he was just going through the motions. The sessions weren't a complete waste, they just seemed more formula than truth. He still hadn't gotten down to the roots of his life.

After the Walk-in, however, Christin became seriously involved in meditation and professionally involved with spiritual counseling. In this way he made a total break with the past.

"I let it all come through and I started to own it," he said. This meant leaving Washington state, his lover, his belongings, and his job as a management trainer to move back to his parents' house in Chicago, where he remained for eight months.

From there, his childhood home, he was ready to start over. He told me: "I was reborn."

"After my Walk-in, I was ready to tap into the energy," he went on. "I had less tolerance for hurting, whether it was hurting myself or others or the environment or the universe. I started to learn about my own reference points. Because in our world, it's too easy to get distracted from your own realities."

His previous soul, as he put it, was addicted to relationships, but in a very short period of time after his Walk-in he lost that need and realized that he didn't have to depend on any other individual. That, says Christin, altered the balance of the relationship with his parents, for instance, who suddenly began to see him as a mature and self-supporting "person." Oddly enough, he said, when his mother went down to Florida for a visit, she brought him back a beautiful crystal without having any idea about the significance of the object. She just felt that somehow it was the right thing to buy for him.

As he was able to "tap into" himself more and more, the demands and chains of the social world started to seem not only less powerful but actually less real. Christin entered training as a spiritual teacher and healer, started extensive reading, and, more important, was now taking himself and his studies seriously.

"I was getting in touch with my deep home, my deep heart," he said. "I was learning to become alive." Such an experience is the ideal achievement of transformation.

For a while Christin published a newsletter that he called *The Spiral Path* because he was particularly excited by that form, the shape of the spiral. That's the shape of the DNA molecule—the double helix—and according to several sources, including C. G. Jung, it can represent the idea of a continuing spiritual search, the Holy Ghost, or simply the play of nonlinear realities: past/present/future, here/there, then/now, all twisting around one another and existing together at the same time.

That notion of the nonlinear, which Christin is now able to live out in his day-to-day experience, is one of the most important gifts of his Walk-in. It's an alteration of reality that let him make the break from his old life. He knows that he exists on many, many levels and feels that others do, as well. Christin utilizes the notion of the spiral in his counseling sessions, seeing it as a perfect symbol of infinity, the eternal present.

And as we were preparing to conclude our interview, Christin summed up his vision of society and the world in what I found to be a very moving coda.

"My outlook is like this," he said,

> I think we're totally graced, each one of us. We each ride on a band of grace. It's totally equal for all of us and there's such an abundance that it really doesn't matter what the form looks like.

Everything is just a different form of reality. So, trust your own process, because there really is no first or second place.

I'VE BEEN BACK THERE

It is really a testament to the Spirit, I think, that true identity so often seems to finally, successfully break free. Nothing can stop its struggle toward the light, sometimes against great odds and sometimes battling fantastic forces, both internal and social. This seems to happen with both Earthly identity and also when that identity is nonordinary or downright radical.

Despite the ridicule of loved ones, the searingly painful self-doubt, and, frequently, the need to tear apart friendships, give up secure employment, and relinquish one's entire social fabric, this out-of-the-ordinary identity, this declaration of a Universal Persona, seems to inevitably make its way into consciousness.

Once it does, the everyday social world begins to loosen its grip without vanishing completely—never evaporating totally as it does in some cases of psychosis or other forms of deep psychological disorganization. What seems to happen is that *another social world is seen* and begins to take its rightful place. Everyday common reality remains as just one possibility, but it's no longer the only touchstone of authority.

Our usually unquestioned "real world" becomes just one frequency on the radio of mind, and we may or may not choose to tune in. The Walk-in or Wanderer begins to remember the "many mansions" available, as Jesus taught.

I'll finish our examination of the social impact of E.T. identity with the story of Betty, whom we met earlier in our chapter on Awakenings.

Betty is the British woman, now in her early sixties, who recognized her extraterrestrial origins while engaged in hypnotherapy. She was deeply regressed during that session and relived an incident from the age of six when she was thought to have died.

One of the elements of Betty's story that interests me is that she comes from a time and place in which social demands, propriety, and well-mannered behavior played a greater role in life than they do in the modern United States.

Betty spent her childhood in the Britain of the 1930s, brought up by conservative parents who were themselves products of the last gasp of the Victorian era. All good citizens were supposed to keep a stiff upper lip, do their duty, remain quiet (if they were women), and never, never, never indulge in behavior that would be sniffed at as eccentric by the neighbors. And, of course, spirituality was considered quite eccentric.

For Betty's mother, this meant never delving too far into her own powers.

Betty, you may recall, told the story of having been pronounced clinically dead while in the hospital, and of how her mother had a "vision"—Betty was talking with someone "all dressed in white," probably an angel—and she knew that Betty was going to make the decision to return to life, which is what happened.

However, when I ventured to say, "Your mother must have been a very spiritual woman," Betty shook her head and answered, "No. From my own knowledge of spirituality now, she was just a very religious woman . . . though she was also what we could call a psychic. But she came from the old fashioned, English, Victorian type of family background where such things were very rarely spoken of."

For her mother—as well as for Betty—it was obviously there, this force, and it wasn't going to fly away just because the entire British Empire was scowling and ordering it to sit still and be quiet. But in such a social climate, these powers can rarely grow to full blossom.

As a child, Betty told me, she could perform some of the "magic" mentioned in the books of Tibetan mysticism: alter the temperature of her body to remain hot in cold weather and cold in the heat, walk in giant nonhuman strides, communicate telepathically, and see people's auras. Sometimes she would blurt out, "He's not telling the truth, Mum!" when she noticed a person's aura shift and she could read what was going through his mind.

But the mystic child Betty just "got on with it," as the British might say. England was still well within the shadow of Queen Victoria, where ideas about E.T.s and cosmic life were completely absent from social dialogue. *Being an E.T. meant being a lunatic.* No more . . . and no less. As Betty explains:

> You see that was the problem at that time in my life. I'm of that generation when these kind of things weren't discussed. *At all.* It was nothing like it is today. If you so much as talked about it, you got put into some mental institution somewhere for being a little bit strange. As a child, I thought it was perfectly normal to go out and talk to the angels, the spirits, and the fairies of nature. I'd come in from playing outdoors and my mother would ask who I'd been playing with and I'd tell her. Well! My grandfather heard about it and said, "We've got to get these things put straight or this child is going to grow up to be odd!" So it was strictly knocked out of me.

Not physically knocked out, Betty said. They used what is perhaps a more insidious method: a kind of inflexible and grim concern, with apparent family kindness, under the guise of helping Betty grow up to be a proper lady. Every mention of spirits, fairies, or otherworldly beings was met with a stern lesson in why her outlook wasn't normal and wouldn't be permitted.

"I became a very reticent child. It was terribly painful," Betty said. "I shut all of this out for a very long time."

Openly identifying herself with other worlds and other realities would have to wait. As an adolescent and young adult, Betty went on to follow what she called her "two great loves": biology, or anything having to do with nature; and music. Soon she was concentrating on music. A scholarship allowed her to earn a graduate degree from the Royal College of Music as a concert singer, and she toured all over England. Eventually, Betty married, had a child, and gave up the nomadic existence of a performer, retraining and settling down for a career as a nurse.

As it turns out, Betty says, this life path was very much in keeping with her extraterrestrial identity.

"As I now know," she said. "I've been informed by some of our planetary elders that most of the initiates do take a choice of either medicine, music, or law. These courses seem to be part of the curriculum for those who are on a given path and choose to be here on this Earth plane." Spending several lifetimes on Earth is a normal part of their higher spiritual training.

As Betty grew older and "thought these things through" for herself, she began to understand that while she had dismissed her mother's approach to the Spirit as being too conventionally religious, her mother *did* possess what Betty called "a gut-level knowledge about these things. She had never been taught, she simply knew, as many Celtic people do."

Well, in terms of time travel it's no distance at all from Victorian England to the modern world of moon shots and extraterrestrials, and so I liked hearing Betty's answer when I asked how she could know for sure that she was really from another planet.

Her response was a perfect blend of British self-confidence and those charming Old World manners of her native England. She laughed and gave me a shrug, with a very confident, "Oh, I absolutely know that I am! And I've been back there!"

Don't call it astral travel, she told me. She doesn't like that term, but during the period that some people call sleep, Betty says she goes back to the planet Venus, which is her base station, though not her extraterrestrial home. As we've said, she identifies her place of origin as Antares, which is part of the constellation Scorpio.

"I absolutely know that," she said. "And I've met a lot of brothers and sisters who are from that same star. These are other human beings—in flesh, like you—but when we look each other in the eye there's no doubt at all. And as soon as we meet we don't speak in words, we speak another language that we know."

Our discussion continued in a very comfortable back and forth. Betty, I believe, demonstrated how the conviction of E.T. identity, once it takes hold, then becomes central, more important than any concern about what the others may say, think, or do—even the king, queen, and empire. She was not only comfortable on the fringe, she had actually found a society of her own. She was aware of its history and organization and was willing to speak about some of the details.

"I can't tell you what my place of origin is like because it's been so long since I've been there," she said, "but I can intimately tell you about my station base on Venus because I go back there regularly."

A lot of the Star People who come in from outer stars use the planets of this solar system as station bases, Betty said. It all depends on the extraterrestrial group.

"There are a number of groups that use Mars and a number of groups that use Venus. And there's a galactic council that uses Saturn—which isn't a mission base, but where the council meets." This group is formally called the Council of Saturn she said, and it's responsible for administering our entire solar system. Interestingly, *The RA Material* speaks of this same group.

For many, said Betty, to be E.T. is to have a specific task or mission to do while on this planet. "And there are those who don't need to come back to this Earth anymore, don't need to incarnate anymore, because they've finished with this school of life and the particular lessons that this school has. And there are others who've elected to come back to help the Earth and the people of Earth." This world is definitely part of the galactic network of evolving life.

I'll speak more about this in our look at why those claiming E.T. identity believe they've arrived here on Earth. More, also, on the final message concerning identity that many extraterrestrials gave me. For now, though, I'd like to end with what Betty viewed as the conclusion of her many years—indeed, many lifetimes—of experience in matters of this planet and elsewhere.

"In the final analysis," she said with the gentlest lilt of a British accent, "it doesn't matter."

> It doesn't matter whether we were born as Earth people or whether we came from some distant star. If we truly believe what we're all trying to understand and learn here—that we're all part of the One Source of all creation—then really, it doesn't matter. All that matters is that you're processing through that path to divinity and learning how to love and be loved. That's all that matters.

Then she smiled, gave a polite nod of the head, and it was time for the interview to end.

7

THE WHOLE (OTHER) WORLD IS WATCHING

E.T.s VIEW THE MEDIA . . . VIEWING E.T.s

The media absolutely love extraterrestrials.

They love E.T.s and spaceships, strange tales of abduction, and weird little green men; they love believers, skeptics, bunkers and debunkers, and almost every character in between.

And with friends like that, you don't need enemies.

Here, for example, is the headline from a recent article in the *New York Times*:

STUDY FINDS NO ABNORMALITY IN THOSE REPORTING UFOS

The story, under the byline of *New York Times* science writer Walter Sullivan (author of the classic study *We Are Not Alone*) goes on to report on research that was conducted by the psychology department of Carleton University in Ottawa, Canada. It says that a study of forty-nine people, all of them claiming to have seen UFOs, "found no tendency toward abnormality, *apart from a pre-*

vious belief that such visitations from beyond the Earth do occur."
(italics mine)

While I obviously take issue with classifying a belief in UFO visitation as "an abnormality," the article, I think, is also a pretty good
example of how the mainstream media—even in the guise of objective news reporting by respected writers—starts from certain, possibly unconscious, assumptions. Crudely stated, the outlook is this:
If you're serious about extraterrestrial alternative reality, *you've got
problems.*

Go a step further and mention 1) that you've seen a UFO or,
heaven forbid, 2) that you happen to be an extraterrestrial! and
the official response is: *You're absolutely nuts!* That's the launch-
pad, the basic assumption, that they're using.

What were the psychologists trying to learn? The article goes
on to say that the university hoped to determine whether UFO sightings had anything to do with "abnormalities of the temporal lobe
of the brain, which figures in memory and learning." Beginning
from a presumption of mental illness, they're doing their best to
ferret out the causes.

No, was the conclusion. Not only that, but the study found that
the UFO sighters "proved slightly more intelligent" than the control group of people who had not had any such experience.

However, this being the psychology department, there were many
other abnormalities they still had to worry about. The researchers
went on to suggest that eventually those who had seen UFOs should
be examined as possible sufferers of "sleep paralysis"—remember,
we said this was a common psychological "explanation." Sleep paralysis is the condition that renders its victims immobile either when
they're falling asleep or when they're awakening and includes hallucinations, a feeling of suffocation, and "the sense of a presence."
The psychologists, apparently, had to find some abnormality to
explain this supposedly "abnormal" experience. Sadly, this is
respected in current, human civilization as *objective science.*

For the mainstream media, when it comes to E.T.s, the presumption is: Something has just *got* to be wrong.

But that's only when information is being presented. When the purpose is entertainment, there's definitely a lot more excitement. . . .

Although we're so reluctant to be open-minded about such notions as soul transfer, Wanderers, Walk-ins, or the evolution of consciousness, we seem to have no trouble at all spending hours and hours transfixed, nearly hypnotized, (paralyzed, maybe) in front of one of our stranger Earth devices: that small box that receives invisible transmissions, assembles them, and redisplays them as images.

Otherwise known as: the television set . . . that hallowed icon of culture.

For some reason, it almost seems natural that when we touch the right button at the right time we see—live and in color—men walking on the moon or drifting in space, images of other planets or of the latest mission by astronauts, who wave hello as they float in zero gravity.

Or what about the popular reruns of *Star Wars*, *Close Encounters*, *Alien Nation*, *E.T.*, or any of the numerous television talk shows that frequently feature the good, the bad, and the abducted? And if we listen closely, we can plot how deeply extraterrestrial terminology has penetrated into the slang of mass communications, the Defense Department, everyday life. *The Star Wars missile defense system. E.T., phone home with your favorite long distance carrier.* . . .

Unfortunately, almost everything the mainstream knows about extraterrestrial comes from the mass media, not from serious wondering or study or investigation or even from a period of deep inner questioning. *Almost everything, broadly speaking, is the product of some form of show business.* And, unfortunately, the profit motive has definitely slanted the portrayal of the E.T. question.

Take this estimation from Vicky—the woman who was so comfortable and enthusiastic about her E.T. identity: She calculated that within one year (1993) TV stations around the United States aired approximately four hundred shows about aliens, and that's not counting commercials that use extraterrestrials as a premise. Vicky even believes that some of these shows were aired as part of a government disinformation campaign, testing the human reaction to the E.T. phenomenon.

In this chapter, however, I'm more interested in how this explosion of material, this mass-media vision of the E.T., UFO, and "contactee" experience, appears to those who seriously and profoundly believe that they're From Elsewhere.

It's not too different from the concerns of almost every other minority group in the United States, as well as of plenty of people who simply think about the world differently.

What is it like, not only to hold a radical sense of identity, but to see yourself constantly reflected in the funhouse mirror of mass communication? Win, lose, or draw, it's always a powerful experience for members of such a group.

People Have Some Goofy Ideas

This is the story of a woman who once worked in the media and walked away from that career after seeing the light . . . literally.

Belinda is an attractive, conservatively dressed woman in her late forties who has always held respectable jobs and who seems very much at ease with herself in society. She's comfortable with authority and is a person solidly in the mainstream and not at all on the fringe.

Except: Belinda is a Wanderer.

For the better part of a decade, she's enjoyed a solid career as a clinical hypnotherapist and "trance channeler." But before her current career, she was a free-lance art director and graphic designer for some of the country's more important advertising firms, a career that she was well satisfied with . . . at least on the surface.

130

In June of 1978, while living in California, Belinda was going through what she called "some personal emotional problems," and one day in midweek, sitting and watching TV as evening approached, she felt the walls starting to close in and decided she couldn't stay home any longer. Belinda got in her car and drove to the home of a man she considered a good friend, explaining to him that she just didn't want to be alone.

"I'm really sorry you're going through all this," he said. "Is there anything I can do?"

"Just hold me," Belinda told him. "And let me know it's all going to be all right."

Her friend put his arms around her. At that moment, Belinda says, she suddenly and unexpectedly went through a series of sensations so strange that they eluded her ability to use words, something she could only describe as a spiritual experience, and which she remembered as "a bright white light and the feeling of lost time." That was all.

Shaken, she returned to her house a few hours later, but on the drive back home she'd resolved to stand by herself, to trust whatever it was that she'd just experienced.

One thing she decided almost immediately: She was, at her center, a very spiritual person who could not find spirituality in the very worldly field of advertising.

She acted on that idea. Belinda began taking courses in all kinds of spiritual disciplines and felt compelled, she said, "to learn everything I could put my hands on." Again, we see an urgent spiritual curiosity common to many E.T. souls awakening to their identity.

Before the night of this mysterious spiritual occurrence at her friend's house, Belinda had no more than a passing interest in astrology; that was the extent of her occult or esoteric interests. Afterward, she began to read voraciously about E.T.s, reincarnation, dreams, and OBEs; always with the odd idea, she told me, that, "Oh, yeah, I'm supposed to remember all this stuff!"

"There were dreams," she said, "*if they were dreams*, that were like being aboard a spaceship. Like real. And the feeling continued into my waking state. I also did automatic writing and read Ruth Montgomery and Edgar Cayce."

I was interested that Belinda considered a lot of this to be *remembering* and I asked her a few more questions. She told me that as a Wanderer, she was, indeed, stripping away layers of her Earth personality to get to something deeper, something that had always been there. One of her stories I found particularly interesting . . .

> When I was four, my parents took me to Michigan on vacation. We were in the country, fishing, walking in the woods. One night, late, I got up and snuck outside all alone to take a walk around the lake where our cabin was. The moonlight was beautiful, reflected on the water. All of a sudden, a tall man appeared by the side of the lake and he seemed to get even taller, and the feeling I got from him was just total sweetness and love.
>
> He said to me, *Can you walk on the moonlight?*
>
> I said, *No, I'm afraid to fall in the water.*
>
> He told me, *If you take my hand we can walk.*
>
> We did. In a few seconds we were in a spaceship. There, I spoke with another man and a woman and they let me play with toys, like you get on Earth, that were lying around on the floor. I remember that. They gave me a light physical examination and then they said, *You're going to be big and strong when you grow up and something special will happen to you. Don't be afraid of it.*

One of the two people aboard the ship, Belinda has come to believe, was actually Belinda herself—a future self, perhaps from the far future. She'd returned to the present to help the child Belinda grow up.

Gradually, over a period of many years, "almost like it was natural to me," Belinda came to realize that her personality was made up of many different parts and that they didn't all fit into an easy definition. Not only was there the human Belinda, but there was something or somebody else, another part that was very difficult to define.

What she came to realize was that she was really an extraterrestrial soul.

Belinda continued to work in advertising while earning a bachelor's degree in metaphysical sciences, after which she was ordained as a spiritualist minister. With more study, she became a clinical hypnotherapist specializing in E.T.s and past lives.

I was picking up on her enthusiasm as she spoke. This reflection of her positive growth was another aspect of her transformation and I enjoyed hearing about it; she seemed so animated and proud in the telling.

Fully realizing she was an E.T., Belinda said, did away with the timid parts of her personality. She was still an artist working in advertising, but now, she said, she'd demand good assignments, and then if the client failed to pay, she'd stand up for herself, making sure she got the money she'd worked for.

And finally, her newfound courage took her to a public convention of the Association for Past Life Research and Therapy (APRT), and there, for the first time, Belinda publicly announced her E.T. identity.

"So," I asked her. "Having been through all this, and having worked in the media, what's your view of the media's presentation of E.T.s?"

Belinda became very businesslike.

"It's a kind of stereotyping," she said. The statement was made without any apparent anger or resentment, but she described the media image of E.T.s as restricted to the realm of cartoons: terrifying, ridiculous, or sometimes just cute. But E.T. identity, she said, is almost never considered to be a subject that needs to be taken seriously. I concurred.

In fact, she went on, you can almost guess which of the skeptics and debunkers they're going to put on the screen.

"They'll bring on Philip Klass (publisher of the *Skeptics UFO Newsletter*) or somebody," she says, "and it's always pretty predictable. And usually they're there to either mystify us or let people snicker." Because, she says, people seem to feel more comfortable if the "experts" allow them to laugh it all away.

The reason? Part of the cause is political, Belinda believes, resulting from the probable withholding of evidence on the part of the government.

But more important, and closer to her own field of interest and training, she focuses on the psychological view. The media portrayal, Belinda says, *has its foundation in the fear of the unknown.* In particular, it is the deeply held and persistent human belief "that the unknown, without exception, always has to be frightening."

That's usually reinforced by the media, which then tighten the leash on readers and viewers, keeping them from opening up to other kinds of experience. It also keeps them from deepening their own inner dialogues.

"People have some really goofy ideas about change," Belinda told me, "that it's evil or bad or downright scary. But really, change goes on all the time."

She said, "If the media and the press and the public in general would embrace the truths about E.T.s and UFO contacts, that they're really occurring, then they'd have to fundamentally change the way they perceive reality. It would no longer be *A-B-C* and black and white."

Too bad, she says. That fear of change keeps people terrified of confronting something that would "move them forward in the evolution of consciousness."

"Which is somewhat confusing," Belinda concluded. "You see it going on and it makes your strongest feeling: *Why on Earth* (literally!) *would they want to do that?*"

SOME OF THE FEAR IS APPROPRIATE

One answer to that question of *why* came from Lucia, the holistic teacher who pioneered a variety of ideas for alternative methods of personal growth after a Walk-In experience in Northern California.

Regarding the media portrayal of E.T.s, Lucia says: Yes, it comes from frightened people who are terrified of facing change, "but some of that fear is appropriate."

"From what I've learned," and Lucia was very definite about this, "there *really are* some E.T.s to be concerned about. There *are* unevolved ones who are harmful and destructive."

But having given that warning, Lucia believes there's far too much attention paid to negative images of those who come From Elsewhere. To rely solely on the picture presented by the media is to rely on a biased and unbalanced view.

"I feel," she says, "that there needs to be more acceptance of the benevolent side of it. There really are good E.T.s. . . ."

When I agreed with her, Lucia went on to quickly point out another important point about media attention: more than worrying about positive or negative images, she said, there needs to be public acceptance that the E.T. experience is a reality: *They exist.* In form. Here and now.

After that, she says, "There needs to be more of a discerning over who are the harmful ones, and there should be more openness to the ones who are helpful." She knows that you can't generalize about all E.T. motives.

And there's one more area where Lucia advises some careful discernment and eyes-open questioning, an area in which people often get away without any scrutiny at all: the skeptics, themselves.

In other words, *be critical of the critics!* Lucia points to one of the most often seen, most popular media forms used on TV: the format that encourages easy drama by forcing a loud, confrontational face-off between someone who claims E.T. reality and some well-known E.T. debunker. The two sides can then play off one another, which is a polite way of saying they can have one of those overheated shouting matches that are ripe for the tube. The real purpose: to utilize extraterrestrials for show after show after show. It keeps people watching. But it's not easy to learn much from a shouting match. . . .

This view, using the example of UFOs, is illustrated admirably by writer Keith Thompson in his book, *Angels and Aliens: UFOs and the Mythic Imagination:*

> All along, debunkers recite their familiar mantra—*hoax, hallucination, mistaken identity*—while pro-UFO researchers keep insisting UFOs *are not only real, they are the most important story in human history.* Thus, players can enter the game knowing which side to root for: ours. Players get to agree on rules: (1) try to be convincing, (2) try harder. And on procedure: each side's referees shall call the plays. And on the goal: to prevail. (Any day now ... this time, finally.)

All of this in the context of an unwritten, unspoken dictate: No one shall prevail.

Ever.

Above all else, the game must go on.

So the questions will never be settled by the usual patterns of debate, and the arguments will go on endlessly—*neither side can prove its position.*

But Lucia suggests that the skeptics are getting off too easy in the public eye. Some skepticism has to be reserved for the skeptics, themselves.

"It's all subjective experience," she says, "and subjective experience is one of the main issues. No one can prove it. No one can prove God, either, and no one can prove soul. It's not a physical thing." In fact, no one can even prove the "you who woke up this morning" is the "you who went to bed last night."

On television, it's usually the debunker who's viewed as serious; it's the skeptic who gets some kind of unspoken, perhaps unconscious, respect. But people who make their living deflating esoteric ways of being, Lucia says, are pretending they have a certainty that, in reality, is impossible to attain. Their self-satisfaction is completely baseless, inappropriate, and unjustified. *The question of proof is still unanswered.* We still have no conclusions.

Echoing the kind of statement I heard many times in interviews with Walk-ins and Wanderers, Lucia told me it all "comes down to honoring everybody's inner knowing of what's what."

Overall, however, she sees a growing acceptance and understanding of the E.T. experience, a wider belief that being From Elsewhere is something more than just sci-fi.

"I think," Lucia concludes, "that we're coming to a time when it will be pretty undeniable."

And many people say this time is coming fast. . . .

THEY'RE AFRAID OF HAVING PEACE: THE POLITICS OF E.T.s

Most of those who took part in my study agreed with Belinda and Lucia: Fear is usually what fuels the common perception of E.T. existence. But quite often, what's out in the open, what we can see and talk about, isn't what frightens us most deeply. What *truly* turns us pale, well, that often gets buried somewhere and goes unseen altogether. Denial is a powerful and most effective human tool.

I heard one opinion, however, that was a variation on the theme that took off to find a frequency all its own. In this particular outlook, fear is definitely placed at the heart of the matter, but according to this perspective, human terror doesn't just spring from nowhere. It has a nice, solid base in human politics.

Why-we-see-what-we-see-when-we-see-it, from this political viewpoint, is wrapped up in the world that's right here under our feet: the world of political corruption, hidden agendas, and the need to maintain order and the status quo.

I heard an outspoken example of this from the woman I've been calling Barrie, a woman who is definitely *not* in the mainstream. A well-known psychic on the East Coast who lectures all over the country, Barrie has always been very much at home with her E.T. identity. Now in her late thirties, she specializes in what she calls "teaching about Star People and the identity-awakening process," a role she finds herself very well-suited for.

What she sees in the media, she told me, makes her very upset.

"If there's a negative, there's also a positive, but all they do is portray the monster side. They just want to scare the public. They don't want to show that E.T.s are here to help the planet in any way."

Listening to this, the question that arose in me was, of course . . . Why? What's the point of such a lopsided portrayal, if that, indeed, is what we're seeing? E.T. bad guys may sell, I said to Barrie, but E.T. good guys can be commercial, too. Steven Spielberg gave us a good example of that. Barrie's answer to me was a little more serious and ventured outside the boundaries of what it means to simply put together a good film or TV drama. She believes there's a lot more than ratings at stake. *If you show the benevolence of those who are From Elsewhere*, Barrie said, it would not only mean accepting the reality of E.T.s, *it would mean actually putting some cracks in the very foundation of our current worldwide political power structure.*

I asked her to explain her view a little more.

Barrie put it this way: How could the world continue on its course of war and famine, social injustice and inequality, fear, suspicion, and hate if it were known that there are beings among us who are in touch with a greater wisdom and, more important, a greater love? Our faith in authority would definitely spring a leak. How could we blithely follow our leaders if we realized there are cosmic beings of immense maturity available to help us right now?

There's an interesting aside to this view. It's related to Brad Steiger's informal 1986 survey (described in his latest book, *Star Born*) in which Steiger identified seventeen hypotheses that are commonly used to explain the UFO phenomenon. One of those ideas, which he termed The Government Conspiracy Hypothesis, goes like this: Washington is keeping mum about a secret plan to acquire advanced alien technology in exchange for allowing a certain number of UFO abductions on Earth so that the evil aliens can conduct medical experiments. (This is actually a common topic on the agenda of UFO conventions in a variety of nations.)

Interestingly, Barrie's view of the conspiracy—from an E.T. position—is that the cover-up is much wider and seeks to obscure the *goodness* of those who are From Elsewhere. *Almost as if true goodness is what the government really fears!* A simple fear of kind power. And a rejection of powerful kindness . . .

"They're afraid of having peace throughout the world," Barrie said, adding that it was her deepest belief that international peace would nevertheless be the eventual result of an official acceptance of those who are From Elsewhere. Many Wanderers deem this inevitable.

But peace, Barrie is convinced, would be a tremendous threat to the status quo: With peace, armies would have to lay down their weapons, police forces would shrink, the entire economic system would have to search for some basis other than war, and, finally, the foundations holding up big government would crumble. For those in power, peace is downright dangerous. A strange idea? There are social activists "down here on the ground" who've said the same. And there is also the global structure of the "ruling elite" (based on power, money, and conflict), which would shatter if humanity really did transfer allegiance to benevolent E.T. groups. No one in power today would want to see their position undermined.

So, the media portrayal of E.T.s, Barrie says, makes her frustrated and a little angry "but most of all, it saddens me."

She told me that all too frequently, when you turn on the TV, you get the little-green-men-are-coming-to-take-you-away view of E.T.s. And it's not helped by the many people who claim to be E.T.s or claim to be authorities on E.T. identity but who are, in Barrie's words, "flakes and phonies and people who are just latching on, searching for something. They make the real E.T.s look like fools."

Again, she cites a political machine at work, an actual government disinformation campaign that is trying to keep the public on the dark side of the moon. Again, fear of the light.

"Not enough people are paying attention," Barrie said with concern; and she then criticized the New Age movement for what she called its often "flaky, weak-minded" understanding of politics and political motivation. The movement doesn't know how the system works and how the system must be changed.

By hiding or running away from that aspect of Earth life, New Agers are missing the mark, says Barrie, because just like any other issue, *the debate over extraterrestrial identity can also be seen as having a political side.* And like any other controversial issue that involves power, money, and politics, there is going to be a good possibility of intrigue: official secrets, disinformation, censorship, spying, and group infiltration, plus a lot of other unsavory activity.

"We shouldn't go on letting them make everyone look like a fake. It's sad. It's just for the power. It keeps them [the people of Earth] from really being able to see themselves. But the truth will come out."

And when the idea of E.T. reality finally breaks through?

Then, Barrie believes, government leaders will be faced with making an embarrassing confession:

We don't know anything about the universe. Our government doesn't know anything—but these Beings DO!

DON'T ATTACH ANY MACHINERY TO ME!

Not all of those who've recognized and accepted that they're From Elsewhere feel so strongly about the media. Not everyone pays particular attention.

Joan, for example, is a heavyset woman in her mid-forties with long, curly black hair who radiates such a powerful and tangible energy field that when I hugged her goodbye at the end of our interview I walked away feeling almost high. It's something she says she's got to be careful about; not everyone appreciates the feeling!

Since childhood Joan has been plagued by a series of health problems, but she says that her most persistent difficulty these days is "simply how to accept being here on this planet and understand what it means to be human." Her E.T. identity broke through to consciousness during a hypnotic regression several years ago.

Joan told me that currently she almost never goes to the movies and doesn't even own a TV. What she has seen, when watching television at her daughter's house, she described as "narrow and very limiting." ("Although," she added with a laugh, "I do like *Star Trek*"—and so do I!)

Again, like many of those claiming to be E.T. souls, Joan doesn't like the fact that when an "alien" shows up on the screen, the Being is almost always evil. It's terribly unfair, she believes, although that kind of evil *is* for real: There *are* some E.T.s who need a lesson in Universal love, in addition to simple human etiquette.

Joan was the center of one unfortunate incident recently at her home in California. She claims to have been the subject of an attempted abduction. Strange E.T.s, she said, without any kind of facial characteristics—weird elongated beings with evil intentions—appeared in her bedroom, surrounded her as she lay sleeping, and briefly tried to connect some type of strange equipment to her body. Joan woke up startled and was determined to confront them.

"Don't attach any machinery to me!" she shouted.

If you've seen too many E.T. movies you might think you know how this turns out, but don't be too sure. The conclusion, Joan says, was somewhat different than even she expected. She told me that with the help of a friend who had been staying over and was sleeping in the next room, she was able to talk to her assailants and convince the evil E.T.s that they had no right to violate her body or go against her will.

"They knew they were transgressing the Law even though they had no human emotions," she told me. "But they seemed to know that the [Divine] Law is over and above even them."

Once bowing to that recognition of Universal Law, the negative E.T.s backed off and left her alone. She had made them cease and desist.

It's just such an experience, Joan said, that makes her not care too much about how E.T.s are portrayed on the tube. Her own attempted abduction is not exactly the kind of experience that would send somebody rushing to the TV set for more escapist fare about spaceships and tiny grey beings with weirdly shaped heads. She knows the power of tapping into the Divine Will.

Another life of intense experiences has been lived by the man I've called Bob. His personal odyssey catapulted him through rage and narcotics addiction to a series of abrupt, explosive spiritual experiences.

And to hear Bob talk about E.T.s in the media is to listen to someone who sounds tolerant, detached, and maybe even slightly bored.

He shrugs it off. "I really don't have any strong feelings about it. I see some of it in a negative light, some of it in a positive light. But whatever it is, it's just someone's subjective feelings about it, how people interpret what they feel. . . . It's good to remember," Bob says, "that whenever you're seeing some image like that on TV, you have to take into account *who's* doing it, *where* it's being done, and *why* . . . all of that."

In other words, recognize and keep in mind that the presentation is usually skewed in one direction or another.

IT TENDS TO PISS ME OFF

Almost like Joan's, Bob's outlook, which seemed to me almost nonchalant, might have grown out of his dramatic Walk-in experience and struggle against drug addiction. Maybe it was that once having seen so much of the darker aspects of human existence, TV images don't really faze him.

And, like Bob, Christin has been touched by life's sharper edges in a journey that includes everything from symptoms of HIV infection to dealing with discrimination against gays to a series of powerful and dazzling energy shifts that led finally to E.T. identity. Christin is no stranger to the extremes of Earthly life, and when I asked about his outlook on the media, he was less serene than most, sounding even a little angry.

"It tends to piss me off," he said.

I told him I could understand his reaction, but I saw that he wanted to be heard, to make sure I was getting down the finer points of what he had to say. He very seriously let me know that he was talking about some important aesthetic questions, ideas about form and content, issues concerning what information can be expressed and how it can be presented.

"Portrayals of E.T.s in the media have to come through the imagination, the minds of human beings," he said. "And the imagination simply *doesn't have the form* to express E.T. identity. That means you get these polarities: good E.T.s, bad E.T.s, E.T.s who end up filtered through the human brain in terms of Earth's physical realities."

This perspective will be familiar to anyone with an interest in Eastern philosophy. Remember the Zen adage that the finger pointing at the moon is not the moon itself? Even our vision of the Moon is that of only one side seen from a great distance. When do we ever see a total picture? Is such a vision possible? A provocative quote from the E.T. group known as RA says, "Understanding is not of your density."

This is a perspective that's not completely absent from Western science, either: the understanding that the viewer changes his experiment by the very act of viewing and that every question influences its answer.

For Christin, all forms of popular entertainment should be seen in just that light. They're imperfect human productions made within the confines of budgets, schedules, ratings, marketing, and a demand that the finished product be some kind of drama or comedy or romance whose main purpose really is: *keep watching*!

In our several interviews, Christin seemed to display a hard-won maturity even while discussing issues that affected him emotionally. His only advice about how to deal with the flawed media vision of E.T.s was to "look within yourself for the answers when you see UFO contacts, E.T.s, or someone who claims to be From Elsewhere." Again—trust your Self.

Because the human imagination lacks a form for the depiction of E.T. identity, most of the portrayals tend to be simplistic. What often occurs, however, is that when Christin watches a film, he'll recognize some particular E.T. quality, and see it as something he knows is true. It's well dramatized even though the larger story is less than perfect.

Christin cited the popular Steven Speilberg film *E.T.,* as an example. That picture, he said, was obviously a piece of popular entertainment and was, of course, still well within the boundaries of human imagination. It did depict, however, a few E.T. qualities that can sometimes be dramatized, such as the ability of some extraterrestrials to heal.

Given the "usual hype," Christin said, it was good to see a film that accurately displayed a positive, healthy aspect of some E.T. experience.

And he added, "This healing . . . I've really seen that happen."

He never throws out the baby with the bathwater—and he has the wisdom to realize that truth is often lodged in fantasy . . . at least here on Earth.

UFO Lands on White House Lawn!

In a culture where fact and fiction are often inseparable, supermarket tabloids—the *Star,* the *National Enquirer, News of the World*—sometimes seem the perfect form of media. Despite their wide appeal and millions upon millions of readers at every social, educational, and economic level, the papers still have a kind of "pink flamingos on the suburban lawn" reputation, disdained as the type of mag you'd find in a strip mall "nail shop." They're a disrespected source of information that a great number of people read in secret—the perfect place for those steamy, bizarre, and fascinating tales of glittering UFOs and terrifying E.T. contacts.

Because of their widespread "coverage" of off-planet matters— the *Enquirer* alone boasts a readership of 3.5 million—I think it's important to include a separate section devoted exclusively to how the nation's tabloid press treats souls from other planets and densities.

On any week, you can open one of the tabloids and find out such interesting information as who E.T.s are supporting for president, how meteors are actually frozen Venutian warriors (an opinion I've entertained more than once!), and how extraterrestrials have a secret food that will let you lose forty pounds without dieting.

It should be noted, also, that American tabloids have assumed a new place in the country's journalistic consciousness because of their aggressive coverage of the O. J. Simpson murder trial. According to those far away on the opposite shore—the *New York Times* (October 22, 1994)—the *National Enquirer* "has broken numerous stories" and was not guilty of reporting much of the erroneous information that continually made its way into more respected outlets. The tabloids, said the *Times*, were having a profound impact on the case.

So, not everything you read, standing there waiting for the cashier, is untrue.

But aliens?

There is a segment of E.T. opinion that sees the tabloids as pushing the discussion of extraterrestrials to the fringe, maintaining the global "laughter curtain" behind which reality may be hidden. But that which is forced into hiding quite often takes its revenge.

"Sensationalism," said the E.T. I'm calling Soren, "is the way unwanted material intrudes into consciousness. Dreams are like that, too. It's looking through a funhouse mirror at something we need to look at. Artists, mystics, crazy people, help in that way, also. All the ways we think of as being on the fringe."

From the perspective of Soren and many others who claim E.T. identity, fantasy is good, tall tales are fine, and pervasive confusion is the "name of the game" on this planet. *It all acts as a catalyst to learning and discovering what really is true.* Some Wanderers even remarked that trusting rationality as the final means to knowledge is absurd and certainly hasn't brought about peace on Earth. They fully realized that a complete and final understanding of anything on Earth is impossible.

So, I'm offering Soren's view as one of the more nicely stated commentaries about the tabloids, and because his views were pretty much mirrored in the comments of others claiming E.T. identity.

Lucia, for instance, said the tabloids diluted the truth and she "didn't resonate to them." She found the papers disturbing and too much in the realm of glamour, something she warned against and was determined to avoid.

There was a similar view from Bob, who said that "a lot of people feed" on the supermarket papers and they're too sensational, which creates a problem: "They make E.T.s too unbelievable for the public. They make it seem so out there, when it should be a normal experience. It's not as traumatic as they make it sound."

Justinian was a little more open to the tabloids because he felt they were "like science fiction movies." In his estimate, about 10 percent of what the tabloids say about E.T.s is true ... and that's 10 percent more than the mainstream media! So Justinian told me that "it puts the word out and the more that happens, good!"

After speaking to a number of E.T.s about the supermarket press, I went back and asked Soren about some of their ideas, about the critique that they glamorize the experience.

"Glamour?" he said. "The world is glamour. Glamour is illusion. What are you going to do, walk away from it? That's the stuff of the world, the glamorous aspect of the Creator."

To Soren, the experience couldn't be easily labeled a simple positive or negative.

"It's another avenue of human experience," he said. "Some of it's fact and some of it's not, but we don't know which is which. Sort of like the experience of Earth life in general."

On the favorable side of the tabloids, Soren called them "the opposite of a scholarly paper and just as valid." Very valuable, he told me, because they pay attention to the emotions, which are not easy to find in the everyday media.

SCHOOLHOUSE EARTH

"It's such an expanded concept for most people that it's truly frightening," declares Inid. "But whether the media shows something as positive or negative, everything is really a lead-up to the New Age that's coming. So it's all perfect."

Vigorous and healthy, Inid is an easygoing woman with light brown hair who was very open about enjoying the sensual aspects of life on Earth. She's the Walk-in who once had the arguable notion that she was the Earth's sole representative of an E.T. confederation. Questioning that idea, however, didn't dim my interest in her other observations.

While drawing a clear line between positive and negative, Inid also believes that the two poles are in a sort of yin-yang relationship, rolling back and forth upon one another, one polarity always affecting the other. Ultimately, she seemed to be saying, it was all in the service of the same process. And ultimately, it all concerned learning. *Our* learning.

Speaking about several well-known representations of E.T.s— movies like *Fire in the Sky*, *Communion*, *E.T.*—Inid said that some of the productions were helpful while others were based in fear, but that all of them were probably "necessary and part of everything." They are all part of a single learning process, as humanity explores its own ideas.

Inid said that even a film which showed a generally negative view "something like *Communion*, which seemed to be more fear-based . . . even that was informational and interesting and different.

147

So there is a positive aspect to it. It's all part of providing hints of awareness so people won't be so frightened. And there does seem to be more and more acceptance that there are other dimensions and other realities."

Positive or negative, she says, it's all a dialogue about something that's real, and something that's important for our planet. All of the debate is on the syllabus of "schoolhouse Earth."

One helpful guideline when you see an E.T. portrayal in the media, Inid advised: Remember they're always concerned with *labels.* And while labels make it much easier to produce a TV program, we might actually get to a deeper and more profound understanding of our lives by setting aside all those labels for a while. The truth is always complex and multilayered and labels are always just sewn on the surface.

And what about the "flakes and phonies and people who are just latching on" that Barrie talked about; squeaky wheels who push themselves to the forefront of attention?

Inid maintained her composure, telling me that "everything is its own learning experience and everyone has something to learn. Because there's so much information and so many dimensions, people can get confused and caught up in the ego of it all, the power of it all. But that's just what we're here to learn." Her viewpoint: *The purpose of being on Earth is to learn.*

From the people who are deluded . . . to the people who are just followers . . . to the people who just feel turned-on by the whole scene . . . to the angry skeptics, Inid says, there's no reason for judgment, animosity, or harsh criticism. She says she doesn't get frustrated or angry, because all our opinions are just steps along the path of acquiring knowledge. And from greater knowledge flows wisdom.

"The people who are being deluded and the people who are making the claims . . . everything is just a kind of dance of learning." The Indian gurus call this the universal play of *lila,* or play

148

of consciousness, and in that view, everything is OK because everything is just the cosmic dance.

And here, Inid offered some thoughts about what it means to take part in that process, especially in an age when so much information is communicated by the mass media. We live in a push-button world that we see on a screen, with a tantalizing vision of easy expertise, quick learning, short cuts, and a no-sweat approach to just about everything—even workshops that promise us enlightenment in three days.

So, keep in mind, she said, that often, but not always, learning can be hard work, but hard work can be incredibly gratifying.

"Whatever you've chosen to learn or be expanded about," she explained, "it sometimes has to come through difficulty." Learning can mean the demand that we face our inner conflicts, that we confront old ways of seeing and reshape them. And conflict, Inid believes, is often at the center of why it's so difficult to learn. Sometimes, the refusal to do anything except simply absorb a tepid TV program is actually a hidden way to hold onto our old beliefs and remain mired in them. The same goes for laughing at E.T. identity. But once that reaction is worked through, the media can also be a springboard to a much more open view. To question our assumptions is a most healthy thing to do.

Asked to sum up her view of the media portrayal of E.T. experience, Inid characterized it simply: interesting, amusing, full of skepticism and joking about extraterrestrials.

"But we often laugh at things we don't understand. If you're nervous, you sometimes make a joke about it. But that's to be expected. It's such a major concept that has to do with people's control issues." We're always afraid of losing control, especially through the collapse of our cherished beliefs.

And that, she believes, is basically what makes people afraid.

"To accept that there are other dimensions," Inid says, "to accept that there are other things going on, that maybe we're even being moved by or are involved in something that's bigger than we understand . . . that can make people very angry. It threatens their sense of control." Anger often sprouts from confused fear.

I liked hearing her say that. I wish that, at the time, I'd had the *New York Times* article with me, the one with which this chapter began, the item detailing how scientists had found no abnormality among the UFO sighters they studied. It would have been nice to have shown that piece to Inid.

So, a last note about that article, which ends with this:

The Carleton psychologists reportedly *did* find something strange and unexpected when they finished their research and compared it to other studies focusing on UFO sightings. In those other investigations (so they are quoted as saying) everyone who claimed to have witnessed a UFO was reported afterward to be under "extreme stress" or was sent into "full-blown trauma"—they all believed in a coming E.T. attack. But in the Carleton study, the article goes on to say, researchers found something that completely negated that kind of trauma. The psychologists are quoted as saying that after the E.T. experience, most of their "UFO subjects were relatively content and anxiety free."

In fact, the article concludes with a statement that would please most of the Wanderers and Walk-ins in my study: In the Carleton experiment, UFO sighters were actually found to be taking comfort "in their belief that space aliens were concerned with, and even guiding, the destiny of mankind."

Perhaps these people met benevolent E.T.s who passed on a message of hope and faith. It would be nice to hear more hope and faith from our doubting *human* media. . . .

8

MISSION

So, Why Are We Here?

PROGRAM 1:

A strange Being from outer space gets off an unusual-shaped flying saucer and makes its way through a typical small town in late 1950s or early 1960s America.

The locals are so terrified of this extraterrestrial Being that they send out search parties packing shotguns and pitchforks, hunt it down and (in a variation on the traditional Welcome Wagon) kill it.

Lo and behold, when they turn over the body, they find some kind of otherworldly writing tablet on which the Being had begun to scribble down some outer space secrets that would have led immediately to world peace, a cure for all disease, and an answer to other tantalizing human problems. It is, to say the least, a tragedy.

PROGRAM 2:

A strange Being from outer space gets off an unusual shaped flying saucer and makes its way through a typical small town in late 1950s or early 1960s America.

Soon, it convinces the locals that it has arrived on a mission of goodwill and shows them a book entitled, *To Serve Man*.

Elated, dozens of grateful men, women, and children rush to climb aboard the otherworldly spacecraft hoping for a pilgrimage to the extraordinary planet of their extraterrestrial benefactor. But as they stand in line, all smiles and goodwill, one of the more skeptical of the locals comes rushing forward toward the crowd, his face twisted in terror, shouting, "*To Serve Man* . . . it's a cookbook!"

The connoisseur of sci-fi will immediately recognize these programs as classic episodes of the eternally popular *Twilight Zone* series, probably one of the major sources of extraterrestrial "information" for several generations of Americans.

They're pretty good illustrations, though, of two competing visions of extraterrestrial visitation. Simply put, *We're here to help,* or, if not . . . then, *We're here to get you.* And in both cases, the assistance or the damage is going to be immense. But even if they're high on entertainment value and low on actual E.T. data, these *Twilight Zone* segments point up one major question that has to be answered when it comes to the presence of extraterrestrials here on Earth.

WHY?

Not *why?* from the point of view of those on the outside, not from the skeptics and debunkers who use *why?* as a weapon to discredit. Instead, let's get an answer from those people who have chosen to live their lives claiming non-Earthly origins, the embodied E.T.s themselves—with many more presumably aboard hovering UFOs or in other spiritual dimensions. Why have these beings from distant worlds decided to visit us?

And there's something else. While most other discussions of personal identity, whether philosophical, psychological, or metaphysical, eventually bring us face-to-face with this question of *Why am I here?* E.T. identity throws some light on another issue. If we're talking about radical identity—Wanderers and Walk-ins—and taking it seriously, then we're not only faced with *Why am* I *here,* but suddenly with a second pressing question, as well, *Why are* we *here?* This is the question of collective mission.

What would possess Beings from another world, planet, galaxy, zone, time-frame, or "slice of reality" to pay a visit to Mother Earth, especially since they seem to be dropping by unannounced, risking life and limb, and arriving, seemingly, uninvited! What's the point of living here on Earth for those who claim to be extraterrestrials? Forget UFOs or flying saucers; why would any otherworldly Being voluntarily go through a soul transfer, Walk-in, or unremembered Wanderer birth so that he or she could live here among us Earthlings—feuding, fighting, polluting, overcrowding, or just desperately trying to decipher nutrition labels? Indeed, Earth is *not* the most hospitable of cosmic vacationlands.

In their book *Star Born,* authors Brad and Sherry Hansen Steiger, after years of research, have distilled seventeen hypotheses about, or possible "reasons" for, E.T. and UFO visitation. These ideas are based on their own interviews and questionnaires and attempt to cover all known reasons as to why extraterrestrials might want to live among us.

In *Star Born* (Berkley, 1992), the Steigers provide an entertaining and useful overview of possible solutions to the question of *why?,* answers that include the following:

E.T. benevolence, E.T. hatred, E.T. indifference to Earth and the plight of Earthlings; E.T.s as American military personnel who've been wrongly identified; E.T.s as part of an evil American government or New World Order conspiracy; E.T.s as time travelers, former residents of Atlantis, or escapees from the center of hollow Earth; E.T.s as Jungian archetypes, elves, angels, demons, messengers of God, changers of reality, or utilizers of some, as yet unknown, physical law. Enough possible explanations to keep the debunkers busy for the next couple of centuries.

Remember the wonderfully cute E.T. of Steven Spielberg's film

or the less-than-wonderful E.T.s of Whitley Strieber's *Communion,*
Bud Hopkins's *The Intruders,* or *Fire in the Sky,* the story of the
Travis Walter abduction case? Recently I even met a retired army
officer who told me that while he personally was not an E.T., he
was certain that outer space Beings had definitely arrived on this
planet and he was convinced they were here for ill and not for good.
This former military man insisted he had "information" that E.T.s
were using Earth as something like a huge garden, or ranch, culti-
vating humans as a kind of food! That was as far as he was willing to take the conversation. Fortunately, none of the E.T.s I interviewed were interested in that type of gardening.

Say the word *extraterrestrial,* however, and everyone has a
theory. Any survey of the literature and the media will turn up a
variety of E.T. purposes ranging from the saintly to the demonic.

What I found through my own conversations with embodied
E.T.s—conscious Walk-ins and Wanderers—was that when it came
to Earthly purpose, those claiming cosmic connections were almost
unanimous in their opinion.

Almost everyone felt that he or she had arrived here on Earth
for the same purpose. They were all part of a collective mission, but
this mission had to be fulfilled in a unique manner. The way the job
was carried out had to be as singular as the life, history, and beliefs
of that one particular Wanderer or Walk-in. The rationale behind
their visit sometimes sounded like an episode of *Twilight Zone,* but
the E.T.s who spoke with me were calm, articulate, and serious when
they talked about their mission. They had the power of conviction.

They were also very hard at work.

I'M HERE TO HELP

Let me give you a sampling of these views selected from several of
the people I was able to interview:

"[E.T. souls] are here for their own personal growth, to serve
and teach humanity, to serve the whole solar system, and as rep-

resentatives of their race and the confederation [a galactic organization of E.T. groups]." (Belinda)

"The spiritual influx of [E.T. souls] is to serve the old without
superiority, [bringing] light into darkness to transform it, needing
to surrender spirit to matter to awaken it [the basic Christ motif]."
(Pauline)

"There will be more and more Awakening for many very
quickly, with genetic triggers going off now and veils lifting—Wanderers all Awakening to themselves, to the higher vibrations." (Julie)

"The human form is necessary to bring the light in and transmute the [negative human] energies; it is necessary to take form
for both the individual [soul] and the whole race, including the
direct link to the angelic order, which aids both the human and
angelic kingdoms' evolution. The angelic beings [now incarnating]
are where Earth and humanity is evolving to: love, peace, and joy."
(Una)

Or, as Vicky told me, "I'm here to help."

In every single interview with someone claiming to be extraterrestrial, I found this same deeply held sense of service and obligation. Planet Earth was often at the center of this mission, but after
that, I frequently heard people say they felt their work involved
the entire galaxy with Earth as just one important cog in a major,
boundless system.

This was almost always wrapped up in a belief that the Earth
is now in the midst of a difficult, tumultuous, and extremely serious shift in consciousness, and that E.T. service is a much needed
ingredient in the ongoing process of evolution. But more on that
later. . . .

Whether Wanderer or Walk-in, the E.T. view of mission is
spoken of in global terms. Moving toward the "spiritualization of
humanity" is what it's about, or so I was told over and over. It's a

project more crucial than the affairs of any one nation, and it has to be placed way above any particular job or social position, and sometimes above personal or family relationships. When the conviction of service and mission is strong, everything else takes a backseat.

Remember, we said that the sense of purpose was collective. Many extraterrestrials told me that this mission to help Earth had to be carried out through individual work, but it was also linked to other extraterrestrial units or E.T. groups. There were many who believed it anchored (and reflected) the subtle work of the beneficent E.T.s associated with some of the UFOs spotted in our skies.

Vicky, who so succinctly stated that she was on Earth "to help," also went on to tell me that "the purpose of non-Earth souls is to counter the darkness here on Earth," which she believed could be done through her work with the Ashtar Command and Federation. She recognized other groups, as well.

Inid, too, thinks of herself as representing an interplanetary confederation and believes that she is not just another spiritual teacher but is here to "bring information to Earth to smooth and prepare the masses for public, mass ship sightings in about seven years." Many E.T.s, in fact, predict much more public, open contacts with UFOs before the end of the decade.

Lucia feels she is here to "midwife the transition, the birth of the new planet," and her friend Una made a similar comment about "serving in the transition time and bringing heaven to Earth." Again, we see a blending here: the practical and concrete mixed with the metaphysical and metaphorical. This is because the real E.T. service is to help uplift awareness, and is the nitty-gritty work of universal, spiritual evolution.

There was also Julie, echoing some of the beliefs found in *The RA Material* (see Appendix 3), which not only explain E.T. purpose as helping the Earth at a time of transition but, in Julie's words, helping to "transmute bodies and personalities from fear-based to love-based, awakening the sense of saving the planet."

Finally, summarizing many of the views I'd heard in my research, there was a comment from Soren who said he, himself, was "responding to the scene of an accident." He often felt like an emergency medical worker, he said, and enjoyed this kind of "crisis work on Earth." Remember, he's been a psychiatric ward technician for many years and the ironic humor of that symbolism wasn't lost on him.

Soren gave me a statement that I was to hear frequently from others in various forms.

> We're all From Elsewhere. And the statement *We are gathering* that I heard during my out-of-body experience means that Wanderers and Walk-ins are here to serve Earth as the Beings most responsive to Earth changes and the activity of the globe. Wanderers, in the past, were like the early fermentation bubbles, leading Earth to a general awareness of shared universal life and love, to allow an outward living in harmony.

So, all of us on Earth are here for one purpose—personal learning through the enrichment of love and wisdom. At the highest levels of thought, all souls are Universal Travelers, never stopping in the Infinite Journey through time and space—which is also the Great Work spoken of by many Western mystics.

We're all headed in one direction, Soren said. It's like the great migrations of the Earth's people that took place in the ancient past; only this time, instead of searching for food, we're moving toward a more conscious way of life. The conscious Walk-ins and Wanderers are simply those who have been to the farther side of our journey—but they, too, are still "on the Path."

THE PLANET WANTS TO KNOW

While this extraterrestrial mission is often explained in cosmic terms, it seems to require some very down-to-Earth work.

That was something else I kept hearing from the people who agreed to speak with me. All of this high-toned cosmic language eventually settled down to some very practical talk about how the "mission on Earth" was going to be carried out. Most of our E.T.s were as comfortable and easygoing with this style of intergalactic chitchat as somebody else might be gossiping around the office water cooler. In fact, in several interviews, I caught a little of that attitude where the "fantastic" was discussed, as if: *Hey, ain't everybody doing it?*

Also, consider this: It's possible, the E.T.s say, that each and every one of us—E.T.s and Earthlings alike—is already, right now, growing and expanding within this very same global, even universal "love-based" consciousness; we only have to open ourselves up to it. The planet is *already* alive within the New Age energies of love and compassion.

It was an attitude that reminded me of something close to the notions of the eighteenth-century English mystic and poet William Blake, who wrote about the infinite consciousness we'd all realize if only our "doors of perception" were cleansed. If we only *learned to see,* he believed, then we'd all be able to view the Infinite—it's not trying to hide from us!

If we allowed it, the esoteric would become the commonplace. And that's true even when one realizes his or her E.T. identity following some kind of extraordinary big-bang happening. It seems natural to develop a broad sense of mission after, say, the strange Awakening of a Walk-in experience. Common sense might assume that Walk-ins, soul exchange, visitation, visions, out-of-body experience, and prophetic dreams are different from the stuff of day-to-day reality, but many of the E.T.s would argue against that outlook.

All it takes, they say, is the ability to listen to yourself.

In fact, *the human personality is not separate from the Universal Self.* It's only a matter of being in tune with greater Being, more responsive to its call, and more fused with its cosmic consciousness. And this is one element that distinguishes E.T. souls from the native human souls. The E.T.s are quite comfortable with this spiritual sensitivity, even to the point of feeling universal fusion. It's just that the E.T.s have fallen under the "veil of forgetting," which usually covers their life on Earth.

Inid, who predicts the mass sighting of benevolent spaceships, lived through an incredibly dramatic Awakening. She started believing in her extraterrestrial mission after a series of events that sounded to me as if they could only have brought her to a single conclusion. She couldn't argue with her own experience.

At the beginning of the 1980s, Inid, whose original name was Kathryn, was thirty-two and living in Los Angeles in the thirteenth year of a marriage that was not so much on-the-rocks as merely drifting. It was, she said, "typical American middle class; married with children and thinking only of money and upward mobility. My husband was my high school boyfriend, so it was a very long-term relationship." She was still fond of her then-husband, but over the years the two of them had veered off onto different paths in life without noticing and without paying much attention to each other. And then one morning they'd awakened to discover a great gulf had opened between them.

At first they tried counseling, but it failed to bridge the gap. Too many emotional wounds had been left untreated for far too long. After a lot of tears and a lot of heartbreak, they decided to split up. It was then that Inid began seeing a therapist who utilized hypnosis.

During these sessions, Inid said, she began to get interested not only in herself and how she was living her life, but she also started wondering about the human mind in general. That was something she wouldn't have allowed herself to do before. Inid now gave herself the freedom to think about who she really was, and she trusted her own feelings about the heady subject of the human spirit.

"Before this," Inid says, "my knowledge about anything extraterrestrial didn't go any farther than what I learned from *Star Trek*, although I was really interested in that outlook." She smiled as she said it. "And I wanted to know more about the theory I saw, about the thinking that I saw on the show."

Without fully understanding why, she put herself through a serious course of home study. She read whatever she could get her hands on about past lives, E.T.s, Buddhism, cosmic consciousness, channeling, the *I-Ching,* psychics, "going from not really having any interest in that world, to delving into every psychospiritual level." She was already moving rapidly into the realms of the Universal, the Self, the Absolute.

Then, about six years ago, she decided to move to the magnificent coastal city of Carmel, California. Again, there was no definite reason; it just seemed right. Inid told me that in Carmel, amid the great beauty of its wooded areas and beach fronts, her consciousness slowly began to change; she could actually feel it.

"There was a lot of time spent walking on the beach," Inid said. "I started having these memories from out of nowhere, like particles of remembrance, about Atlantis. *It was like remembering something that you sort of already know.* Knowing but not knowing. And I spontaneously started drawing symbols on the beach, even though I wasn't sure what they were."

That evening of the mysterious beach walk, Inid said, she went out driving to the grocery store to do her week's shopping on what should have been a mundane trip. But the day had already put her in a very different frame of mind. Something was ready to give. As she drove along the tree-lined road that night, Inid looked up at the clear night sky and could make out what she describes as "an extraterrestrial ship up there," darting, moving quickly up and down and over and back, swift movements. Nothing incredibly vivid or dramatic, mind you; a small disc-like ship with a few lights around the edges.

Inid was exuberant: "I was delighted, very excited. I suddenly felt so happy to see it."

As she observed the ship's swift movements, Inid became aware that she was shifting into another dimension and somehow contacting whoever it was up there on the craft. She was feeling that she was in actual communication with the E.T.s aboard. Shortly afterward, however, she seemed to lose whatever message they may have conveyed.

But this UFO sighting was only the beginning. On the morning after, it was followed by a vision.

That morning Inid went to a small office just off the main street in Carmel to have an accupressure session, and as she lay there relaxing on the therapist's massage table, the various points on her body pressed and soothed, she suddenly saw a kind of blank space open before her, and right there, a tall, muscular man suddenly appeared, dressed in a helmet and leather protective clothing similar to that of a Roman centurion.

I'm in charge of you, he intoned. *You're under my command.*

No, I'm not, Inid answered. *I'm not doing that.*

She glared at him. It was a fearless stare, even if she secretly was very afraid, and it lasted for a long time until, she says, a second vision materialized. This time, it was an image she recognized from her childhood. Without warning, behind the soldier, there was an unexplained display of mist and lights, and when it settled, Jesus appeared. He set his hand gently on the Roman's shoulder, peered down at Inid and then quietly told the centurion, *It's all right. It's okay.*

Inid was afraid to tell the therapist what had happened, and when the accupressure was finished, she got up with a weak smile and simply left the room.

These visions, says Inid, were only a warm-up.

But as startling as they may seem, they came to her without any feeling of death or rebirth and with no sense of any tremendous break with the past. The reason for that, Inid was to discover later on, was that these experiences were actually happening to another soul; a soul that eventually departed from Inid. Her name was Kathryn, the original "inhabitant" born along with her body. Her pre-Walk-in self.

That original soul, Inid says, had arrived in her body to help smooth the way for Inid's mission on Earth. But first it had to deal with a series of past lives and memories involving Atlantis, Rome, and various levels of higher consciousness. There was also an incident of sexual abuse that this previous soul had to "work out" (in Inid's words), and, finally, one morning while she was meditating, it came to her—or again, to the soul named Kathryn: she was an extraterrestrial Walk-in.

But Kathryn wasn't quite ready to understand that.

"At the time," Inid says, "this was an isolated insight. Kathryn couldn't handle that revelation yet, so nothing happened right away. There was still a lot work to be done."

That work, she told me, involved several years of "releasing trauma from this current lifetime, working on self-esteem, inner-child work, unwinding victimization and abuse, and introspection. It was very difficult and there was a lot of mourning, a lot of sorrow and exhaustion."

In addition to those therapies, Kathryn took a job working for a church poverty program, helping to feed the homeless.

What allowed the soul named Kathryn to finish this project on herself and finally depart, was a series of hypnotherapy sessions with a psychologist in the Southwest, a specialist in the hypnosis techniques of Milton Erickson. After four days of treatment, she was able to unravel the last of her "self-esteem and abuse issues." That completed, Kathryn once again was able to push the edge of her E.T. awareness.

"Fully realizing that identity, though, would have blown the circuits at that point," Inid said. "The time still wasn't right." She understood only later how difficult the Walk-in (and walking-out) process had been.

A few days later, there followed what Inid calls "the most fantastically wonderful experience" of her life—an occurrence that really marked the beginning of her self-conscious E.T. identity.

It was Christmas Eve. Inid had not been drinking alcohol or coffee and she went to bed feeling happy and extremely healthy. As Inid (or, as she says, Kathryn) lay in bed, her body began suddenly to shake and tremble and there was no way she could stop. Soon she felt her body lifted up until she was raised to a sitting position. In the corner of the room, she had the distinct feeling of a presence, something like "a Being's energy" but she couldn't quite see what it was—"I wasn't ready," she repeats—but outside the window, she saw another hovering spacecraft, similar to the craft she'd seen in Carmel.

"I looked out there," Inid says, "and I just knew that that craft was *home*. My real home." It was an intuitive shock of recognition.

She was telling the story so enthusiastically it was difficult for me not to pick up on her feelings.

"What a wonderful Christmas present!" Inid said then. "There was no fear involved, it was the coolest thing anybody could have happen to them. It was absolutely, perfectly wonderful!"

One of the elements of Inid's story that interested me most was that everything she learned about herself came *after* these large, dramatic visions and spaceship sightings—the real self-knowledge came to her in a steady series of small insights, instants of heightened awareness at odd times of the day: driving, walking, or sitting in her car and waiting for the light to change. The Walk-in "fireworks" were just the moving of "big blocks"—the real work took place over years of careful, thoughtful introspection.

Her sense of E.T. mission also arrived gradually. Inid feels there wasn't any one single, major moment that snapped everything into place.

A few years after the second ship sighting, Inid had a very clear dream that she says helped to make yet another profound change in her life. It was a fairly simple dream of meeting a woman who she understood would assist her on a journey toward a deeper and more complete understanding of her identity. The woman was a Los Angeles psychologist and hypnotherapist with a large clientele of Walk-ins.

"I emerged from the dream very tired and shaky," Inid said, "but not emotionally shaky. Just knowing that I'd been through something terribly profound." She heeded the dream's advice, called up the therapist, and made an appointment.

During the initial sessions, the therapist used a combination of hypnosis and channeling to ask the trance-state Inid when she'd had her first contact with extraterrestrials.

The answer was surprising.

"Age three," Inid said.

"When was your last encounter?"

"Just a few days ago."

Then there was a series of questions that Inid believes she was either "not allowed to hear or wasn't permitted to answer." It's also possible, she says, that she simply wasn't able to reply. In any event, Inid became irritated.

"Who are you talking to?" Still in a trance, she began shaking her head against the back of the chair where she was reclining. "I could answer your questions better if I knew who you thought you were speaking to."

It was at this moment that Inid began to realize that something had drastically changed: the soul named Kathryn had departed. There had been a soul-exchange. Inid could now recognize herself as an E.T. soul "and step into my new life completely." She had at last passed through a phase of "alternating personalities" and arrived at a state where, she stated, the old self had simply vanished. This is the classic scenario of a Walk-in soul transfer.

So, for Inid, it was a long trip from a conventional, worldly view to expanded consciousness, and although there were obviously miraculous moments, the journey wasn't always easy. Listening to her tell me this story, I was left with the question of why Inid felt she had been put through these kinds of trials: unexplained UFO sightings, dramatic visions, a piecemeal soul exchange. It was quite an ordeal.

The answer, again: Extraterrestrials are here to help. Giving assistance is a very subtle art, requiring vast experience of human life and consciousness. That was Inid's feeling, and it echoed the sentiments of many others I interviewed.

"I've been through this to make me real and to make me human and to make me understand," she said. "Now I can understand the gamut of abuse issues, monetary issues, family issues, taking care of children, what it all feels like. It wouldn't serve any purpose for me to come here and give people suggestions on how to be if I didn't first understand what it was to live here on Earth."

I asked her how you know when you've learned enough.

"People sometimes think that extraterrestrials already know everything," Inid answered, "but that's not true. For everybody, it's all just a constant growth cycle—growing and learning, spiritually, and on all levels. This planet has been relating to extraterrestrial life for some time." And both have been growing together.

In the past, says Inid, it was enough for E.T.s to work behind the scenes of Earth history (what Soren called "the fermentation bubbles just starting to rise"). *Many of the great artists, statesmen, thinkers, and leaders that we read about were actually extraterrestrials,* she believes, and in days gone by it was enough for them to work "undercover." Today, though, the pace of history has quickened and the Earth is in an unprecedented state of crisis. There is a need for help that's far beyond urgent. And since the planet is on the verge of opening up to a more universal vision, it is right and good that E.T.s now come before the public view.

So each soul-exchange, each Wanderer and Walk-in, Inid feels, has his or her individual way to lend a hand. Whether it's in small or large ways doesn't really matter; each E.T. has some very particular information to share and a different area that could almost be said to be targeted for help.

Inid's vision, I think, goes even further than that. To some extent, she was breaking down the artificial barriers between "Earth natives" and our "E.T. visitors." The Earth is a giant melting pot for the many races of several galaxies, she said, and *each one of us is a soul whose origin is completely spiritual, not a product of Earth or any other planet at all.* All beings, then, have a cosmically attuned Self. And each soul exists at a different stage in the development of consciousness—some quite Earthly, others more universal.

Which means, of course, that we are all developing ourselves in greater consciousness according to our abilities. By doing so, we'll be continually deepening our humanity and the enrichment of Earth—and the Universe.

"People are waking up," Inid told me. "People are becoming aware and as they do, they're being given more and more information. That's one of our purposes for being here. And it's happening. We're communicating. *People's souls will be drawn to whatever it is they need to know.* Because now, the planet wants to know the Truth. The Soul wants the Awakening." It is the Soul—the Self in all of us—which is more available for communion than ever before in the history of this planet.

Thus, the E.T.s are here . . .

NOTHING SPECIAL

All of which sounds like quite a large order to fill.

If it does, you should know that these explanations—which seem to concern such a monumental, universally important job—usually come wrapped in a very humble understanding. Being E.T. and assisting the planet in its evolution are really "nothing special." Walk-ins and Wanderers usually leave their trumpets at home.

For example, Belinda, working as a hypnotherapist, wanted me to understand that there was "nothing so special" about her extraterrestrial origin. She said "[What is more important is] my interest in spiritual information, channeling, automatic writing, and sharing my views—that helps to serve, and it teaches people to get in touch with their inner powers and spiritual soul intelligence." Again, telling people you are an E.T. is not the main service at all.

As for Christin, he said he'd arrived at a place in his life where every minute was nothing less than an answer to the question, "So, how are we going to go into the light?" In other words, he continually reflected on how he could use each moment, each particular action, to deepen himself and help the planet. That was how he determined all of his actions and judgments. This seemed to me to be the ultimate in self-sacrifice for the good of the whole.

I frequently got this kind of answer in my interviews: "You've got to remember it's nothing special," or, as Linda told me, "Don't try to appear special, just help others see their own spiritual empowerment and help others express their own gifts and talents." All of those who follow the "path of unity" emphasize the importance of working together and trusting inner process. At some point this becomes like "second nature."

Delve into the philosophies of the East and you often get the same advice. From my own experience meditating in Buddhist monasteries in the United States and Asia, from my own reading of many Zen Buddhist texts, I've often come across something like:

What is enlightenment?

Nothing special.

What was it like after you became enlightened?

Nothing special.

This kind of talk definitely rings with the sound of one hand clapping, and, as is often stated, "Zen is everyday mind." There is that wonderful image of the Buddha transmitting everything he's realized in one moment of silence when he smiles and hands a single flower to his disciple. This is considered the height of "mind to mind transmission"—utter simplicity and purity. *The all in all.*

If seeing the great and the small in the single phrase *nothing special* seems like a paradox, that's probably because we're approaching it through the limited, dualistic, intellectual mode of rational thought. It's not a bad mode, mind you, it's a tool that has certain excellent uses. But the paradox appears when you use the tool for something that it wasn't meant to be used for. When you begin to give yourself permission to see the world *as it is,* when you stop worrying so much about getting it all straight about explanations and fixed language and rely, instead, on inner recognition and personal experience, the paradox disappears.

And you can work at it. That's what the E.T.s seemed to be suggesting. We can give up our need to grasp control of information using the everyday conscious mind and let the Higher Self through. The voice of the Inner Self (another term for the Higher Self), however, can only speak through your own quiet, calmed, alert personality, because emotional static drowns out its call. It takes some effort to develop this stillness of mind.

There is always the discipline of suffering through the veils of a conditioned, false sense of self, full of fear, conflict, and opinions. Only when these squawkings have been silenced can we hear the True Voice Within, and this practice of self-mastery often takes years.

In Earth terms, this inner peace is related to what's usually called, "going with the flow." That's a style of living I heard of from both Wanderers and Walk-ins. Instead of being nailed down by fixed ideas and rigid schemes, they were developing a style of feeling, thinking, and living based on relaxation and the ability to just follow the course of events, both "within the self" and "outside in the world." Of course, at a certain level of awareness, the duality of "inside and outside" disappears—and then the flow really gets going!

I don't mean to say that they didn't have definite goals, employment routines, or specific topics to present when they were involved in teaching; it was more that they "trusted the process," as one Wanderer put it. It was almost as if they heard another, higher voice within themselves and then identified with that voice. As Inid said, "I don't need to know everything; it's all planned and orchestrated and I'm an instrument of this plan." She didn't see herself as a puppet and she wasn't surrendering to fatalistic nihilism. She just realized *there was a larger pattern of changes that her daily affairs were a part of.* This brought her comfort and ease.

Which brings me to another seeming paradox.

Most of those I spoke with recognized the necessity of "doing it their own way," of choosing settings and jobs and social roles in which they felt comfortable. Some people might call that a "selfish" way of living but the E.T.s say that "suiting yourself" is usually the toughest task of all; and until we please ourselves, we have no real hope of pleasing anyone else.

Pleasing themselves was the first job because that's what let them heed the call to global responsibility. To assist in the work of the world required a great deal of personal decision and continued work on the self. As one of them told me, "helping the world does not mean feeling put upon or manipulated by others." It has to come from inner directives with which one can *resonate*, and then, even difficult tasks can be undertaken willingly.

This is the kind of "message" many of them shared. As Linda said: "Being an E.T. is not as important as making contact with the Higher Self." In the end, spiritual work is the same for all of us.

Actually, I was somewhat surprised to hear that from Linda, given the nature of her experiences and all the personal and social turmoil she'd gone through in recognizing that she was extraterrestrial. But Linda seemed to think that was all secondary, that "what's important is to get beyond time-space definitions of self and beyond the simple thinking that so-and-so is an extraterrestrial from such-and-such a planet." This is just clinging to "name and form," to quote an old Buddhist teaching.

Everyone, said Linda, is an aspect of divinity. "Every act counts for service," she assured me, "and each person is important. I see my role basically as just trying to keep that hope alive."

The true human being (whether E.T. or otherwise), Linda said, is no different at all from the Infinite Creator.

We are One.

DO YOUR OWN THING

The E.T. soul I've called Matthew supplied one of the few answers that was slightly outside the normal equation that visiting Earth means offering help.

When I asked Matthew why he thought E.T.s had come to Earth, he threw me a little by answering, "I don't know," and then he said the question was far too broad for a simple response. "I can't speak for anyone else, it's up to the individual. Some E.T.s, you know, really might not be so positive. Maybe they're not actively negative, but there are E.T.s who are always throwing a monkey wrench in there. I don't think our own simplistic ideas about who's here for what purposes necessarily holds in all cases."

Personally, he said, he was working to eliminate "Earth-centeredness" by writing a book (now completed) concerning UFO links to some recent research about Mars. He wanted to help society see that ours is not the summit of intelligent social organization in the universe ... apparently a very difficult lesson for Earth to learn.

Matthew is a man who lived through several UFO sightings as a child in New Jersey, experienced all kinds of dreams and visions, and asked all kinds of philosophical questions. Also, and this was somewhat common among those I met, as a child he was certain that the people around him "didn't look right." He thought that they should have elongated faces, very high foreheads, extremely smooth and simple bodies, and perfectly symmetrical feet!

But Matthew didn't take any of this very seriously until he reached his mid-twenties.

At that point, he said, something popped. It was like a sudden insight had come up from behind and hit him on the top of the head. Matthew told me he was abruptly taken with the idea that "Life here is not as it appears. It's not as circumscribed as we may believe it to be. It extends way beyond the familiar."

Matthew began paying close attention to his dreams, because

for years he'd experienced a searing and intense longing for the beautiful landscapes and cities that came to him at night. These were places that were obviously other planets, with trees planted in strange patterns, rising towers with pagoda tops, everything bathed in a kind of other-worldly light. In the morning, he'd wake up weeping with a terrible feeling of homesickness.

As Matthew began looking closer at the dreams, he started experiencing odd moments of memory recall while awake; remembering scenes that common sense would say he'd never really seen before.

"Once, I was in downtown Harrisburg, Pennsylvania," Matthew told me, "and I was looking at a group of government buildings. Just staring at them. Then, all of a sudden, I was taken with this feeling that they reminded me of another time and place, and I remembered a similar city with human-like creatures, but it was definitely not on Earth and it was definitely not now." This was a "bleed-through" from an E.T. past life. I'm sure many children have this type of experience but don't report it for fear of criticism from narrow-minded parents.

In Matthew's words: "This was spontaneous knowledge. It seemed totally gripping and totally true." A burst of inner knowing . . .

As I've said before, Matthew accepted his E.T. identity with gracious ease and without any single, shocking incident to propel him to alter his life, saying, "My experiences have always been more recollection than revelation." His is the tale of a Wanderer gradually piercing the veil of forgetting to return to the awareness he once had . . . *before incarnating on Earth.* Matthew, like all Wanderers, had agreed to memory loss as part of his contract. This is done to help protect the free-will of ordinary Earth humans, those not ready to accept the reality of E.T.s and other worlds.

Slowly, on his own, Matthew began "teaching" himself to open his mind to possibilities that, in the past, he would never even have imagined. He'd get up in the morning and suddenly understand, for instance, that all time here is measured by the span of a human lifetime, and then he would let that realization take root and grow in his consciousness.

"The measurement of time [on Earth] is just for convenience," Matthew believes. "Because one day I woke up and in an instant I experienced *all of having been*. From that point on, I found it easy to feel myself *as always having been,* in an eternity that isn't chopped up in little increments of time." He was actually experiencing himself as a timeless Being.

That view gave Matthew what he thinks of as a definite affinity with time travel as well as space travel, but he surprised me by wrapping up the statement this way: "I don't pay a lot of attention to it."

"What do you mean?" I asked. "Explain that a little more." Was this also "no big deal"?

"When that kind of stuff comes up," Matthew said, "the ego will always grab onto it. That's the melodrama of the ego. It gets to be a distraction."

Again: *Nothing special.* Speaking here about his E.T. mission on Earth, I thought Matthew brought together beautifully a great deal of what I'd heard from the other E.T.s. "You know, when you're *really* in that situation [as an extraterrestrial], even if you're commander of one of the ships, it's pretty unglamorous. When the specter of glamour creeps into anything, I tend to back off and get real discriminating about what feels right, and think *why is this person telling me that?* Being glamorous is an easy way to avoid being present."

Being "glamorous" means getting caught up in any kind of grandiose fantasy, while being "present" means staying clear, open, and nongrasping *in the present moment.*

To Matthew, some statements of E.T. mission were too exaggerated, others too self-denying, with some people lying about it and some telling the truth. He went on to say that while we may never be able to explain what all extraterrestrials are doing here, "Whatever else they are, they are all definitely [acting as] a catalyst for human awareness." Wanderers and Walk-ins hope to spur the process, expanding and refining it.

> E.T.s are a historical inevitability. Eventually, we're going to have to realize that we on Earth are not alone. And E.T.s can help anyone who's open to it also understand this: Life and consciousness are not ego, and we can find our place in the scheme of things without having to be the top dog in the universe.

Feeling superior is actually a tremendous hindrance to gaining universal vision.

During this part of the waking-up process, Matthew went on to say, we're going to have to disengage from what we'd always thought was just the "ordinary mundane world." The true boundaries of our experience are a lot broader. As we start to let go, we may feel adrift for a while, or to put it in E.T. terms, we may feel as though we're wandering about. But by being open to our experience, we can relax a bit more during the process of spiritual realignment, which means "returning" to the vibrations of the Higher Self, our Universal Awareness.

He finished with this idea about one thing E.T.s are here to teach: *a lesson in how to remain unfixed and unstuck.*

"Any realm is a distortion," Matthew said. "You can play the game of dancing or navigating through the different levels of distortion or, as some people prefer to do, just cut right through all that and go straight to your deepest identity . . . which is without borders." Don't get stuck calling yourself "Earth native" or "E.T. soul," he said, but instead, realize your Infinite Nature.

"In other words," I said, "at some level, everyone is the *One* but we're just not aware of it."

"Exactly," he replied. "It's not a matter of achieving something which you're not. *It's a matter of pulling yourself out of all the cues that you're taking in*—because those cues are illusions. They keep telling you you're not who you basically are. And if you let them, those illusions will cut off your ability to believe in yourself."

He was stressing the importance of inner knowing—the same route by which all Walk-ins and Wanderers come to realize their origins. If we trust our deepest self, and seek to be free from self-limiting patterns, we will walk with confidence along the path to greater awareness. These E.T.s are not here to "save us"—only to point us back to our inner selves.

Again, it is not a matter of constructing anything or achieving some special state of awareness. It would be more helpful to think of it as removing all the barriers to the realization of What Is.

We are already saved.

9

DEATH

FROM ELSEWHERE TO ETERNITY

Death, it seems, is the human mystery without end.

It captivates—has always captivated—the human imagination and marks the boundary beyond which one map is just as good as any other . . . which may be just as good as no map at all. In the oft repeated quote from Shakespeare's *Hamlet*, death is seen as "the undiscover'd country from whose bourn no traveler returns."

So, perhaps there are only questions. Absolute end or eternity? One life or many? A straight line from unique beginning to finite end? The cyclical course of turn and return? Or none of these?

One of the most popular motifs in the arts, the question of death and of "life afterward"—or not—now and then even makes its way into the mainstream press. The *New York Daily News*, on November 13, 1994, reviewed an item it published seventy-five years earlier: the story of an East 33rd Street woman named Ella Smith Lawson, who, in 1919, kept the city fascinated with her story that she had died and "gone to the fourth dimension." Ms. Lawson apparently believed that someday everyone would learn to do the same, and that people would begin making the interdimensional trip routinely.

So, how does this tie into our discussion? Well, throughout this book we've been looking at the phenomenon of E.T. identity—which doesn't exactly leave our world the way it was before. We've been talking about a completely different approach to reality. The presence of extraterrestrials on Earth may require us to begin looking at life—and death—with new eyes and start rethinking our centuries of Western philosophy. Perhaps it is possible, when we consider death, to understand it not in the romantic terms to which we've become accustomed, no matter how great the poetry, but rather, to consider it more akin to what we'd hear channeled through the words of an E.T. civilization, such as RA.

They tell us: "There is no end to beingness." And if we find that somewhat difficult to comprehend, we have our Walk-ins and Wanderers here to help us. . . .

DISTRACTION, ANONYMITY, AND SLEEP

"Dealing with death is key," said Soren, "particularly for Wanderers. But really, for everybody. On an individual, social, and planetary level. Sex and death. Union and separation."

On an individual level, Soren says, death is something that must be dealt with because "it's something that all people who think they're human must face."

On a social level, it must be dealt with because "everyone has such a bugaboo about it."

And on a planetary level, it must be dealt with because truly dealing with death can bring about so much greater harmony, for all nations.

Indeed, peering into the experience of separation and loss is something that can transform consciousness for anyone.

For Soren, who is an experienced ocean surfer and survivor of three suicide attempts, this "dealing with death" came in a series of incidents that brought him to the edge of his human being. The dramatic happenings he underwent may not be necessary if one is to "deal with death," but of all the E.T. souls I interviewed, Soren was one of the few who had undergone both out-of-body experiences (OBE) and near-death-experiences (NDE). As you might guess, these experiences left him with a profoundly altered outlook, something very close to one E.T. group's assessment of Earth as a place that's characterized by "distraction, anonymity, and sleep."

Because of his experiences as a child, Soren knew from an early age—although he didn't fully understand—that there was another state of being and that this planet was not the only place to be. He already knew that what most of us take to be the only possible reality is just a relative state, a single frequency on an endless band of signals.

He told me the story of one of his earliest experiences with an altered state of mind. When he was six or seven years old, Soren stepped up on an old wooden box that helped him climb a tree near his home, and while he was playing up in the branches, he had "a transformation of consciousness"—although it came about in a manner that's not highly recommended. As in every parent's nightmare, the young Soren lost his grip. He tumbled out of the tree and landed on the ground below in a sitting position with the base of his skull jammed against the wooden corner of the crate.

It's possible, Soren said, that what happened was no accident: It might have been "arranged" by some outside force or entity because as Soren described it, "It was like *falling into place.*"

"It brought me up short in a very strange way I'll never forget," he said. "It was like my spine was at full extension. That brought about this moment—it was almost like *kundalini,* an energy transformation. Like a meditation experience."

He never forgot it.

How could he? As if he needed any help remembering, ten years later there was another "accident" that seemed to build on that feeling of liberated energy. This time, Soren was sixteen. He was surfing off the Hawaiian coast in some fairly rough water when all of a sudden, he wiped out. The waves came crashing down, holding him beneath the surface. As the sea bubbled white and swirled powerfully around him, Soren struggled to break free, to breathe, but no matter how strong he was and how hard he fought the riptide, he couldn't make it. Submerged, he was starting to get that dreamy feeling—a sure sign of oxygen deprivation.

"I then lost all interest in trying to get back to the surface," he told me. "I wasn't feeling suicidal. It just didn't make any difference anymore."

Under the surf, he felt himself changing form.

"I became this spherical ball of light, this sphere of light and radiance. I could see in all directions, more than something like a life review, I could see everything, everything—including my life."

What was really odd, Soren noted, was that during this time in his adolescence, he was in a period of positive energy. He had not yet tried to take his own life, he was not using drugs, and he felt that "everything was going very well." But the experience dovetailed, he said, with the earlier transformation of consciousness, that childhood *kundalini*-rocking fall from a tree, as well as several earlier OBEs. These were several boyhood incidents in which he experienced himself floating outside his body, able to look down on his physical form lying there below. There were also those trips he took as a child, when he would go off on "voyages" with Martians. All of these feelings of buoyancy and nonphysicality were no longer foreign to him.

So, as the aftermath of the surfing "accident" worked on him, it began to remold his consciousness and his view of life and death.

"That state [the nonphysical] was more real to me than anything else," Soren said. *"Compared to that state, the waking state was like a dream."* In the "normal" waking state, he found, "There's a lack of realness and a much more abbreviated sensory array." He'd been given a vivid demonstration of what was possible when he surpassed the boundaries of physical form and ordinary consciousness.

According to Dr. Ken Ring, author of *Life at Death*, those who undergo an NDE are put through a series of similar and identifiable stages. There is a dropping away of fear and, along with an awareness of dying, an acceptance of the end of human life. This involves the loss of physical sensation, so it's actually a painless process. And along with the loss of the physical comes a deep and profound silence, although some reports speak of hearing something like the wind or a strange buzzing right before you separate from your body—and then a feeling of hovering, and a view of your own bodily form. Some of those who go through an NDE have reported hearing and seeing themselves pronounced dead by emergency medical staff.

Afterward, there is the stage that has been so often popularized: a passing into a totally different realm of reality. This is the dramatic journey through a dark tunnel, still with incredible peace, until some "presence" is encountered. With this meeting, there begins a review of one's entire life. It takes place without the usual emotions of fear, judgment, or blame; and when it's over, the person is asked whether he or she wishes to continue on or to reinhabit the body. For those who are able to tell of their NDE, obviously, the decision has been made to return to our world . . . at which point, the person often comes back to waking consciousness with a great deal of pain from injuries or medical procedures.

What is consistent, Dr. Ring writes, is the survivors' conviction that the experience was real and that it was the most profound thing that has ever happened to them. Also consistent is the almost predictable view that it's impossible to capture in words the intensity of the experience.

So, an NDE taught Soren something about death. When he was younger, this Wanderer went through a period of dizziness and a pronounced fear of heights, and would sometimes go into states of vertigo when he was on bridges or in tall buildings. That could be associated to an early fear of death, but Soren explained that the problem went away when he began meditating. Aside from these episodes of vertigo he'd never experienced a deep fear of dying.

In Soren's view, "It's facile to say that death doesn't exist, but that's part of the truth. The other part is to say: It really has nothing to do with me. I don't die. *The reality to me is that people can't die.* And I look forward to it the way people look forward to peeling off an uncomfortable suit of clothes at the end of a workday."

This is something like the longing for release that a hyperactive child might feel in church—that's how Soren described it. He said it was like being forced to sit still, wear an uncomfortable suit, and be attentive to the sermon, all the while dreaming about the pleasure of finally getting home and taking off the confining garments.

And after death? Soren believes that E.T. souls go back to where they are originally from, although somewhat altered by the experience on Earth. They've also been touched by the changes that, in their apparent "absence," might have taken place at home. E.T. souls who hail from planets filled with love, return to those same planets, able to help the home group evolve even more.

Death, it seems, is a gateway to another reality, but one that must *come in its own time.* In Soren's case, the youthful suicide attempts can be seen not so much as self-destruction but more as an unfortunate method, the only means he knew, of reexperiencing a heightened state of awareness, a far different reality. He had no intention of "hurting" himself, he simply needed to "save" himself.

Because he remained alive, Soren was able to begin meditation, learning how to ground, deepen, and integrate his states of higher awareness. At that point, he had no need to escape the physical form—*because it was no longer limiting.*

> Dealing with death, Soren says, is a gateway back to a higher state of awareness, a state that the E.T. soul has become separated from and which he or she needs to be reunited with, to live a full life here.

For the E.T., death can also be taken symbolically as a mirror, reflecting the lives that Walk-ins and Wanderers are living right now, here on Earth. Death can represent *a death to the old self*, a death to what's apparently real (which means life in the realm of the body). Coming consciously face-to-face with the limitations and pains of life is a kind of dying. Our suffering is epitomized by death, because it is the ultimate process of change in this world and the great example that for everything created, there is eventually a time it must break apart. However, this is *not* what happens on the home planets from which the E.T. souls come. The realities of Earth life confront vague memories of the past and the meeting is a painful one.

"You suffer," says Soren, "to whatever extent you identify with your body, with your emotions, with your thoughts."

But, of course, when you are not identified with any of those "personality elements," you are more free to make contact with your deeper self. It's that attitude of detachment that I often heard expressed by the E.T.s, an attitude that I already knew well through my own study and personal experience of Eastern religion, metaphysics, and psychology. It's a very delicate balance that needs to be achieved: seeing death as simply a returning home, and understanding that there is far too much work to do here on Earth to make that return too quickly.

But there's a time for everything: for toil and learning on Earth and for release and homecoming. For our employer as well as for the Creator, we have a job to do ... and it's unfair to cut out of work too soon.

GOING HOME

This feeling of death as a "returning home" was also familiar to Lucia, the woman whose Awakening began during a shower with the inner announcement, *You are going to have a Walk-in today.* In the case of Walk-ins, Lucia agreed that it's like they've already faced a kind of "identity death," and that the Walk-in experience often occurs—as you might remember—at a time when the person feels "I can't go on, I need to die."

"What's important," Lucia said, "is piercing the illusion of death. Because nothing dies. The consciousness which animates the body continues. There's nothing to fear. *We just shed the body. The body is just an instrument.*"

And, like most of the E.T.s I interviewed, Lucia also expressed the feeling that "you must deal with death to fully understand your spiritual nature and the meaning of life."

"Returning home," however, is usually balanced by something else. For Justinian, any sense of homesickness took a backseat to the feeling there was too much still to be done. According to Justinian, "In those who are strongly aware of their E.T. identity, the sense of purpose is so powerful that they feel filled with purpose. They don't want to die, even if they feel death is a kind of return."

The "longing to leave" is certainly there, he said, but it's softened by the driving force of purpose—which is strengthened even more when the E.T. soul is closely identified with the True Self. It's also important to remember that this sense of purpose need not hurl the E.T. into the world vainly trying to advertise him or herself as a "helper."

Justinian, as a spiritual counselor, teacher of metaphysics, and a Walk-In, feels that of the two "types" of E.T.s we've identified, it's usually the Wanderers who have the greatest struggle with this longing for home. Walk-Ins are newer souls and have, in a sense, volunteered for a later soul-exchange operation, so they're still brimming with purpose; it's a fresher experience.

Justinian said it wasn't a near-death experience but rather an out-of-body experience, several of them, that eventually dissolved his fear of death. In fact, he told me that by the time of his sudden Walk-In, he had already "made peace with death" and had grown accustomed to "conceptual dying," by which he meant the inevitable losses of cherished attachments during life. That probably made the acceptance of a new E.T. soul somewhat easier. He already knew what it meant to surrender.

In their book, *The Star People*, Brad and Francie Steiger put together a wealth of information on the transcending of the physical body experienced by those who claim E.T. identity and those who do not:

> Dr. Dale Ironson, assistant professor of psychology at Franklin Pierce College in Rindge, New Hampshire, has suggested that as many as 30 percent of the "normal healthy population" have had an out-of-body experience (OBE) at least once in their lifetime.
>
> In a study conducted by Dr. Charles Tart at the University of California, 44 percent of 150 students reported having OBEs.
>
> In a similar study carried out by the late Dr. Hornell Hart of Duke University, the figure of those having OBEs was 27 percent.
>
> Dr. Stanley Krippner, a psychologist and a former director of the Maimonides Dream Laboratory in New York, commented that the two studies cited by Dr. Ironson, together with a third conducted by Dr. John Palmer at the University of Virginia, indicated that as many as three out of ten people have had OBEs. This ratio makes it probable that well over sixty million Americans have had out-of-body experiences.
>
> Among Star People, the ratio of those who have OBEs would probably be as high as seven out or eight out of ten. And a great number of them claim to be able to experience them at will.

Each of Justinian's OBEs took him outside of his body, while still leaving him with the ability "to see." He became aware of himself hovering over his physical form, staring down at the corporeal self, his body. While in this suspended state, Justinian says he was able to remember not only past lives, but to go far beyond that state, to "meditate on my whole time track, remembering back to various evolutionary existences."

Every time he repeated this experience, the fear of death dissolved even further.

The lesson of this meditation, stated here all too simply, of course, can be put this way: *I am not this temporary physical vehicle*. This body is something I've taken on and that I'm using.

With that realization, Justinian said, he was able to let go of a fear of death that had filled him with terror and confusion since childhood. He emphasized that spiritual practice was partly to thank for this; so was the understanding that when he traced his evolutionary path, it led him back, far beyond his present life here on planet Earth.

For those who come From Elsewhere, there is also the complex matter of Going Somewhere when all work on the Earthly plane is through. The unusual concentration of OBEs that helped him dissolve death fears, eventually gave Justinian a very detailed conception of what happens *after death*. He talked about it as a kind of spiritual progression.

Basically, he said, there are three deaths:

A physical body death, which leaves the person existing in his or her astral body . . .

An astral death in which an astral or emotional body dies; this leaves only the mental body as the final "sheath of personality". . . . The mental body, is considered a non-physical form surrounding the visible body, responsible for the workings of intellect.

Then comes the death of this mental body, which means the person is completely absorbed into the soul. This absorption, says Justinian, is not a loss of self-consciousness but, instead, *an increase*. One is regaining one's *true spiritual birthright*, which is usually possible only after death.

We find somewhat similar imagery in the *Bardo Thodol*, the Tibetan Book of the Dead. There also, three different levels of existence are described: a physical, Earthly realm; then a realm of pure form; and, finally, a level that's beyond language or symbolism. Here, we can only say that there is pure energy or spirit. This is the most exhilarating realm and is usually described as a realm of light.

For E.T. souls, however, according to Justinian, "there is a unique energy configuration. With death, the human elements that they've become identified with, or were strongly influenced by, by being in a human incarnation, are cast aside and they come much more powerfully into their true extraterrestrial identity, uncloaked by any human characteristics."

And also, when an E.T. "dies," not all the human patterns fall away. The E.T.s take with them the most important human qualities or elements that they've discovered while in human form and human consciousness. They are distilled and retained, as one part of the experience of the whole universe.

This means that to some extent, an E.T. soul can never regain full consciousness of his or her original identity while still in human form because, as long as human life lasts, there will be some amount of conditioning. There will also be the "veiling," which was agreed to, as part of the privilege of serving Earth through human incarnation. Birth, childhood, and the other Earthbound experiences most definitely leave their mark. So, there is a ceiling to how much the Wanderer or Walk-in can recover.

"E.T.'s are limited to a certain extent," Justinian noted, and agreed with me when I suggested that only through extensive and intense spiritual practice here on Earth could one recover this original consciousness. It's something like saying: If you're able to become a Buddha, then you'll have it all anyway! But interestingly, I've found that very few Walk-ins and Wanderers make the effort to launch into serious practice of this sort. It's possible they're somewhat comfortable just accepting the limitations with which they're living. They may also be at home with the idea of just making some kind of positive social contribution.

But as Justinian said: "Yes, if a person can go into deep states of *samahdi*, totally abstract from the personality, then they gain a much greater sense of their identity." So, again, it depends on the spiritual efforts that are made here on Earth.

Samahdi, difficult to describe in words, can be imagined as a remarkable and profound state of mind in which consciousness is absolutely silent and absolutely still, free of all constrictions including those of time and space. It is a state that can usually be reached only through meditation practice.

After death, then, the E.T. soul comes into wider consciousness and greater understanding of what the sojourn on Earth was really all about in the first place, and almost every E.T. I spoke with believed that death will be their true Great Awakening.

EASY WAY OUT

"Death to me," Bob said, "is an adventure."

That's one lesson he's learned from being E.T.. While it may sound morbid or almost like a longing for "the end," Bob denied that he's looking forward to death. Instead, he said, he thinks of himself as "curious" and accepts the fact that life on Earth, in human form, is finite.

Bob's serious drug habit before his Walk-in left him well acquainted with the eventuality of death. Before his E.T. experience, he says, he was sometimes an agnostic and sometimes an atheist, but at all times he was close to despair and suicide.

"It was easier to die," he said, "That's what I thought. It was harder to stay on this plane and go on."

This was the lowest point of his life, he told me, a time when he was virtually ready to give up. Then, "something happened," he had his Walk-in—"or some sort of intervention," he says—along with its unexpected influx of energy and ideas. At that point, says Bob, "meaning hit me over the head like a lightning bolt." Afterward, *there was meaning to his life without question;* he felt it, thought it, and knew it. That sense of value reversed what he saw as the relentless plunge toward death.

Bob says he wasn't seeking out any change at the time, he'd just assumed that his life was dropping into a downward spiral—that he would crash and die, inevitably, never to return or go on. He'd already given up hope.

186

But today, becoming comfortable with his E.T. identity, Bob admits he has no definite knowledge of what happens after death, and expects to be asking questions about the process of death for the rest of his life.

Bob isn't looking forward to death because he still has things he wants to do. His expectations are that the end of his tenure here on Earth will be, as he puts it, still a mystery but "better than the birth process." I appeciate his dry humor.

Perhaps we can close our discussion of extraterrestrial views on death with an insight from the Russian philosopher P. D. Ouspensky. Hopefully, it will give us a larger sense of perspective.

In his book *Tertium Organum*, Ouspensky writes of the great attraction of death for the imagination, especially in those areas that we would call mystical or religious. The problem of love, however, is usually accepted by philosophers as something that's merely given, which is strange, he says, because love is just as great a mystery for human beings. For Ouspensky, this is not a psychological or emotional state of love that's being discussed, but rather "that contact with the eternal and the infinite which it holds for man." In this view, love is a gateway to the timeless realms of Spirit and True Self.

Giving death too much importance in our thinking, Ouspensky writes, is to miss what actually binds the Universe:

In reality love is a *cosmic phenomenon*, in which people, mankind, are merely accidental; a cosmic phenomenon as little concerned with either the lives or the souls of men as the sun is concerned in shining so that, by its light, men may go about their trivial affairs and use it for their own ends. If men could understand this, be it only with one part of their consciousness, a new world would open up before them and it would become very strange for them to look at life from all the usual angles.

They would understand then that love is something quite different, and of a different order from the small events of earthly life.

For Ouspensky, love really should be written *Love*—a cosmic event, a magical quality, an essential state of being whose exploration can bring us tremendous insight. Likewise, for the Wanderers and Walk-ins I met, death should really be written *Death*—a doorway to their spiritual birthright and long-forgotten homeplanets, a reunion with their Higher Self, and the piercing of the veil under which they have labored so long. Yet, they also say that death is "a great adventure," and beckon us all to put aside fears and stop to consider the meaning of our lives—here, today—in light of the "Great Portal"—there tomorrow.

10

VISION

COMING ATTRACTIONS OF THE WORLD TO COME

We end our book with a beginning.

Although we're about to finish this examination of extraterrestrial life on Earth, the journey revealed to us by Walk-ins and Wanderers is actually at its starting point.

If you've traveled with me this far, along the way you must have picked up more than a few questions raised by the strange claims of our extraterrestrials—questions about the state of the Earth, about the human race, about the path on which Earth seems to be headed. And, if the E.T.s say they're here to help, what is it exactly they plan to help us with? And what do they see ahead of us?

I offer a quote from Hans Holtzer, from his book *The UFO-nauts*:

> We are dealing here with the basic issues, concerning not merely a marginal aspect of our lives, but fundamental concepts and problems concerning the very core of our existence and future. The subject of extraterrestrials, therefore, cannot be taken lightly, nor must it be left to cultists and irrational dreamers, but must be rescued from the hands of partisan claimants and placed upon

189

a rational platform where the general public can view it dispassionately and make up its own mind. At the same time, the very complicated problems of extraterrestrial relationships must not be allowed to be drowned by hostile scientific factions or governmental agencies in the mistaken notion that such knowledge might upset the emotional balance of the populace.

The men and women whose stories compose my research would heartily agree. For them, the extraterrestrial question is most serious and yet, most open to discussion. For those who've fully integrated their E.T. identity, understanding our world can't be confined within the bounds of what common social opinion sees as normal.

There was, first of all, overwhelming agreement about what could be called a *hidden world process*, or at least, a process hidden to most people, veiled to those who have no desire to seek. This hidden process is said to affect every aspect of humanity and civilization. Most E.T.s admit they have only partial knowledge of these workings, but they say there are enough "signs" available pointing to the "hidden plan" for anyone aware and sensitive who wishes to search.

You can find this kind of outlook elsewhere, in the metaphysics usually associated with New Age literature and in some Eastern religions, Theosophy, UFO studies, and in various forms of millenialism. And, as a reminder: These Walk-ins and Wanderers *do not* claim to be privy to special information that has been given them by virtue of non-Earthly origins. The difference between their recognition and others' skepticism is that the E.T.s trust their self-validation, their "subjective knowing." They've affirmed a type of global and historical dynamics (the historical progress of human civilization and the growth of increasing awareness and sensitivity to greater meaning in life), one that is intimately bound up with such issues as identity, the nature of self, and extraterrestrial life.

To begin, I think it's worthwhile to isolate a few of the more general remarks made by the E.T.s I interviewed, because they underline how those who claim to be from all points of the universe share quite a few visions:

"Earth is in major transition." (Vicky)
"a global energetic transformation" (Belinda)
"planetary consciousness upgrading" (Barbara)
"change in global spirituality to come" (Barrie)
"The Earth consciousness is evolving rapidly." (Pauline)

However, *it isn't enough* to simply say: E.T.s feel the Earth is going through some changes and will soon be entering a New Age. In one or two interviews, of course, that kind of simplistic answer was given, but the majority of those with off-planet origins expressed concepts far more complex and multifaceted.

Together, the weight of their combined testimony paints a vivid picture of Earth's near future—a future of unprecedented, drastic, and dizzying change.

In the words of Tomas, who believed himself to be at One with the Elohim of Peace: "The Earth experiment is completed, it is returning to Essence—in the [upcoming] dimensional shift, the old dimension [and ways of being] will cease to work, and the world will be far different from how it used to be."

Consider these other, possible, events that might be upcoming, according to the Wanderers and Walk-ins:

Sightings, contacts, and public discussion about UFOs will all increase dramatically, leading to some sort of public disclosure by governments or the United Nations, regarding evidence of "genuine alien interaction." This may be used as a ploy to institute a "global police state," or it may signify the start of constructive cooperation between benevolent E.T. groups and a newly awakened humanity.

In the next twenty years, the Earth's total population will be greatly reduced as a result of natural disasters and man-made conflict. By the year 2010, at the end of what the E.T.s consider the present cycle of civilization, the population may be reduced by 50 percent or more. The total size of humanity after the predicted changeover to "a new heaven and Earth"—the metaphysical transformation deemed to be the New Age—may be less than 500 million. Indeed, one source claims that the human population may be so small that it will have to be supplemented by extraterrestrials who will lend a hand in the reconstruction of society.

Few of the E.T.s were able to completely outline their vision. But what they saw when they reported on the future was an Earth in total transformation, going through changes that can barely be imagined. A few relied solely on apocalyptic imagery, speaking about an impending ecological catastrophe. But there was a paradox: Such a disaster would set the stage for unprecedented individual growth, they said. Views of our present Earth situation, presented repeatedly by Wanderers and Walk-ins, are echoed by much of the literature available in New Age bookstores, except that the E.T.s' ideas were definitely not centered on planet Earth. They saw themselves as concerned visitors, not natives to the transformation, and simply (in the words of Matthew) "as part of the global salvage and assistance project."

The "author" of such a project? The central force was always considered to be the Infinite Creator, namely the *Universe-As-It-Is*.

A Personal Darkness and Light

All of this, though, is only the basic foundation. These ideas are the building blocks upon which to construct a much more advanced and more personal idea of where the Earth is headed.

Indeed, most of the E.T.s I interviewed taught workshops or made use of these ideas in private counseling. Christin, for example, recognized what he called a "global resurrection and the entering of Spirit to Earth at the present time, with a gravitational shifting in DNA codes and energies that will cause a stoppage of time and new life in bodies, approaching deathlessness. This evolution is occurring both in Earth and the human species."

As a witness to this process, he shared with his clients the energy shifts he experienced in his own body, a living example of the collective process of death, rebirth, and resurrection.

Another E.T. who used similar imagery was Betty, who saw "a clear course of evolution for Earth and humanity, requiring transition into an Ascension, a higher state of being [which is] planetary initiation."

Which is to say: *What was happening globally, in the present, mirrored their own spiritual challenges.* What the Earth as a whole was undergoing was exactly what they were experiencing personally. Like the Wanderers, gradually unveiling their true spiritual identity, Earth itself was awakening to the basic purity of love. And, like the Walk-in's abrupt, traumatic influx of Divine potency, the Earth was going through a death to old ways and rebirth into a higher intensity of light.

Julie, who works to help clients who are in the midst of psychospiritual transformation, expanded on some of these ideas. She said, "Humanity's transformation has never been done on Earth. . . . In the planetary graduation it will be more filled with light with no more darkness [and] many cycles are coming to a close now."

The old dysfunctional patterns are going to be released, she said, and Earth will embrace the Light of love and compassion. The New Age is all about a *greater intensity of light.*

Light and *darkness.* I heard those descriptive terms again and again. This symbolism can be dated back to ancient Mesopotamia, and, according to the studies of one scholar, J. E. Cirlot, it involves a belief in the eventual synthesis of the All, a union of "opposites" sometimes equated with Spirit. Perhaps it is also this light that we hope to find at "the end of the tunnel."

Darkness, then, is not necessarily identified with evil, but rather with ignorance and the *illusion of separation.* Darkness and light play off one another, and we must continually make choices to find our way to the "greater light."

Una, for example, who spoke from an angelic (or "extracelestial") perspective, said she recognized "Earth in transition, with angelic kingdom entrants here to help Earth and humanity; [but] Earth is going through infusions of light, and all of humanity is going through them, too, which is difficult since it sheds the light into the darkness and all [sorts of negativity] come into the open."

Una believed that this was the reason for much of the social and psychological disease at the present: All sorts of negativity "coming to light" in the new climate of "greater light." She expressed her vision in terms that sounded like a proud parent, saying with a certain degree of innocence, "I feel so thrilled for the Earth, it will evolve as a planet, and all the extraterrestrials are coming here to assist in its growth." Obviously, she wasn't speaking of those E.T.s who are better known for abductions, cattle mutilations, and other terrifying contacts.

And as we've touched upon, those hostile E.T.s do exist, as well. There's a reason for their appearance on Earth, and I think it's worth an explanation as we go deeper into the vision of Walk-ins and Wanderers.

In the Chinese Buddhist tradition, they use a witty phrase to describe the mix of monks living side-by-side in a temple: "Dragons and snakes commingle." You get the good with the bad, the sincere with the dishonest. In Chinese culture, the dragon is a symbol of benevolent strength and grandeur, while the snake is considered to be an animal of hidden motives, tricky and selfish. So, young monks be warned: Be careful not to assume good intentions on the part of your comrades.

This is true, of course, for any gathering of people. And as the E.T.s will tell us, it's true for extraterrestrials, too. The reason? *Earth is a schoolhouse for many races throughout the universe who have not yet learned to love.* That causes a chronic hostility, and while many E.T.s and Earthlings *are* practicing love and compassion, the small but powerful minority that does not want to love is consciously committed to securing their own dominance at any cost.

So say many of the Wanderers and Walk-ins. They told me that Earth is unusual as a planet in its mix of galactic "races" and that our globe is a great melting pot in which many groups have settled, coming from scattered points throughout the galaxies. This makes for an amazing, stellar diversity, but it also means that we are not "one people" except at that most essential level at which all beings are one. For this reason, again, the E.T.s counsel love and respect for differentness, the ability to learn from others, and the pleasures of an open mind.

The E.T.s I spoke with believed that this could mean unimagined opportunities for those of us on Earth, no matter where our point of origin. Like many E.T.s, Una considered this to be an unparalleled time in the annals of Earth's history, but acknowledged that only a few were able to speak about it with such intimacy.

Una's measured optimism was heard from other E.T.s. There were some Walk-ins and Wanderers, of course, who took a more muted view, especially when they focused on the fragile ecology of planet Earth.

GOODBYE, CALIFORNIA?

We can go deeper into the connection between personal spiritual change and the transformation of the planet. For many E.T.s, it's a story of imminent disaster . . . if the current ways continue.

For instance, the fate of the Earth, ecologically, is a story of things getting worse before they get better. According to Matthew (who also spoke in terms of light and dark), "The planet is going down the tubes and it will get much more difficult before it gets easier—ecological disaster is quite likely."

Barrie told me she also foresees "earthquakes with many people dying" but did not believe there would be a devastating "pole shift," with the exchange of magnetic north and south poles, anticipated by some.

And Pauline felt that "Earth will survive intact—but not necessarily all the people. The Earth changes and disasters are to cleanse
the planet."

Cleanse it of what? I asked her. And she told me: Cleanse it of
the negativity, hatred, greed, and selfish aggression that have built
up over the millenia.

Most of these prophesies were presented to me with an attitude and tone of dispassion and detachment. There were some
exceptions, though. Bob, for instance, spoke in a voice of lament
when he said, "Man is destroying Earth, and there will be a purification if humanity does not change. I think there will be catastrophic changes between 1991 and 2003, with California going
into the sea, much loss of life, and a lower population to sustain
life on Earth. There will be a spanking. I have dreams and feelings
[about this happening.]"

Una agreed: "I know that the humans, instead of caretaking [the
Earth], have harmed it."

And Linda sees "a series of happenings to alert people about
the catastrophic and destructive Earth changes to come. . . . Humanity is in so much indulgence, placing most importance on human
life and plans, rejecting the spiritual chain of evolution and life.
. . . *Earth is now in great crisis.*"

Linda, by the way, is the founder of an alternative community
in Oklahoma, and these ideas about cataclysm, survival, and personal responsibility were very much in her mind when she founded
the group. That's one reason she dedicates her life to such teachings in expectation of a great upheaval. Her message seems to be:
Recognize the urgency of the times, make the appropriate changes
. . . and *survive.*

Christin, in his teaching, also talks about the link between the
transformations of persons and planet. Wanderers and Walk-ins,
he says, consider themselves to be interdimensional agents in favor
of "lightening the load"—reducing human conflict while intensify-
ing the Light already dawning. As for the prophesy of devastating

196

Earth changes, Christin explains, "The less dense our awareness, the less catastrophic our transition . . . there is a self-correcting function on Earth, so it will start over [shedding its human burden] if it is too dense. Thus there is an acceleration in all beings to lighten up through love and the acceptance of diversity [i.e., mutual cooperation among peoples and races.]"

And from Lisanne, a similar comment: "The potentials of the Earth Changes are not definite, and depend on human ideas and spirituality."

This is an extremely important element of the E.T. metaphysic. The cataclysm is *not* inevitable—it is seen as the product of human behavior, and humans have the chance to change its wrath or even reverse it altogether.

So, we come full circle. The approaching changes in the planet are connected to possible ecological disasters, which are laid at the door of human responsibility, and that leads to an urgent call to awaken, to transform ourselves, to heal our collective hidden traumas. We can learn to cooperate with the changes that the Earth *must* go through. As usual, free will reigns supreme. The quality of the Earth's transformation depends upon human counsciousness.

And whether it's in the rarified air of their homeplanets or in the circling UFO ships or "down here on the ground," all of the benevolent E.T.s seek to support greater consciousness, more and more infused with love and wisdom.

HIGH ENERGY, HIGH OPPORTUNITY

We can think of the process of human consciousness evolution as "an organic feedback loop" between humanity and its home orb. The cosmic cycles continue to turn, and so the planet must now switch to a new frequency. And because of the disharmony of the human situation, this shift could very well turn out to be catastrophic—unless individuals take advantage of the higher energies available.

If, however, we are willing to avail ourselves of the "higher energies," the change will be much smoother. More people will then awaken to their spiritual nature, *which is actually what the planet itself is doing.* We'd do well to remember that while global transformation may be cosmically ordained, timed by forces beyond human motivation, human consciousness and our personal behavior still exert a powerful effect, and we can lessen or magnify the Earth's physical upheaval.

It's precisely this "call to consciousness" that the E.T.s in my study have been urging us to heed as they play the role of "visiting spokespeople helping the transition." What that eventually comes down to is this: supporting both individual and collective awareness to help soften what threatens to be a severe cataclysm.

As Pauline told me, it's "the need for beings of higher frequency to aid the Earth Changes." It is not an exaggeration to state that almost all of the people with whom I spoke believed some type of planetary apocalypse could be upon us within their Earth lifetimes, if not within the next twenty years.

But doom and gloom wasn't their response, even though others—without the aid of metaphysics—might be thrown into inconsolable depression or despair by a similar outlook. Switching to a higher frequency, opening the awareness of love, heeding wisdom—all of this was seen as possible by the E.T.s. Over and over I heard them describe the coming years as a "tremendous opportunity" for themselves *and humanity* (when considering themselves as distinguished from humanity.)

Linda, for instance, said she thought the next few decades would bring unforeseen opportunities "for humanity to grow in consciousness . . . as the energies available to Earth are special [now], [coming] from astrological and ray influences and the transitional cycles."

There were many who defined the opportunities as a time for "awakening." That phrase was used in various ways and not always with precision, but the common theme that seemed to unite the use of the term was the development of unconditional love, self-understanding, wisdom, and a sense of unity. Soren, I thought, gave a pretty good definition: "Earth awakening is part of Earth's awakening to its spiritual identity and the purpose of all life."

Looked at in this way, potential Earth catastrophes, sweeping changes, and even unprecedented UFO phenomena could all be considered an effort to help people "wake up." This is how Matthew explained it: "UFO's are a catalyst for people to realize a new view of the world and the universe. The global shift is now in play, with the crop circles chip being played and the world process occurring. So, people pay attention to more important things and leave off others."

The crop circles are those mysterious UFO-related shapes seen on the ground in many countries. These unexplained crop impressions, Matthew believed, pointed to the process of an Earth cycle change that was going to lead inexorably toward apocalypse and the New Age—and he also believed the process was already far advanced. "Signs" are being given to humanity to help us develop greater consciousness and universal vision.

If Matthew's picture is correct, it means that *cosmically ordained events are stimulating the human condition*, a thought that was voiced by most of the other E.T.s as well. As Belinda told me, there is "increased E.T. activity and more information about positive [i.e., benevolent] E.T. groups to balance the negativity. Therefore people will ask more about E.T. identity and go within, since the shift into the new dimension will facilitate awakening to individual light and love."

In other words: Cycle change itself spurs higher consciousness . . . or at least it does for those who take the challenge of greater awareness, who awaken to universal principles, who open to love and understanding.

According to Lisanne, one of the many spiritual teachers I interviewed, this personal change requires the end of human fear:

> The global awakening, the evolutionary threshold all over the world—the talk about E.T. connections, the vast interest and concern . . . As Earth goes through large changes more will feel fool-

ish to deny [E.T. existence]. There will be healing of the global, astral, [emotional] body and the threshold of a new species of humanity without fear. . . . This is the end of one level and the beginning of the next, [and] the E.T.s are seeking to help Earth expand its holographic understanding [of universal-spiritual reality.]

She went on to explain that, to her,

The planet is asking for help, so new information is being given to help Earth. People are waking up, and when you are ready to know more, you are given more—humanity wants to know more about its truth . . . the *soul* of humanity wants to know more.

The awakening of humanity is going on at the same time and is completely connected to the transformation of planet Earth. Our personal reactions matter—they all help determine the fate of our globe.

This was a view held by most of the extraterrestrials—a vision rich with feelings, celebrating the specific link that joins Earth's New Age with the development of higher consciousness. The real question remaining, then, is: *Who exactly has the courage to grow with these planetary changes?*

A TIME OF HARVEST

So, there is an intricate weaving of Earthly need, human desire, and the opportunities offered by a higher agency. Here's Lucia's explanation:

There are many new means of advancement possible for Earth and they are [only] allowed to come when the collective is at the place of needing a universal perspective and the tools [to grow]. The transition is a spiritual New World order, learning how to exist in a co-creative way to make heaven on Earth.

If humanity truly desires to grow, the E.T.s say, it will be given the means to do so. Lucia, in fact, widens her outlook to say she "doesn't feel particular to E.T. souls," and that "everyone is awakened who has gone through a soul realization, personalized soul integrity, finding the Higher Self."

"We're just teething right now," Lucia says, "but there are major changes ahead. I resonate with all the prophecies which tell us that things will get significantly different."

Which brings us to another aspect of this vision: Wanderers and Walk-ins believe that they've not only arrived on the planet to share their wisdom, but also in response to a mass human calling, a sub-consious urge for change and higher levels of awareness. Those who claim E.T. identity believe themselves to be *specifically called by the planet itself, as well as by a near-slumbering humanity.* Humanity sent out a distress call.

In their words:

"The E.T.s always come in times of need on different worlds." (Barrie)

"Earth put out the call for Wanderers, as it is a crucial time to be here." (Soren)

"All the Wanderers and Walk-ins are coming to assist Earth in its growth and change." (Una)

"There are *many* beings here from the multidimensions to avert the destruction of Earth and the surrounding sector. There are many on the planet and in space. *The Walk-in phenomenon is due to the Earth transformation.*" (Pauline) [italics added]

"It is important for humanity to realize the hierarchy of spiritual beings available to serve Earth and human evolution, to advance Earth civilization ... thus the E.T. groups and the Walk-ins are here, as midwives." (Lucia)

So, what is ultimately at stake? When I put the question to Christin, he answered by relying heavily on Christian and Christological symbolism, summarizing his view of the changes to come with this prediction: "I see an approaching Planetary Pentecost at 2012, an individual enlightenment expressed collectively."

That date, or its close approximation, was to be heard again and again, with many of the E.T.s saying that this was the date by which only those of sufficiently pure and spiritualized consciousness will remain on Earth.

This coincides with the end of the Mayan calendar and is also discussed in *The RA Material*, where the prophesy is set for 2010. That year is seen as "the time of harvest" when Earth completely enters "the density of love and understanding" and the next epoch of global harmony begins. Almost every one of the E.T.s I spoke with agreed with these views and considered themselves as doing their part to aid the planet as it passes through inevitable changes of civilization and consciousness.

Well, that much stated, we're well into the heart of New Age thinking. It's an outlook shared by many others who do not assert E.T. identity, but what's different for the Walk-ins and Wanderers is that each of them claims to be a *direct representative* of the metaphysical, galactic philosophy that's usually associated with New Age thought. Stated simply: *They believe themselves to be from the other side, from the realms of awareness toward which Earth is headed.* They are, then, like "messengers from our destiny."

They not only agree with the current evidence of millenialism, but by their realized E.T. identity and life purpose, they seek to bear witness to its claims, using their very lives and central senses of self to express these ideas. They seek to become living examples of a future, widened vision.

And what about those of us who feel we're an extraterrestrial part of this process? Or who suspect that our true identities are veiled, that we're among what could be millions of Sleeping Wanderers?

Some thoughts on the matter were given by Justinian. This is his advice to those who feel themselves to be E.T.s but aren't quite certain, or who feel strangely curious about their identity:

> Fervently follow a spiritual path to fuse with the Higher Self. Learn to disidentify from the physical, emotional, and mental levels

and become your soul. Discover why you're here. Fulfill that purpose fervently.

The effect of this, he hopes, will be people who are more open to accepting their ego patterns and by knowing how to be humble who, by doing so, can disidentify from them.

"It's very challenging," Justinian said. "Don't be at war with your personality patterns."

And don't be an "E.T. separatist," he said, because that's an ego trap, too. It's more important to "learn to identify with the one life that we all are."

Then he laughed and advised, "Get going!" before reminding any potential E.T. that "service is the reason we're here."

HISTORY AND THE FAR SIDE

For all of those people who claim off-planet origins, the whole discussion of extraterrestrials popping up on Earth is set within history. They believe that contact between those from Earth and those From Elsewhere has been going on for some time . . . if not for all time. It is an actual process, and it's to be taken into account whenever we try to understand the Earth's history:

> "I see a lot of E.T. activity, not all benevolent, and there is a glamour that E.T. equals goodness . . . but a lot of E.T. contact claims are delusive, from negative entities." (Lucia)

> "There is a great band of E.T.s here to aid Earth as part of the plan—[as it was] in past, present, and future." (Joan)

> "The Earth is seeded, and has been developed from other beings coming here. . . . The Earth would not have survived if not for continual E.T. aid." (Inid)

But regardless of wrestling aliens, angels, and E.T.s, almost all of those who spoke with me believed in the ultimate triumph of love and wisdom: *The Earth will be saved, no matter how bad things get in the next few years.* No matter how many people die in ecological or geological disasters, or how many fail to awaken and choose instead a heedless materialistic indulgence, intellectual skepticism, or drugged slumber ... *compassion, they predict, will prevail.*

For those who had seriously and thoroughly examined their beliefs, the future—no matter how difficult the journey—was thought to yield a golden age, an age marked by social harmony, interplanetary exchange, and advanced technologies that will be put to use in strictly humanitarian ways.

This overview is not so different from the visions reported by John Mack, M.D., from his sessions with those he believes to be UFO abductees. As for Earthlings who've had close encounters, Mack eloquently states in his book *Abduction*:

> What is the vision of the possible human future that the abductees have brought back to us from their journey? UFO abductions have to do, I think, with the evolution of consciousness and the collapse of a worldview that has placed humankind at a kind of epicenter of intelligence in a cosmos perceived as largely lifeless and meaningless. As we, like the abductees, permit ourselves to surrender the illusion of control and mastery of our world, we might discover our place as one species among many whose special gifts include unusual capacities for caring, rational thought, and self-awareness. As we suspend the notion of our pre-eminent and dominating intelligence, we might open to a universe filled with life-forms different from ourselves to whom we might be connected in ways we do not yet comprehend.

Don't forget that the life-forms most often met in abduction cases are scary and invasive—they'd definitely be considered hostile by most Walk-ins and Wanderers.

In my study, those who claim E.T. identity haven't simply met extraterrestrials; *they say that they themselves are actually from the other side*, from civilizations and states of being already in alignment with universal, metaphysical principles. Abduction, invasion, and fear are definitely not their purpose.

When Wanderers and Walk-ins are labeled From Elsewhere, they want us to realize that the "where" from which they come is actually the place where Earth is now headed—a state of greater understanding and unity with all creation. Like other believers in the future New Age, the E.T.s were far more comfortable with thoughts of an interplanetary future, with ideas of an expanded galactic community, then they were with the spiritless realities of current society. Perhaps that's part of what accounts for their "flakiness" or "spaciness" in the eyes of the mainstream.

This is not an idle observation, however. In many ways, those who claim to be extraterrestrials are not adjusted to present society, and, moreover and more important, *they don't seek to be.* The world they believe they herald is, in their view, far superior to what presently exists. And almost all of them are working concretely to bring this about, engaging themselves in social action instead of in cloudy abstract thought. They are practical idealists, holding most radical and unusual cosmic beliefs, but still deeply concerned with the fate of our planet and the people living here. This global vision, more than anything else, makes their existence meaningful and important, although they are living among us as strangers.

They see themselves as working for a bright future. I heard dire predictions of destruction, of course, but they were only relevant for the short-term, perhaps the next twenty years.

And through inevitable periods of loneliness, alienation, sadness, and social disconnection as conscious souls, these E.T.s have found strength and sustenance in a global vision that provides a wider outlook on everything: life, death, evolution, and the place of Earth in the greater universe. It is a vision we cannot afford to miss.

APPENDIX I

A Brief Quiz for Sleeping Wanderers

The following quiz basically indicates what I look for when determining if someone is an E.T. soul. It's a very subjective measurement based on my own experience, neither authoritative nor statistical. Please take it as simply a broadstroke portrait of E.T. Wanderers (or Star People), and a novel type of road map to assist your journey towards the shrouded citadel of Self.

You are most likely an E.T. Wanderer if . . .

1. You were often lost in daydreams of E.T.s, UFOs, other worlds, space travel and utopian societies as a child. Your family thought you were "a bit odd," without knowing quite why.

2. You always felt like your parents were not your true parents, that your real family was far away and hidden. Perhaps you thought things around you were somehow "not the way they should be," and reminded you of life somewhere "far away." These beliefs may have caused you a great deal of pain and sorrow. You felt "out of place."

3. You've had one or more vivid UF0 experiences (in a dream or during waking hours) which dramatically changed your life: they helped resolve doubts, inspired confidence and hope, and gave you meaning and greater purpose. From then on, you knew you were a different person. Like a spiritual wake-up call, it changed your life.

4. You are genuinely kind, gentle, harmless, peaceful, and non-aggressive (not just sometimes, but almost always). You are not

much interested in money and possessions, so if "someone must do without," it is usually you—such is your habitual self-sacrifice. Acts of human cruelty, violence and perpetual global warfare seem really strange (shall we say, alien?). You just can't figure out all this anger, rage and competition.

5. You have a hard time recognizing evil and trickery: some people call you naive (and they're right!). When you do perceive genuine negativity in your midst, you recoil in horror and may feel shocked that "some people really do things like that." In a subtle way, you actually feel confused. Perhaps you vaguely sense having known a world free of such disharmony.

6. The essence of your life is serving others (be they family, friends, or in a profession), and you cherish great ideals, which may also be somewhat innocent and naive (in worldly terms). But you sincerely, deeply hope to improve the world. A lot of disappointment and frustration comes when such hopes and dreams don't materialize.

7. You completely embrace the scientific temperament, with a cool, reasonable, and measured approach to life. Human passion and red hot desire seem strange: *you are baffled*. Romance and the entire world of feelings are truly foreign to your natural way. You always analyze experiences, and so people say you're always in your head—which is true! [Note: This type of Wanderer is less common, and probably wouldn't be reading this book—their skepticism would be too great! Such an "odd bird" is probably a brilliant scientist.]

8. You easily get lost in science fiction, medieval epic fantasy (like *The Hobbit*) and visionary art. Given a choice, you'd much prefer to live in your dreams of the past or future than in the present. Sometimes you consider your Earth life boring and meaningless, and wish you could go to a perfect, exciting world. Such dreams have been with you a long time.

9. You have an insatiable interest in UFOs, life on other worlds or previous Earth civilizations such as Atlantis or Lemuria. Sometimes you feel like you've really been there, and may even go back someday. There may be quite a few of such books on your bookshelves. (Actually, this question is a give-away, since only Wanderers and Walk-ins have profound, undying curiosity about worlds beyond—and for good reason!)

10. You have a strong interest in mystic spirituality (East or West), both theory and practice, with a deep sense that you *used to have greater powers and somehow lost them.* You may feel it's unnecessary to discipline yourself since "you've already been there," but somehow forgot what you used to know. People may doubt your resolve, but you know it's not that simple.

11. You have become a conscious channel for E.T.s or some other non-Earth source—and you realize that the purpose of your life is to help others grow and evolve. (Most likely, you're no longer sleeping, Wanderer!)

12. You feel, and *perhaps all your life have felt* tremendous alienation and a sense of never quite fitting in. Maybe you hope to be like others, try your best to be "normal," or imagine yourself like everyone else—but the bottom line is that *you simply feel different* and always have. There is a very real fear of never finding a place in this world. (Which you might not! Note: This is *the* classic profile of Wanderers.)

Of course, my questionnaire is not exhaustive, and simply answering "yes" to any one point doesn't necessarily mean you are From Elsewhere. Although some questions are pretty good E.T.-indicators, such as number 3 (if your E.T. contact was clear and overwhelmingly positive), and the combination of numbers 1 and 12 (a classic profile), there are no guarantees. (And I assume no legal liabilities, please!) Only you can determine whether or not you are an E.T. soul, coming from the depths of intimate self-understanding.

In most cultures, external sources determine right and wrong, true and false, with subtle yet rigid standards for what "normal people say and think." So if you're seriously wondering whether or not you're a Wanderer, an E.T. soul just visiting Planet Earth (which seems more like *Planet Hollywood* every day!), don't expect support and a fair hearing from everyone. If you've remember, many marriages were broken on the rocks of E.T.-announcement (and E.T.-musings as well). Be careful to whom you turn for feedback and guidance, since some people will surely freak out, or question your sanity.

If you do conclude *it really is possible* to be sure of something as radical as E.T.-identity (which, however, is not radical to some people), *then you have to see if through to the end.* Plainly stated, if you can't stop wondering then you must make a commitment to finding the answer. Otherwise, your doubts will consume you and fill your life with anxiety and uncertainty.

Don't let skeptics and jokers flood you with negativity, but try to use their criticism to clarify your own thinking. I think it's a good idea to give every opinion a hearing, compare perspectives and possibilities, then let it all settle down into the roots of mind. When everything is integrated and processed (which may take years), it will emerge as a set of well-reasoned, balanced beliefs, which may still include uncertainty! *If you truly relax into your natural mind,* then I assure you, the dubious will fall away, and only the real will remain. Have faith in your self: it's none other than the Voice of the Universe, if you can be still enough to really listen.

APPENDIX 2

Wandering Journey: My Personal Path

It all comes down to an acceptance of something you can't measure in a conventional way.
—ROBERT MONROE
quoted in the *Wall Street Journal*
September 20, 1994

Like the E.T.s in our study, you've probably arrived at this last chapter in one of two ways:

As a Wanderer, who gradually reads through the entire book and then slowly, comfortably, reaches the point of realization. . . .

Or, like a Walk-in . . . suddenly! Someone who, as soon as you hit the sentence that mentioned that *I, too, am From Elsewhere* in the Foreword, turned right to this chapter, immediately. Either way, it's an interplanetary nonstop trip, and I hope you've been hurtling between worlds.

While this book was never intended to be an autobiographical study, my own recognition of Wanderer identity obviously warrants a few explanations—to say the least.

Perhaps I can explain how it felt for me to personally arrive at the odd conclusion: *I, too, am a Wanderer.*

Trained as an academic in psychology, comparative religion, and personal counseling, I've studied in both Western and Eastern traditions and don't really have any fascination with claims that are zealous, unduly emotional, or poorly reasoned. Even so, my thinking has always been outside the mainstream. E.T.s, UFOs, interplanetary life, soul-exchange, cosmic purpose—these ideas never seemed so strange to me, and that's fairly typical of Wanderers. Because we live through a kind of "unveiling" of E.T. identity—uncovering something that's been present since birth—the discovery of being an E.T. soul isn't that much of a shock.

Possibly, you're a little more surprised.

Remember, though, each of us must ultimately deal with the questions: *Who am I? Who and what am I, really, as a conscious human being? What does it mean to be human?*

And the answers to those questions, which take us into the deepest areas of identity, can only be found through our own efforts. It's a puzzle that requires a different answer for every person who attempts a solution.

For me, the puzzle began as it does for most Wanderers: as an attempt to ease a terrible, personal pain and to find out what was causing it. Materially comfortable as a child in New York City, I was aware even as a youngster that this comfort was mere surface. Underneath, I felt a searing, essential loneliness, a sense that I was different in a way that couldn't be accounted for. Nothing helped. Nothing explained what I was going through. Standard procedures such as mainstream psychotherapy gave standard answers, and while these answers sometimes fit, they never satisfied. The pain continued to grow ever more intense.

All during my early schooling, I could find only one source of comfort, a single "sanctuary" where everything snapped together, and where there seemed to be more respite, at least for a little while. This was in a serious reading of religion and philosophy: Chinese and Indian Buddhism, Taoism, and the *I Ching*, a book of divination.

Before my eighteenth birthday, I'd made a home for myself in the philosophies of the East. I wasn't alone—there were many others who wanted what the West couldn't provide. In fact, one of my favorite childhood friends was already reading Gandhi at the age of twelve and went on to become a scholar in Chinese studies.

A serious encounter with Eastern philosophy can be an incredible liberation. If you've ever been swept away by these works of existential religion, you know how exciting it can be, how heady the experience is of first coming upon these ideas. Even in the writings of the more commercial authors, a young person first discovering Zen and Taoism starts to feel that he's suddenly been given some precious secret; as if he's finally gained "permission" to be who he is, the person he felt himself to be all along. And all this, without having to ask anyone "May I?" The only authority is within.

What I failed to appreciate as a young man, was that these ideas require much more than a simple reading. They need to be realized, embodied. They demand devotion. I didn't yet understand just how arduous that process would be and how far it was going to take me.

So, although I'd stumbled onto some of the greatest gifts of the East, I was only slightly closer to finding out who I was and why I felt as I did.

It was in that state of confusion that I went away to college, and there, the real force of my existential angst hit with the power of a mountain landslide, piling on top of me with a thunderous roar.

At Oberlin College, in Ohio, all the pain of childhood that had been repressed; all the nights of primal, faceless loneliness; all the rage; all the discomfort of not joining in and not wanting to join, of hating the basis of society; all of this came crashing down on me. I was overwhelmed. I lived every day feeling torn apart by a suffering whose origin I couldn't find. It was a period of deep, deep misery that weighed on every moment of my life. I had never before faced such pain.

And what really saved me was meditation.

During my first semester at Oberlin, I'd happened into a sort of unofficial course in Eastern religion. At the first class meeting, our student-teacher taught us how to sit *zazen*, the basic Japanese Buddhist meditation practice. I'd tried this before on my own, teaching myself from books, but there was something different about this live instruction. The teacher, Jay—who later became a good friend—was the real thing. An ardent meditator and social activist, he'd organized temple protests in Sri Lanka and was passing on knowledge gained through his own experience. Anyway, something clicked. Meditation was to become an extremely intensive, lifelong pursuit. Today, when I think back on it, I'm actually grateful that this period of difficulty unfolded itself so early in life, because it provided a "path" that I could follow onto a "boulevard of liberation." It's something I often reflect upon and appreciate to this day.

But things got worse before they got better.

Day-to-day, I sat in meditation trying to still the pain and remain aware of my breathing, concentrating on truly knowing each breath as it went in, then out. Soon, however, I started to experience a widening split in consciousness. It opened like a fault line in the earth, showing me the sharp contrast between the brilliant, joyous tapestry of meditation and the whole drab cloth of college life, the mundane studying and planning for "the future." It touched off a severe conflict between the lukewarm student world and my own ardent fantasies that were built upon deepening meditation, Himalayan mysteries, and ancient forest asceticism—along with a healthy dose of youthful imagination. The sides were being drawn up: I'd pitted myself against the world.

What I didn't know then was that I was rushing headlong into the deep wellsprings of serious religious practice.

And everything started to crumble.

My studies became meaningless. The only thing that seemed important was this compelling need to meditate, to cool the raging fires of emotional shattering and mental distress, to somehow settle the ever-present suffering in my mind. And the anger! It was enormous: against society, my family, parts of myself. And, always, running like a hidden stream beneath everything else, the most serious questions for me continued to be: *How can I become free? How is it possible for me to live in this world? How is it possible for anyone? What is my life all about and what am I doing here?*

What was plain was that I was going to have to make some essential changes in myself, alter the actual *quality* of my mind—meditation had taught me that this was possible. The basic tenet of all Buddhist practice might be summed up as precisely this: It is possible to realize—*to make real*—the intrinsic freedom that is hidden by the confusion of ordinary mind. I knew that with work, I could do it.

So, while the meditation practice I'd adopted was good, it wasn't good enough. I felt myself wasting precious time, and the strain of remaining in place was driving me downward. I left college, began seeking out formal Zen training, and finally chose a temple in upstate New York.

This was a Rinzai Zen Japanese temple called Dai Bosatsu Zendo. A touch of Japan in the Catskill Mountains: ceramic tiled roof; thick wooden beams on the ceiling; beautiful oak floors, a long, cold meditation hall with a simple Buddha at the front; and harsh, very harsh; born out of the most martial of the Japanese Buddhist sects. Just what I thought I wanted! For three months of intensive training, I put myself in the hands of those old-school monks who taught Zen stillness with the swift smack of a stick for anyone who slept, nodded off, or so much as stirred on the cushion. And if you meditated with what they thought was a smug expression? They hit your for that, too.

Up at 4:30 in the morning to the sound of a gong, then a quick wash, no talking, and it was on to *kinhin*, or walking meditation, where we sought to become one with the sounds and feelings of our bodies in motion. After much ceremony and chanting, we engaged in a period of sitting meditation and, following that, some other forms. The ideal was that everything you did would eventually become meditation. In every thought and action, it was hoped, we would be concentrated and focused on that single moment and nothing else. From such concentration, it's held, spontaneous insight arises.

One common misunderstanding about meditative practice is that you're not going to be thinking at all, which usually results in your mind rigidly grabbing onto anything it can find. Better, I think, is for meditation to help you focus awareness on exactly what you're doing in that instant, rather than being caught up in fantasy—fantasies of eating, friends, sex, what you're going to do when you leave the monastery, or what it might be like to be the teacher. You just stay in the here and now.

As this is developed, psychological pain is free to rise up and pass away. . . .

But even as I meditated, I wanted something more.

Over the next year or so, I returned to the monastery for several intensive retreats, but I still wasn't satisfied. The ordinary routes available to interested Western students seemed to be lacking in rigor. There was so much social chatter, so much downtime outside the practice hall, so many confused young Americans. It was just what I was trying to escape. I wanted a "real" practice environment where meditation alone was paramount. The problem, as I saw it, wasn't the hard-core discipline of the Rinzai priests. Instead, it was that this kind of Zen training was way too soft!

Through some friends I'd made at the temple, I got in contact with a Thai teacher of Theravada-style Buddhism, a "way" that is said to be much closer to the ancient path of the historical Buddha in India. Theravadan Buddhism demands a form of concentration that is gentle, yet intense and free of cultural overlay, unlike Japanese Zen. The teacher had a temple in Denver that not only had the reputation of being austere but, if I was interested in going, I'd also be the only non-Thai, non-monk who lived there.

It sounded perfect, exactly what I was searching for.

I was twenty-one. I'd been temporarily living at home. Without any other warning, I left my parents a note saying little more than "Thanks," and telling them how much I appreciated all they'd done for me. No forwarding address. No phone number. No word on where I was headed. I was thinking that I was through with being the child of my parents and my plan was to practice at the Denver temple for a while, then move on to Thailand. I was going to take my dreams literally. I would actually become one of those wandering forest hermits—they still have them in Southeast Asia. I wanted vows of poverty. I wanted to live clothed in tree bark, to eat only once a day, shave my head, follow in the path of those ancients who sang such praises as, "Oh, glorious monk, how wonderful to have the sky above your head. ...." These guys, I believed, cared only for liberation, they were way beyond the common need for ego gratifications. They were afraid of nothing, and I envied them.

So, I took off for the temple in Colorado feeling that it would be my last stop in America. I was prepared never to return, angry that my country seemed a land of empty materialism and useless worldly pursuit.

At this point, I was done with the more popular Zen primers of authors like Alan Watts and Suzuki Roshi and had begun working my way through far more esoteric material, becoming seriously immersed in Victorian translations of original Pali texts. And I kept up my practice, convinced that meditation was the flame that would finally burn away my ignorance—my fears, desires, pain, and confusion.

At the temple in Denver, I dove into the sober, blank Theravadan path of meditation eight hours a day. Alone. There were several monks in residence there, but to my surprise not one of them chose to take part. In fact, they preferred to watch TV and hang out! They didn't feel the same kind of burning discontent that I was going through. I was driven to practice, feeling guilty if I spent my time in less concentrated activities, and angry at myself if I chose not to meditate.

The Theravadan form of practice means sitting motionless in the lotus or half-lotus position with eyes half-open and mouth closed, concentrating your attention on the tip of the nose, becoming aware of nothing but the passage of breath going in and out. Eventually, this process brings you to higher states of consciousness along a path that goes something like this:

In the first state, you become "permeable" to any psychological issues that have been denied. You deal with pain, upset, and confusion as well as fear and memories. It can take quite a while, but when the mind clears, and you become quiet, there's a much higher state in which you experience a kind of bliss in your body and what I can only call "radiant mind," a sense of joy, love, and happiness. No object external to you creates this—it arises naturally, by itself, when all the psychological debris has peeled away.

Eventually, your breath goes very slowly and your mind becomes even more clear and open. In this state, it's possible to feel that you're expanding beyond your body and beyond the room where you're sitting. Often, you can see visions of what might be called past lives. Deeper insights freely come to you: the nature of personality, the nature of self, the process of birth and death.

The result for me? Something like an out-of-body experience. More than one, in fact, a series of them. I'd be sitting in meditation in the Denver temple and slowly feel that I'd become light and carefree, separated from all physical form, floating. Then, afterward, I'd finally come back to myself.

This experience briefly dulled the inner pain, but the suffering would always return. When it did, it was excruciating, even though my practice had exhausted me enough to feel the hurt less keenly. I began thinking about it as a subtle torture, like an army of faceless demons attacking me when I had nothing left to hold onto, or hide behind. Then one day, after meditation in Denver, when I got back to my room, there was a surprise awaiting me. A phone call from New York.

My parents had discovered my whereabouts. They wanted to come out to Colorado for a visit.

Their anxiety was completely understandable. Here they were, watching someone from a well-to-do modern urban upbringing put all his energy and aspirations into becoming an ascetic, forest monk. They thought I was crazy, feared that maybe I'd inherited some kind of mental illness or was the victim of some psychogenic chemical imbalance. Please, they said, would I agree to go back to New York and undergo a battery of standard psychological tests? To which I answered: Yes, I would.

I was definitely feeling like a martyr at the time. And like any good martyr, I was ready and willing to do whatever anyone asked of me without complaining. If someone wanted to examine my psyche, spread it out on the expert's examining table. I didn't mind. It was their problem. And anyway, the sense of self is an illusion.

So, it was back to Manhattan, where I was put through several testing sessions with a psychologist. After the process was completed, we sat together in her office where she looked at me sternly across her desk and warned, in no uncertain terms, that if I didn't enter intensive therapy right away, I might have what she called, "a break." A psychotic episode is what she meant, a break with what's conventionally meant by "reality."

What I heard her saying, was that it was time for me to shape up and start getting along, play the game, see the world in ways that psychologists believe to be true, grow up and stop all this bizarre religious stuff.

I was secretly pleased. I couldn't tell her that "a break" was exactly what I was hoping for—not a psychotic break, of course, rather, a spiritual transformation that would lead me out of my suffering.

I thanked the psychologist for her conclusions and my parents for their kindness, and decided it was time for me to move on: I headed for the jungles of southern Thailand.

It was in Southeast Asia that the break I so desperately wanted began to take place.

The Denver temple set up the trip for me, and I soon found myself peering through the window of a jet as it prepared for our landing in Bangkok. I can still see how that countryside appeared from the air—dense, thickly green, so green it seemed to turn black in some sections, with mountains rising up like the incredible visions you often see in Asian woodcuts and line drawings. The countryside lay there below me as impenetrable and difficult to cut through as the illusions of mind, and I had a real moment of excitement as we touched down, figuring that I had, at last, arrived at my life's destination.

Southern Thailand ... I went off to live in a forest *wat*, a monastery, in the middle of a lush, perfumed jungle. We were surrounded by rubber plantations and the heat was at least 80 degrees during the winter days, with probably 100 percent humidity. Immense, slithering lizards crawled over the trees and there was the constant sound of chattering monkeys. Alone, I took up residence in a raised *kuti*, or hut, and at night huge, flying cockroaches would propel themselves into my thin, sheet-metal door. All night I'd hear them, a constant *ping*! *pang*! as these immense roaches smacked against the entrance, and in the morning the metal would be covered with tiny dents.

This, I thought, was the perfect place to forget everything. And very rapidly, *I really did begin to forget*—my previous life, New York, my family; all those memories began to dim.

Not one other seeker on that trip spoke English, and, while our teacher was able to speak the language, he much preferred smiling to saying anything at all. Also, if I'd thought our practice in the Denver temple had been rugged, it was nothing compared to the effort we made in Thailand, with that Southeast Asian heat wrapping itself around us like a giant snake, squeezing so hard it was difficult to breathe, as we sat and sat and meditated. Muscles aching, legs tired, spine sometimes screaming for relief. All day. At last, there was nothing but meditation.

I was able now, through meditation, to visualize a colored ball hanging in the air in front of my face and slowly, with a lot of work, I could actually see it not as a figure of the mind but as a real *thing* bobbing in front of me. Whether this was a product of imagination or whether I was actually materializing an object outside my body, I still don't know.

Eventually, I traveled to Sarnath in India and meditated at the *stupa*, the holy structure, where the Buddha gave the first of his teachings. But travel only brought on frustration. I wasn't a tourist and I wasn't about to start acting like one. This wasn't why I'd come to Asia, to take photos of holy sites. I couldn't wait to get back to Thailand and intensify my practice.

That's when I experienced the vivid beginning of what was to be my "break." I'm not sure why. Maybe it was the temple where I was staying—the Garden of Liberation, which existed for no other purpose than exactly that, the liberation of the mind. Maybe it was all the work I'd done previously and, then again, maybe it was just that the time was right. I could also go along with the Zen masters who sometimes say, "I don't know and it doesn't matter," meaning there's no real explanation. Whatever the answer, while meditating and living in such lush, exotic surroundings, my mind suddenly became clearer, and, finally, I felt at ease. There was no struggle left in me.

The natural state of mind—self-luminous and absolutely free—came shining forth.

I felt so liberated that when my visa expired I was perfectly satisfied to go back to the United States. Why not? An enlightened mind is an enlightened mind anywhere, not just in the jungles of Thailand.

So, not only did I return to America, but I felt liberated enough to even go back to school. And for several months, everything seemed just fine. Then, one morning I awoke again with that awful, heavy sense of meaninglessness that pressed on me like some dark weight. I didn't know why it had returned or where it had come from, but fortunately I knew what to do about it. I needed some intensive Zen practice. The best place for it, ultimately, turned out to be in Rhode Island.

Like a parched man finding water, I entered the monastery of a Korean Zen master named Seung Sahn Sa Nim for a three-month silent meditation. There was a wonderful atmosphere in that monastery: relaxed and disciplined, supportive and yet still allowing ample time for individual work.

And there, in Rhode Island, I finally completed my break-through. I smashed what remained of my block, what was keeping me from living in the world. I got rid of the old, tearing emotional pain that I'd felt so deeply, for so long.

Sitting in meditation and in question-and-answer sessions with the Zen master, all the reading, studying, and inner work I'd been doing, all the practice in the United States and abroad, *everything* suddenly fell into place and was realized.

I'd been following that old Zen path, the one that says "You should meditate like your head's on fire" or like you've "swallowed a red hot iron ball and can't spit it out," meaning to focus your aspiration for enlightenment to a point of complete dedication. I'd watched a close friend grind himself down with too much practice and sort of "go crazy." I'd been told by a mental health professional that I was losing my mind. And although I didn't worry very much about insanity, I did wonder whether I'd ever "see the light" on the other side of the struggle.

And then, one day in this Rhode Island monastery . . . I just allowed myself to die on the cushion.

I went to an empty space. No breathing. No movement. No thinking. Just silence—with awareness and clarity.

What I came to realize, was this: The natural state of mind is rest and ease, and that's a very tangible experience. What keeps us from enjoying it is a fear of death, or maybe, more accurately, a fear of the "death of personality." But in that empty space, I discovered that *this fear is itself just an empty shadow.* Once the fear is realized to be empty itself, you can relax profoundly in the quiet of a basic "mind-ground" that is beyond thought. And when thoughts arise, they are as fleeting and insubstantial as a light wind.

But if you fear that state? Then you begin to believe that you'll be led into death or some vaguely imagined annihilation—a fear of losing your self. In meditation, it came to me: This was only fear! Nothing else. And if you can pass through that fear, just be with it and not run from it, it goes away, and then, there's no problem at all. The fear of emptiness can be seen as nothing but a ghost, and when it goes, all that remains is silence and peace. It's almost impossible to convey what a sense of freedom this brought me.

Now, I understood that it was OK to live in regular, everyday society; not only OK, it was *virtuous*. From 1980 to 1985, during my most arduous period of practice, I'd lived with this awful, enormous hatred of everything social and worldly, and I'd removed myself from society, finding it despicable. I'd been eating like a monk and I'd grown terribly thin. I'd had a few girlfriends during that time, but no real taste for intimacy, feeling that I was so confused on my own, why would I want to take on anyone else's confusion? I already had more than my share!

But now? A major transformation. My life was completely altered. The split between the spiritual and the worldly was rapidly healing.

What I didn't understand at that moment was that what I took to be the end of my journey was actually the very beginning.

With my practice "in my heart, not in my robes," I left the Zen monastery in Rhode Island and took the train back to New York where I was looking forward to trying out this new way of life.

In the city, I signed up for the perfect "Zen practice" job: I became a dishwasher for a macrobiotic restaurant. And that was fine . . . for a little while, anyway. Sooner than I'd expected, though, Zen or no Zen, breakthrough or not, the sound of both hands washing became tiresome, the job started to seem pointless. I had to admit that I was still clutching onto a role, the role of the (apparently) Enlightened Man. I wasn't remaining true to my changed direction. Something felt incomplete. I needed a different kind of experience.

It was time to move on.

For this trip, it was back to beautiful Colorado, but not to the temple in Denver. Instead, I decided to finish college and was accepted at the Naropa Institute in Boulder for a degree program in Buddhist Studies. Naropa, started by a Western-trained Tibetan master, was said to have one of the best blends of East-West teaching in the country and the students who attended were very lively, very spiritually aware.

During my two years there, I made many friends, very interesting people, one of whom introduced me to the ways of the South American native mystics, something similar to what's found in Carlos Castaneda's writings. This was an extremely important contact, one that continues to influence my life. It was also during my Buddhist studies in Boulder that I first discovered *The RA Material*. And it was there that I began to have my first extremely vivid experiences with extraterrestrials.

When I walked through the entrance of the Naropa Institute, I was hoping only to wrap up my Buddhist practice and it never occurred to me that I'd conclude these studies with the colors of a rich, complex E.T. tapestry. But that was before I'd been through one of the most remarkable experiences I can relate, which took place during a winter vacation, at a session at Robert Monroe's place in the Blue Ridge Mountains of Virginia.

Monroe (before his recent death) was something of a swashbuckling astro-traveler, and according to the *Wall Street Journal*, the more than seven thousand graduates of his program come from backgrounds as mainstream as business, industry, and the military. The army has experimented with his techniques, and companies like DuPont have reportedly sent dozens of executives to his institute.

Monroe had developed a technique he calls Hemi-Sync, or Hemispheric Synchronization. It utilizes a series of different frequency tones that are played into a set of headphones while you lie face-up in a kind of Pullman car sleeping berth. It feels something like lying in a "capsule-bed to forever." The varying tones harmonize the hemispheres of the brain, which throws you into a different state, a higher level of consciousness. By the time I got there, Monroe was already doing a lot of work in areas like E.T. channeling, Earth prophecies, UFO studies, out-of-body travel, and future contacts with extraterrestrials.

Since I'd had a great deal of previous training and practice by this time, when I lay down and slipped on the headset, *I was actually doing meditation on the tones.* Concentrating my mind. Going into the sounds, deeper and deeper. Instead of *thinking about* what was happening, I was becoming completely absorbed into it.

The total energy level of my body changed. I went into another cycle, into a different level of clarity. I passed beyond the Earth. This wasn't a visual experience, it was totally kinesthetic: I felt my naked body moving through space, being lifted, then powerfully thrown through a membrane, a shockingly cold area, until I finally came into a place where there was this *instinctive knowing* that, all around me, there was a group of beings who were *my* group and were loving me. This was my actual, real family. Knowledge of this arrived with a certainty so unquestionable that it was like knowing without the senses. I had no doubt at all about its reality.

After that, I felt an immediate rushing sensation, a kind of interpenetration and, once again, the feeling that somehow *these are my people.* At that point, I knew that I was not alone. And I knew I would never again be alone on Earth.

Everything would be OK, I was sure of it. There was no longer a need to worry about my life—I was being taken care of, but, also, I could be my own support on this strange, confused sphere.

Right around this time, I started to have a series of strange dreams. There were many of them but this one, I think, is a good example:

One night when I'd been reading a great deal about Earth Changes and prophesies of geological upheaval, I went to bed feeling afraid. Soon, as I dreamed, I was in New York City on the very day the world was going to end. There was no argument about it, everyone knew it was happening. There I was on 14th Street, and beneath me the ground was shaking, buildings were falling down, there was thunder and lightning, people screaming, everybody running around. Nothing less than absolute panic!

Then, in the sky, unexpectedly, I saw dozens of UFO airships organized in a flying formation. They weren't panicked at all. One came right up and hovered over my head while a conical vortex of light was placed around me. But instead of some horrifying abduction, I was brought to what felt like a place of safety behind police lines where there were many other people who were also being protected. All of us were made to feel safe and secure, and, while I was there, somebody even washed my feet. At that point, I knew I'd be OK and whatever apocalypse might happen to Earth, I knew I wouldn't be harmed.

As is mentioned in much E.T. literature (notably *The RA Material*) the most common type of benevolent E.T. contact with Sleeping Wanderers is just this kind of dream. Dreams are the primary mode of alerting veiled E.T.s that they are, indeed, galactic citizens and not true denizens of Earth. Veiled E.T.s are just short-time visitors.

For me, the dream was pivotal. It was this experience that led me to take seriously the idea of extraterrestrial identity and led me to the understanding that I might actually be a Wanderer. But I still hadn't completely unveiled myself.

This was 1987. Awarded my degree from Naropa that year, I went back to New York once again, grappling with this new sensation of E.T. soul and imagining that I could keep my spiritual direction while following what I conceived of as a very romantic occupation: a New York businessman.

Another perfect Zen job, I thought, so at least I hadn't lost my sense of humor. I went to work for my stepfather who runs a pest control company called Bliss. It was even located in the same building as a national distributor of bronze Buddha statues. What could be better? I was going to work at Bliss in the Buddha building!

But bliss it wasn't.

And the world of New York business was less than sympathetic to someone who had put in five years practicing the path of no-self and was starting to make contact with a discarnate group of E.T.s. I lasted less than six months.

So, what to do? Luckily, as my fascination with business split apart, I came to appreciate my college studies of psychology more and more. And as I meditated on the question of where best to study the subject and where I would feel most comfortable, the answer that came to mind was: San Francisco.

Supported by the openness of the city itself, I went deeper into New Age ideas. I started graduate work in counseling at the California Institute of Integral Studies, a school that was started by a student of the famous Indian philosopher, Sri Aurobindo, himself one of the early colleagues of Alan Watts. I began looking more seriously into UFOs, channeling, and the teachings of Theosophy. I was giving lectures and workshops in all of those subjects along with metaphysics, and some cross-cultural training for foreign students.

And all this time, I was living through intense dreams of being on UFO craft and visiting other worlds, dreams that often came with a feeling of *that's my (E.T.) group*, while, in other dreams, I would experience myself teaching on board a ship, or channeling deep within the caverns of Earth; mystical dreams. I started to keep a night journal by my pillow—as well as a voice-activated tape recorder to catch any strange utterances spoken during my "sleep." In the morning, I'd be surprised to play back a recording of my own voice, speaking in some strange, unearthly dialects. To this day, I don't know what these instances of "speaking in dream-tongues" were really all about.

There was an overall feeling in many dreams that I had a definite role to play helping people through the coming changes. It reinforced my sense of inner security and my sense of purpose here. Slowly, I was realizing my affinity with the "global salvage project" (in the words of one E.T. I interviewed). I now realize that this purpose is intimately related to the publication of this book.

But it was *The RA Material* that really reshaped my thinking. It put my whole life into much clearer focus.

These are texts totalling four books, approximately 100 pages each, that were channeled by an extraterrestrial group that claims to have been serving Earth since early Egyptian times. They say they are one of many different members of the Confederation of Planets in the Service of the One Creator. Something like the federation in the *Star Trek* series, this is a collective organization of interplanetary civilizations, dedicated primarily to the growth of awareness in love and wisdom throughout the universe.

The RA Material details Earth history and historical E.T. influences, showing a scheme of galactic evolution through what's termed the "seven densities" (levels of consciousness) and the two paths of unity and separation, what we commonly call "good and evil." In doing so, they go a long way in explaining the nature and function of all the self-serving negativity we see on Earth.

The RA Material teaches that some sixty-plus million ordinary Earthlings are really Wanderers—E.T. souls who've been here on Earth for as many as twenty-five thousand years, while others have been here just a short period of time. (Some of those more recent arrivals are really quite naive about Earth life!)

Studying that work, making an effort to understand the deeper meaning, and feeling just how right it was for me, I came to realize that perhaps I'd been here on Earth for a long, long time (a twenty-five-thousand-year contract man, we call it) and my E.T. roots had long been buried beyond awareness. Now, though, I was able to retrieve the hidden treasure—and I could tell that my contract was coming up. Understanding all these dynamics put into perspective both my intimate familiarity with various cultures at different periods of history, as well as my more cosmic inclinations, and also explained my overwhelming sense of not really belonging here.

And so it is with most Wanderers. Our progress is gradual. There isn't a single, dramatic *Ah Ha!* experience.

Eastern religion, I now realize, was the primary path that I had followed for many lifetimes, and it finally brought me to the state of clear, pure awareness. It allowed me to break through my delusive personality level—delusive because it is ever shifting, ever in flux—to appreciate a more universal vision. Buddhism and Taoism are important paths of enlightenment, and they're not at all in conflict with E.T. ideas. And obviously, you don't have to be into Eastern philosophy, E.T.s, or any kind of New Age thinking for a taste of enlightenment. There are many paths. Indeed, it's all a matter of sincerity, effort, and compassion; of finding the true Self at the heart of Being so that the vision will naturally reveal its splendor. The true Self is always available for contact.

I actually don't want to make a big thing out of this. I've found that in most situations concerning spiritual matters, it's easier not to talk about such complicated things. And, in most situations, it's totally unnecessary. Try seriously discussing True Mind, E.T. souls, past life experiences—most people, if they're listening, will immediately get their circuits jammed. But remember, all that really counts for service to be rendered and received is for us to share our goodwill, intelligence, and kindness.

Sometimes, though, if I let down my guard and speak my mind, *something* will come out. One time, I remember, I was talking to some friends who were unaware of my E.T. ideas and I heard myself say, "How strange these Earth people are!" And at other times, "Earth is a crazy place!" (a thought that many natives would probably agree with). My Wanderer awareness is never far from the surface.

Most of my acquaintances, however—from here or From Elsewhere—hold some kind of wider consciousness. For those of you who don't, I ask only that you please understand there's really nothing remarkable about it. The E.T. incarnate and the more universal perspective are here for service, to help people, to aid Earth. And that's just the way of the world . . . or, more correctly, the way of the worlds. It's like water, which flows from a place of greater volume to another place in need of it.

I appreciate how strange all this may sound. One problem that makes it even more difficult, as all New Agers know, is that some of those who espouse New Age ideas are really, without a doubt, extremely flaky. Because of the unprovable nature of most esoteric matters, the movement attracts charlatans and others with a weak sense of self; those who find comfort parroting ideas they've heard or read; those who consider it romantic to be from another star, at least for the moment. The proof is in the way they live their lives. If they seem to be power-hungry leaders, or confused followers, that's probably just what they are.

And many people who say they're serving Earth don't do anything of the sort. They don't have much training. They don't put in much effort. They just like to hear themselves talk. Or perhaps they take secret pleasure in feeling so special "serving humanity."

Then again, there are others, *saying the same things, who have done the work on themselves.* It's not so much what people say they believe that's critical, it's how they conduct themselves and what their motivations are.

You see, the fulfillment of realizing E.T. identity on Earth is actually this: the spiritual integration of the human personality. The realization of being From Elsewhere must blend with a person's own particular Earthly sense of self. The personal and the cosmic move alongside one another in a Universal dance, and there emerges a unique expression of unified divinity—what we call "an individual soul." To accomplish this, a person needs a strong self-supporting function and the assurance to boldly walk alone when necessary. One first has to recognize that few can understand this greater perspective, and then become comfortable with the fact that being understood by others is not the most important thing. It's OK to work more or less in solitude. It's OK to be patient and await the reunion with the E.T. family ... after all the work on Earth has been completed.

More important, I think, is to be present and available; to be of service as much as possible. "Being an E.T." is simply a command to benevolent action. And, in any case, what we really are is so much more than either E.T. or human being. . . .

Which brings me to this:

Please don't think of E.T.s as being special, superior, or some kind of elite group. *This has absolutely nothing to do with any concept of an elite.* And please don't condemn them to the margins of society as useless or "insane." If you don't accept their beliefs, at least give them a hearing without being intolerant or rejecting Universal notions that seem way too far out. Keep in mind that some of these notions might someday be the key to your own unfoldment.

Remember, dreamers were once scorned for imagining a walk on the moon, intercontinental wireless communication, and global satellites. What today is deemed impossible is often accomplished tomorrow.

Above all, don't be afraid of finding out the truth. Realize that the truth—whatever it is—will give you a much better grounding in your life. Because—for all of us—the basic work is to find the meaning of our lives. If you're not afraid to listen to yourself and your own experience, then you'll eventually discover it. Truth often surprises, but always heals. In time, whatever is false or superfluous will always fall away. . . .

And again: being E.T. or not E.T. isn't that vital. *Every one of us is really divine spiritual essence embodied here on Earth.*

What is vital is the process of choosing what's right and true for us, and thereby making deeper and deeper connections with our True Self (which in Buddhism, is the same as self-luminous emptiness, pure consciousness without subject-object). This is the process of eternal learning, of growing awareness into more and more perfect harmony, expanding the reach of mind and heart so they can embrace all aspects of experience. This is the magnum opus, what our Medieval alchemists called the Great Work. It is the work of Self-refinement through the cauldron of life.

Don't be in a hurry. Don't forget to listen to your inner voice. With balance, fearlessness, and insight you can see through whatever conflicts you have within your personality and with your world.

When you learn to long for an ever-deepening rapport with your own self, the truth, whatever its shape or form, will always come clear.

APPENDIX 3

The RA Material

Without a doubt *The RA Material* is the single most important source of written teaching I've ever encountered. *The RA Material* is the first of four volumes of channeled text, organized into 100 question-and-answer sessions over a two and a half year period.

Having said this, it becomes difficult to organize my thoughts on a subject whose personal influence has been so tremendous, such a revolutionizing and redefining experience. For anyone interested or sympathetic to the extraterrestrial perspective, I believe it's difficult to come into contact with *The RA Material* without its having a profound impact on one's personal civilization and feelings. Indeed, I believe one's complete outlook on the universe will be altered. Perhaps the greatest gift bestowed is its effect as an aid to self-recognition, which, in my case, led directly to the realization of being a Wanderer here on Earth.

From the time I read and began to integrate these teachings, everything changed—or should I say, "everything became clear"?

The RA Material and the three subsequent volumes of *The Law of One*, are the product of twenty years of previous "experiments" by Don Elkins, a former airline pilot and University of Louisville physics professor. He was trying to communicate with extraterrestrial intelligence and was later joined by Carla Rueckert, who ultimately became the "instrument," or full-trance channel, for the contacts with the RA group.

The RA Group began in 1961 with a group of interested students and academics, and came to understand over many years of trial and error what the group needed to know to accurately receive and assess telepathic material. After Jim McCarty arrived in Kentucky to help support their ongoing spiritual studies, they were contacted by a source calling itself RA, and the quality of the information they were receiving changed dramatically. The clarity and potency of their material took a quantum leap forward.

From 1981 through 1984, Elkins, Rueckert, and McCarty formed the core group dedicated to a full-time channeling contact with RA, an ET group (a unified society) that claims to have given early mystery teaching to the ancient Egyptians (hence the name RA, which was the Egyptians name for the sun god.) In these sessions, which numbered over one hundred and took place several times a week, Don Elkins acted as the questioner, Carla Rueckert as the receiver (the vocal channel), and Jim McCarty as the "scribe," transcribing the many notes and "closing the circle" of the three of them.

They received an enormous amount of information about a wide range of subjects, including Wanderers, the paths of good and evil, the past and immediate future of Earth, and the fundamentals of human evolution—the evolution of consciousness, moving through individuality to union with the Creator, which is the Infinite, the All. From the beginning, RA considered itself "a humble messenger of the Law of One"—the basic nature of all things beyond our mistaken notions of duality—seeking to "lessen the distortions" generated by their earlier attempts to help Earth. These were later perverted for elitist purposes and co-opted by a corrupt priestly hierarchy in those earlier times.

The RA group was not into feeding the egos of anyone in the group of three, and repeatedly chided them when their questions strayed into matters of "transient importance" (such as who was who in past lives and what percentage of planets are at the level of Earth's awareness). RA always stressed the primacy of our seeking for greater truth and self-development. Even their language was most carefully chosen (often far beyond the recognized vocabulary of anyone in the room) so that their awareness of unity was preserved. This contact is anything but watered down, as even the casual reader will quickly see. In fact, I know many people who had a hard time "getting into it" because the ideas presented were so far beyond our ordinary way of thinking. *The RA Material*'s sophistication, in my opinion, far surpasses most of the common New Age "feel good, curiosity-feeding" literature you usually find.

From RA's perspective—as they say, their group is about two billion years older than Earth humanity—the many conflicts we see around us, and within us, are only superficial. At their level of awareness, "there is no disharmony, no imperfection: all is complete and whole and perfect"[1] This is the basic message of the Law of One, and it can certainly be found at the higher levels of Eastern philosophy, embodied in mystic Hinduism, Buddhism, Taoism, and Sufism. This most certainly does not mean that human cruelty, inequity, and suffering are "all well and good," but rather that there is a more unified perspective available, which resolves all apparent polarities.

For RA, there is only one game in town—on any planet, at any level of awareness in the infinite creation—and they teach that "the original desire is that entities seek and become one"[2] This "original desire" is the basic impulse of the Creator, the fundamental reason for all existence anywhere, and certainly "the meaning of life." All other divergent pursuits may or may not lead us toward realization of this unity—it all depends on how we use and learn from experience, and our personal desires. The Law of One is considered the fundamental nature of the universe, not exactly a "law" but rather "the way things are"—and the dividing line between people is simply that some of us realize that life is about learning and self-unfoldment, while most do not.

If you speak with anyone who considers him or herself to be

[1] Elkins, D., C. Rueckert, and J. McCarty. *The Ra Material*, volume 1 (Louisville: L/L Research, 1984), p. 86.
[2] Ibid. p. 188.

an ET soul, you will always be told that human experience is simply the catalyst to greater learning: which means Self-realization and the gradual expression of our intrinsic perfection. The purpose of all conscious Wanderers and Walk-ins—as well as of all teachers of nonsectarian spirituality—is just this same unfoldment, and then its careful application in service to others.

In addition to opening my eyes (perhaps I should say "reopening") to a greater vision about the universe, the RA sessions spoke at length about the current state of affairs on Earth and contrasted them with life at other levels of consciousness throughout the universe. The social and individual conflicts and struggles that run a constant thread through our history—and are a source of much anguish to most Wanderers—are very much the product of humanity's growing selfhood, and while they are somewhat "normal" at this level of civilization, they are completely absent in older planetary cultures, the "homeplanets" of all ET souls. So much of what is considered "normal" here, is certainly *not* normal elsewhere—which was certainly a comforting thought when I first encountered it. Nevertheless, we now find ourselves here, and productive integration into society—whatever that means to each of us—is as important to ET souls as it is to anyone else.

It is not my purpose to outline RA's voluminous teachings—the four volumes speak for themselves. Sharing a bit of what these books are all about, and how they were pivotal influences in my intellectual and spiritual development, is really all I want to do at this point. If you are interested, you can probably find them in, or order them from, your local spiritual, New Age–type bookstore, or write directly to the Louisville group at:

L/L Research
P.O. Box 5195
Louisville, KY 40255-0195

I want to close this appendix with a final quotation from RA, which points to their basic message: that human beings are, in truth, far more glorious, far more noble Divine creatures than we imagine, and most assuredly possess a grand potential that far surpasses what our Earth leaders tell us. When you begin to do the meditation work of self-cultivation, and aspire to deepen your life moment by moment through love and inner wisdom, these words will ring out with an undying sound:

> *Each entity is only superficially that which blooms and dies. In the deeper sense, there is no end to being-ness.*

LIST OF INFORMANTS

Barbara—A health-care administrator in her mid-forties, who claims to have had a total of three successive Walk-in experiences over a period of several years. She has also written about the Walk-in phenomenon. *Walk-in*.

Barrie—A lecturer, psychic, and group facilitator on the East Coast in her late thirties. Her special area of teaching is Star People and the Awakening process. *Wanderer*.

Belinda—A nurse in her late thirties, who announced her extraterrestrial identity for the first time before a public convention of the Association for Past Life Therapy and Research. *Wanderer*.

Betty—Born and raised in England, a former nurse and professional singer, currently a spiritual teacher. In her early sixties, has traveled worldwide giving lectures. *Walk-in*.

Bob—In his mid-thirties, presently unemployed and previously a drug addict for over twenty years. His narcotics use abruptly ended after his Walk-in spiritual transformation, effecting a reversal of self-destructive personality traits. *Walk-in*.

Christin—A teacher, counselor, and principal administrator in a global peace organization, in his late thirties. Had initial symptomatology of HIV infection before his Walk-in experience, and has progressed through extensive bodily healing in the years since. *Walk-in*.

Erika—A legal specialist in environmental policy work, in her mid-thirties. Still unsure about her E.T. identity, although she has had a series of profound dreams and OBE contacts. *Wanderer*.

Inid—Amidst career change, divorced mother in her mid-forties. Realized identity through hypnotic regression and claims to be the sole representative of her confederation of extraterrestrial races. She has written a long essay on the dynamics of soul exchange. *Walk-in.*

Joan—In her mid-forties, presently unemployed and concerned with persistently ailing health. Recognized a childhood Walk-in through hypnotic regression, and had been involuntarily hospitalized in her twenties because of conflict with college authorities and unwise use of numerous psychic powers. *Walk-in.*

Julie—In her mid-forties, divorced mother and administrator-counselor at holistic spiritual healing center. Claims extensive direct and channeling contact with Jesus Sananda (Christ) and with an E.T. confederation commander (Ashtar). *Wanderer.*

Justinian—Metaphysical teacher, counselor, and developer of subtle energy technologies for healing and spiritual growth, late thirties. Has extensive training in occult/Theosophical systems and considers most Walk-ins actually a "fragment exchange"—infusion from a more spiritualized aspect of Self. *Walk-in.*

Linda—International lecturer, counselor, author, and leader of a spiritual community in Oklahoma, in her mid-forties. Actively engaged in public dialogue about the role of Walk-ins in the New Age, and the need for community and social collectives. *Walk-in.*

Lisanne—International author, teacher, counselor, and director of a holistic spiritual healing center, in her early forties. Has worked with many individuals facilitating identity recognition and "multi-incarnational clearing." *Wanderer.*

Lucia—A holistic teacher, writer, therapist, and organizer of New Age seminars, in her late thirties. Has led support groups for Walk-ins and pioneered a variety of alternative personal growth practices, including spiritual parenting and energetic healing. *Walk-in.*

Matthew—In his mid-forties, wrote a book on Martian archaeology and possible ancient civilizations. Had extensive childhood extraterrestrial experiences and visions, and espouses a philosophical view of non-Earthly identity transcending time-space definition. *Wanderer*.

Pauline—In her early forties. Walk-in type experiences over several years, culminating in newfound teaching abilities and personal psychological healing. Presently leads a quasi-nomadic life, going where she feels she is needed to aid others. *Walk-in*.

Peter—Professional architect in his mid-thirties. Had a series of paranormal visitations later recognized as a type of Walk-in transfer, associated with extreme cognitive-social disorientation, which resulted in development of broad philosophical system regarding the structure of consciousness. *Walk-in*.

Soren—Psychiatric hospital technician in his mid-thirties. While growing up he suffered extreme social alienation and made three suicide attempts, resulting in temporary residence in psychiatric halfway house. Extensive study of New Age systems, especially *The RA Material*, in identity-awakening process. *Wanderer*.

Tomas—Eastern European living in America, in his late twenties. Has chosen extremely hermetic lifestyle with little social contact and claims intensive relationship with Jesus Christ (Sananda) and Maitreya (World Savior), as well as special world-service responsibilities. *Wanderer*.

Una—A visual artist in her early fifties, widowed mother of two. Claims to be incarnated from angelic kingdom, lives a somewhat isolated life and feels special affinity with plants and animals. Collaborator with Justinian and Lucia on angelic technologies projects. *Walk-in*.

Vicky—Body worker and therapist in her mid-thirties. Claims extensive relationship with E.T. confederation (Ashtar Command), and evidences great self-confidence in recognition of identity and role on Earth. *Wanderer*.

Vikram—Housepainter and screenwriter in his late thirties. Claims extensive relationship with E.T. confederation and considers his present writing project contractually determined by association with Ashtar Command. *Wanderer.*

INFORMANTS NOT INCLUDED IN THE THESIS:

Elizabeth—Occupation not specified, in her early thirties. The only informant who seemed psychologically unstable, she claimed she was from the "Cat Planet" and realized she was an extraterrestrial because the initials of her name spelled *E.T.*. Not included because her answers to questions were generally too vague, and evidenced a diffuse sense of identity.

Helen—New Age teacher and holistic healer in her late thirties. Considers herself an extracelestial (EC) or soul transfer from the angelic kingdom. Not included because interview tape was damaged and no retaping was proposed due to mutual agreement.

GLOSSARY OF TERMS

Abduction—Forcible involuntary capture by negatively-oriented (self-serving) extraterrestrials, claimants called "abductees." Increasingly discussed aspect of UFO phenomenon with therapeutic implications. (See also: *Hypnotic Regression, UFO*)

Akashic Records—Records of all past deeds, thoughts, and potential future scenarios for Earth, encoded on a nonphysical subtle energy plane, available to be "read" by those appropriately trained. Considered by some the "Great Hall of Records." (See also: *Channeling*)

Angelic Kingdom—Denotes an evolutionary line of nonphysical Beings, parallel and interactive but independent of the human. Responsible for maintenance of the planet/solar system and the development of consciousness. (See also: *Extracelestial*)

Ashtar Command—Title used to describe an intergalactic federation of benevolent extraterrestrials under the supreme jurisdiction of Ashtar, a ship commander with whom many New Age channels claim to be in contact. (See also: *Confederation of Planets in Service to the Infinite Creator*)

Channeling—Considered a form of interdimensional communication in which a nonphysical intelligence speaks through a human being in some degree of trance. Responsible for a significant amount of New Age literature. (See also: *Psychic Powers, Space Brothers*)

Chakra—Sanskrit term for quasiphysical energy centers in the human subtle body that develop in tandem with spiritual-material evolution, foci for many Eastern meditative practices. Also called centers or wheels of energy, as they are said to rotate increasingly with heightened consciousness. (See also: *Kundalini*)

242

Confederation of Planets in Service to the Infinite Creator—Term used in *The RA Material* channeled text that denotes an intergalactic collective of benevolently-oriented extraterrestrial races, said to be serving Earth at present during Harvest transition time. Comparable to Ashtar Command. (See also: *Ashtar Command, Harvest*)

Contactees—Individuals claiming direct contact with UFO groups and E.T. beings. Used variably with "abductees." Generally reserved for friendly and constructive communication for humanitarian, healing, and world service purposes. (See also: *E.T., Space Brothers, UFO*)

Cosmic Christ—The essential, universal Christic principle: unconditional love blended with wisdom in unity. Term used in different ways by spiritual writers, also identified with Maitreya. (See also: *Maitreya*)

Densification—Process whereby nonphysical spiritual energies, ideas, and tendencies become anchored in the physical body and personality. Common for Walk-in processes during which new qualities are integrated. (See also: *Walk-in*)

Extracelestial—EC. Coined by E.T. Earth Mission teachers, denotes a Walk-in soul transfer incarnating from the Angelic Kingdom to the human to serve the evolution of humanity. (See also: *Angelic Kingdom, E.T.*)

Elohim of Peace—Comparable to Cosmic Christ, indicating transcendental spiritual being/principle of universal peace and harmony, considered able to overshadow or inspire particular individuals. (See also: *Cosmic Christ*)

ESP—Extrasensory perception. Term used to describe range of nonordinary powers and abilities that suggest usage of sensory faculties transcending the physical range of five senses. (See also: *Channeling, Psychic Powers*)

E.T.—Extraterrestrial. Broadly used to describe individuals and races originating from beyond the physical Earth sphere; associated with

UFO phenomenon, channeling, and New Age philosophy. (See also: *Space Brothers*, *Wanderer*, *Walk-in*)

Fragment Exchange—FE. Alternate term used by some to explain Walk-in phenomenon, indicating transfer of independent aspect of total Higher Self into personality consciousness (in contradistinction to new soul entering). (See also: *Extracelestial*, *Higher Self*, *Soul Braid*, *Soul Exchange*, *Soul Transfer*, *Walk-in*)

Harvest—Term used in *The RA Material* text to denote impending cycle change on Earth in which only those of the consciousness of benevolent love and understanding will remain on the planet. Presence of Wanderers is considered due to their desire to serve humanity during Harvest transition. (See also: *Confederation of Planets in Service to the Infinite Creator*, *Wanderers*)

Higher Self—Term for the essential, monadic core of human body-mind-spirit complex, possessing full knowledge of past events and future development, and available guidance and aid. (See also: *Fragment Exchange*)

Hypnotic Regression—Therapeutic technique of inducing hypnosis with guided imagery to recall forgotten memories and experiences. Used with some Walk-ins to revivify identity, and also with UFO abductees. (See also: *Abduction*, *UFO*)

Kundalini—Sanskrit term expressing basic intelligence of universal energy, manifesting in human beings through *chakras* and energetic flows refining spiritual awareness and cosmic consciousness. Associated with many Walk-in experiences. (See also: *Chakra*, *Walk-in*)

Lucid Dreams—Vivid dream-like experiences in which person has waking awareness and some degree of control over elements of dream imagery and narrative sequence. (See also: *OBE*)

Maitreya—Buddhist-Sanskrit title and name for World Savior to come, comparable in definition and purpose to Cosmic Christ. Channeled by some in New Age movement, awaited as "the return of the Christ" or "the Buddha to come." (See also: *Cosmic Christ*)

Multidimensional Clearing—Indicates purification and release of conflict and disharmony from all aspects of human beings, on all subtle energy levels of energy, emotion, thought, and past experience. (See also: *Hypnotic Regression, Past Lives, Subtle Energy Technologies*)

New Age—Term applied in various ways to denote impending change of civilization, consciousness, and matter on Earth. Associated with various spiritual artifacts and philosophical tenets, congruent with planetary Harvest said to usher in new cycle of human existence. (See also: *Channeling, Harvest*)

NDE—Near-death-experience. Indicates experience of conscious separation from physical body under circumstances approaching death and dying processes. Often associated with spiritual-transcendental visions, insights, and meetings with benevolent nonphysical beings. (See also: *OBE*)

OBE—Out-of-body experience (also called OOB: "out-of-body"). Experience of conscious separation from physical body in which person has full waking awareness; like NDE, also associated with various spiritual experiences. (See also: *NDE*)

Past Lives—Category of experiences claimed to originate in an individual's past lives, assuming continuity of consciousness and identity throughout the cycle of incarnation, death and rebirth/reincarnation. Often accessed through meditative exercises and regression therapy. (See also: *Hypnotic Regression*)

Psychic Powers—General appellation for spectrum of extrasensory, transcendent, nonordinary abilities and functions, including clairvoyance, clairaudience, metal bending, and channeling. (See also: *Channeling*)

Soul Braid—Alternate term used by some to describe fragment exchange, in which new aspect of total Higher Self enters personality and dense body, resembling Walk-in transfers and catalyzing comparable life changes. (See also: *Fragment Exchange, Higher Self, Walk-in*)

Soul Exchange—Another term for the Walk-in process in which two different souls voluntarily exchange residence in a human body-personality consciousness for the purpose of release for the departing and greater potential for service to humanity for the entering soul (usually an E.T.). (See also: *Extracelestial, Fragment Exchange, E.T., Soul Braid, Soul Transfer, Walk-in*)

Soul Transfer—Another term for general Walk-in and Wanderer claimants, in which an E.T. soul enters into human body and personality consciousness either at birth or in midincarnation. (See also: *E.T., Fragment Exchange, Soul Exchange, Walk-in*)

Space Brothers—Alternate term for benevolent extraterrestrial races, allied in service to various planets and Earth humanity. Popularized in 1950s by science fiction writers, UFO researchers, contactees, and channels. (See also: *Ashtar Command, Confederation of Planets in Service to the Infinite Creator, Contactees, E.T., UFO*)

Subtle Energy Technologies—Recently developed technologies utilizing vibrational processes of various types, including pyramid energies, radionics, focused electromagnetic waves, insert gases, and flower or gem preparations. Often used for integrated physical-mental-spiritual healing and transformation. (See also: *Chakras, Multi-dimensional Clearing*)

UFO—Unidentified flying object. Denotes any nonordinary flying object, usually associated with E.T. phenomenon and discussion of Beings from outside the Earth sphere and civilization. (See also: *E.T., Space Brothers*)

Walk-in—Descriptive term for interdimensional-interplanetary soul transfer in which being from a more evolved E.T. or Angelic civilization (or greater spiritual evolvement, but of Earth origins) enters the voluntarily surrendered body-personality consciousness of a human being, for the purpose of service to humanity and the planet. Comparable phenomenology to the fragment exchange or soul braid process. (See also: *Extracelestial, E.T., Fragment Exchange, Soul Braid, Soul Exchange, Soul Transfer*)

Wanderer—Descriptive term for interdimensional-interplanetary soul transfer in which a being from a more evolved E.T. civilization incarnates at birth, voluntarily losing memory of identity or origins. Purpose is usually service to humanity and the planet, although there are self-serving Wanderers. (See also: *E.T., Soul Transfer*)

REFERENCES

Agar, M. 1980. *The Professional Stranger*. New York: Academic.

Anka, D. 1990. *Bashar: Blueprint for Change*. Simi Valley, California: New Solutions.

Bailey, A. A. 1925. *A Treatise on Cosmic Fire*. New York: Lucis.

———. 1942. *Esoteric Psychology II*. New York: Lucis.

Berreman, G. D. 1966. Emic and etic analysis in social anthropology. *American Anthropologist*. 68:346–354.

Bramley, W. 1989. *The Gods of Eden*. San Jose, California: Dahlin Family.

Bullard, T. E. 1987 *UFO Abductions: The Measure of a Mystery*. Mt. Rainier, Maryland: Fund for UFO Research.

Capra, Fritjof. 1988. *Uncommon Wisdom*. New York: Simon and Schuster.

Cirlot, J. E. 1962. *A Dictionary of Symbols*. New York: Philosophical Library.

Cosmic Awareness. 1991. The Wanderer's Dilemma, What to do About the Aliens. *Revelations of Awareness*. 384 (91–99): 15–17.

Elkins, D. and C. Rueckert 1977. *Secrets of the UFO*. Louisville: L/L Research.

Elkins, D., C. Rueckert and J. McCarty 1982. *The Law of One*, vol. II. Louisville: L/L Research.

———. 1982. *The Law of One*, vol. III. Louisville: L/L Research.

———. 1983 *The Law of One*, vol. IV. Louisville: L/L Research.

———. 1984 *The RA Material*. Louisville: L/L Research.

Gatti, A. 1978. *UFO Encounters of the Fourth Kind?* New York: Kingston.

Harrison, A. A. 1990. Psychology and the search for extraterrestrial intelligence. *Behavioral Science*. 35 (3): 207–218.

Holzer, Hans. 1976. *The UFO-nauts*. New York: Fawcett Publications.

Hopkins, B. 1987. *Intruders: The Incredible Visitations at Copley Woods*. New York: Random House.

Jung, C. G. 1959. *Flying Saucers: A Modern Myth of Things Seen in the Sky*, (R.F.C. Hull, trans.) London: Routledge and Kegan Paul.

———. 1964 *Man and His Symbols*. New York: Doubleday.

Kathlyn. 1990. Mikha'el's Point of View: On Walk-ins. *Free Spirit*. VIII (3): 24–37.

———1990. Mikha'el's Point of View: On Walk-ins. *Free Spirit*. VIII (4): 26–28.

Keel, J. A. 1975. *The Eighth Tower*. New York: Dutton.

Kirk, J. and M. L. Miller 1986. *Reliability and Validity in Qualitative Research*. Newbury Park, California: Sage.

Koteen, J. 1991. *UFOs and the Nature of Reality*. East Sound, Washington: Indelible Ink.

Light Speed. 1991. 1(7).

Luminare, C. n. d. *What, on Earth, is a Walk-in?* (private.)

Lundberg, G. A. 1926. Casework and the statistical method. *Social Forces*. 5:61–65.

Luppi, D. 1990. *ET 101, The Cosmic Instruction Manual*. Santa Fe: Intergalactic Council.

Mack, J. E. 1994. *Abduction*. New York: Scribner's

Malinowski, B. 1922. *Argonauts of the Western Pacific*. London: Routledge.

Meier, E. B. 1979. *Message From the Pleiades*, vol. I. (Stevens, ed.). Munds Park, Arizona: Genesis III.

———. 1990. *Message From the Pleiades*, vol. II. (Stevens, ed.). Munds Park, Arizona: Genesis III.

Montgomery, R. 1979. *Strangers Among Us*. New York: Ballantine.

———. 1985. *Aliens Among Us*. New York: Ballantine.

Murray, H. A. 1955. Introduction. In A. Burton and R. Harris (eds.), *Clinical Studies of Personality*, vol. I. New York: Harper and Row.

Ouspensky, P. D. 1981. *Tertium Organum*. New York: Knopf

Parrish-Harra, C. W. 1983. *Messengers of Hope*. Black Mountain, North Carolina: New Age.

Pelto, P. J. 1970. *Anthropological Research: The Structure of Inquiry*. New York: Harper and Row.

Ring, K. 1980. *Life at Death*. New York: Cowan, McGann and Gohegan.

Ring, K. and C. Rosing 1990. The Omega Project. *Journal of UFO Studies*. 2: 59–98.

Rogo, D. S. (ed.). 1980. *UFO Abductions*. New York: New American Library.

Rojcewicz, P. M. 1988. Signals of Transcendence; The Human-UFO Equation. *Journal of UFO Studies*. 1 (new series).

———. 1988. Strange Bedfellows: The Folklore of Other-sex. *Critique*. 29:8–12.

Royal, L. and K. Priest 1989. *The Prism of Lyra*. Scottsdale, Arizona: Light Technology and Royal Priest Research.

Runyan, W. M. 1982. *Life Histories and Psychobiography*. New York: Oxford University.

Sagan, C. and I. S. Shklovskii 1966. *Intelligent Life in the Universe*. New York: Dell.

Sitchin, Z. 1991. *The Twelfth Planet.* New York: Bear and Company.

Slusser, G. E. and E. S. Rabkin (eds.). n. d. *Aliens, the Anthropology of Science Fiction.* Carbondale, Illinois: Southern Illinois University.

Solara. 1991. *El-An-Ra: The Healing of Orion.* Virginia: Starborn Unlimited.

Spradley, J. P. 1980. *Participant Observation.* New York: Holt, Reinhart, and Winston.

Steiger, B. and S. H. 1992. *Star Born.* New York: Berkley.

Steiger, B. and F. 1981. *The Star People.* New York: Berkley.

Steiger, B. 1990. *Star People Statistical Update.* Phoenix: Timewalker.

———. n. d. American Indians and the Star People. *Connecting Link.* 1 (3):10–12.

———. n. d. *Star People Are Among Us!* (private).

———. n. d. The Star People and the Pleiades Connection. *Connecting Link.* 1 (5): 16–18.

Stevens, W. and B. Hermann 1989. *UFO Contact from Reticulum: An Update.* Munds Park, Arizona: Genesis III.

Suzuki, D. T. 1962. *The Essentials of Zen Buddhism.* New York: E.P. Dutton.

Temple, R. K. G. 1976. *The Sirius Mystery.* Rochester, Vermont: Destiny.

Thompson, K. 1991. *Angels and Aliens.* Reading, MA: Addison-Wesley.

Van Maanen, J. (ed.). 1983. *Qualitative Methodology.* Beverly Hills: Sage.

Wilhelm, R. (trans.). 1950. *The I Ching or Book of Changes.* Princeton: Bollingen/Princeton University.

Zonatar. (n. d.) *Soul Exchange.* (private).

FROM ELSEWHERE: THE E.T. JOURNAL

If you enjoyed *From Elsewhere: Being E.T. in America*, you'll certainly want *The E.T. Journal*. Covering all subjects of interest to E.T. souls, seekers, and the curious, each issue includes:

- Questions and Answers
- Regular Feature Columns
- In-Depth Essays
- Reader Mailbox

Some of the topics we'll cover:

- Experiences of Walk-ins and Sleeping Wanderers
- Star Wars for Real: Cosmic Good and Evil
- Meditation, Reincarnation, and Life Lessons
- The Little Ones: E.T. Children on Earth
- Psychologists, Skeptics, and the Media
- The *RA* Column: UFOs and Evolution
- The New Age: E.T. Predictions and Prophecy

Cost for a one-year subscription of 6 issues (published bi-monthly) is $24.95 (USD $34.95 for addresses outside the U.S.A.), payable by check or money order to Scott Mandelker. Public lectures, workshops, and private counseling (including telephone sessions) are also available. Group teachings can be tailored, and your personal concerns addressed in a one-to-one format. Please write for more information (include SASE, self-addressed, stamped envelope, with written requests).

PLEASE SEND ORDERS AND CORRESPONDENCE TO:
The E.T. Journal, c/o Scott Mandelker, Ph.D.
2130 Fillmore Street, #201; San Francisco, CA 94115 USA

—— Yes, I want *FROM ELSEWHERE: THE E.T. JOURNAL*. My payment is enclosed.

—— Please send me information on workshops, lectures, and private counseling sessions. (SASE)

My special interests: _____

_____

Name: _____

Address: _____

City, State, Zip: _____

Telephone and/or Fax (optional): _____

INDEX

Abduction, 55, 204
Alien Nation, 129
Alienation, and extraterrestrials on
    earth, 3–4, 11–15, 17, 65–66,
    78–79, 106, 205, 212, 213
"Amnesia," and extraterrestrials on
    Earth, 18, 185
Angels and Aliens: UFOs and the
    Mythic Imagination, 136
Apparitions. *See* Visions, and
    extraterrestrials on Earth
Ashtar Command, 23, 24, 51, 70–71,
    109–10
Astral projection. *See* Out-of-body
    experiences (OBE)

Bardo Thodol, 184
Base stations, planetary, 124, 125
Blake, William, 158
Buddhism
    Theravadan, 216–18
    Tibetan, 27, 122
    Zen, 167, 213–16, 221–23

Capra, Fritjof, 42
Carleton University UFO study,
    127–28, 150
Cirlot, J. E., 193
Close Encounters of the Third Kind,
    129
Communion, 147–48, 153
Confederation, the, 41–42, 228
Council of Saturn, 125
Council of Twelve, 70–71
Crop circles, 199

Death, and extraterrestrials on Earth,
    175–77, 184–88
    fear of death, 59, 222–23

near-death-experiences (NDE),
    27–28, 177–79
and out-of-body experiences
    (OBE), 182–84
as "returning home," 180–82
Denzer, Jeffrey L., 58
Drake, Frank, 60
Dreams, and extraterrestrials on
    Earth, 12, 23, 48–50, 74–76,
    132–33, 163, 170–71, 225–26,
    117

"Earth changes," 191–92, 195–97,
    198
Eastern philosophy, 27, 122, 167,
    211–18, 219–24, 228–29
Elkins, Don, 233–34
Emotions, and extraterrestrials on
    Earth, 87, 88–90, 98–99, 119.
    See also Alienation, and
    extraterrestrials on Earth
Essentials of Zen Buddhism, The, 38
E.T., 58–59, 129, 144, 147
E.T. Earth Mission group, 31
"*E.T.*: An Odyssey of Loss," 58
Extraterrestrials on Earth. *See also*
    UFOs
    alienation and, 3–4, 11–15, 17,
    65–66, 78–79, 106, 205, 212,
    213
    allergies and, 3, 4
    dreams and, 12, 23, 48–50, 74–76,
    132–33, 163, 170–71, 225–26,
    117
    dual nature of, 104–106, 111–13,
    115–21, 230
    general characteristics of, 3, 8,
    66–67, 94, 106, 118, 124,
    168–69, 207–10

and the government, 137–40, 191
hostile, 135, 141–42, 147, 194–95, 204
hypnosis and, 27–28, 122, 162, 164
identity, validating, 33–47, 51–53, 87
out-of-body experiences (OBE) and, 14, 15, 26, 30, 124, 178, 182–84, 218, 225
quiz for, 207–10
telepathic communications and, 20, 25–26, 29–30, 31–32
throughout history, 203–28
types of. See Walk-ins; Wanderers
visions and, 22, 74–76, 108–11, 123, 132, 161
Extraterrestrials on Earth, case histories
Barbara, 80–88, 191, 238
Barrie, 101, 114, 137–40, 191, 195, 201, 238
Belinda, 130–34, 154–55, 166, 191, 199, 238
Betty, 26–29, 121–26, 193, 238
Bob, 19–21, 33, 44, 65, 100–101, 142, 146, 186–87, 196, 238
Christin, 24–26, 101, 118–20, 142–44, 167, 191, 196–97, 201, 238
Elizabeth, 241
Erika, 65, 238
Helen, 241
Inid, 91–92, 102–103, 113–14, 147–50, 156, 159–66, 168–69, 203, 238–39
Joan, 140–42, 203, 239
Julie, 107–13, 155, 156, 193, 239
Justinian, 114–18, 146, 182–85, 202–203, 239
Linda, 34, 43, 167, 169, 196, 198, 239
Lisanne, 65, 89–90, 197, 199–200, 239
Lucia, 31–33, 102, 114, 134–37, 146, 156, 181–82, 200–201, 203, 239

Mandelker, Scott, 211–32
Matthew, 94–96, 170–74, 195, 199, 239–40
Pauline, 29–31, 96–99, 155, 191, 196, 198, 201, 240
Peter, 21, 33–34, 64–65, 240
Soren, 12–17, 93–94, 145–47, 157, 176–81, 198–99, 201, 240
Tomas, 72–77, 191, 240
Una, 44–45, 155, 156, 193–94, 195, 196, 201, 240
Vicky, 23, 45–53, 129–30, 155, 156, 191, 240
Vikram, 67–72, 73, 105, 240–41
Extraterrestrials on Earth, and Earth's future, 189–91, 203–205. See also Extraterrestrials on Earth, mission of
and "Earth changes," 191–92, 195–97, 198
and the "hidden world process," 190
and millenialism, 201–202
and population reduction, 191–92
and spiritual evolution, 192–94, 197–202
and UFOs, 191, 199, 204
Extraterrestrials on Earth, mission of, xi–xii, 5–6, 15, 38, 67, 112–13, 152–57, 164–66. See also Extraterrestrials on Earth, and Earth's future
E.T.s view of, 166–74, 196–98, 201–202
Extraterrestrials on Earth, and relationships. See also Alienation, and extraterrestrials on Earth.
and disclosure of E.T. identity, 73–74, 85–86, 91, 92–95
emotional detachment and, 87, 88–90, 98–99, 119
family, 86–87, 88, 92–94, 116–17, 122–23

friendships, 105–106, 113–14, 116, 121
romantic relationships, 78–79, 85–86, 88, 91–92, 105–106, 113–14, 116–17
and sexuality, 99–103
walk-ins and, 66, 78–79, 85–88, 89–90, 96–103
wanderers and, 78–79, 89, 101
Extraterrestrials, on other planets, 60–61

Fire in the Sky, 147, 154
Franklin, Benjamin, 5

Galactic Brotherhood of Light, 70
Government, and extraterrestrials on Earth, 137–40, 191
Grof, Stanislav, 42–43

Hart, Hornell, 183
Hemispheric Synchronization technique, 224–25
"Hidden world process," the, 190
Holzer, Hans, 63, 189–90
Hypnosis, 27–28, 122, 162, 164

Incest, 57–58, 88
Ironson, Dale, 183

Jefferson, Thomas, 5
Jung, Carl G., 50, 57, 120

Klass, Philip, 133
Krippner, Stanley, 183

Lawson, Ella Smith, 175–76
Life at Death, 179
Lilly, John Cunningham, 35

Mack, John, 54, 55–56, 204
Maitreya the World Savior, 75–77
Mars, 125
Mayan calendar, 202
McCarty, Jim, 234
Media, and extraterrestrials on Earth, 147–50

media view of, 127–28, 133–37, 142–44
politics and, 137–40
popular television, 129–30, 141–42
tabloids, 144–47
and UFOs, 127–28, 136, 145
Meditation, 213–18, 220–23
Millenialism, 201–202
Monroe, Robert, 211, 224–25
Montgomery, Ruth, 19

National Enquirer, 144–47
Near-death-experiences (NDE), 27–28, 177–79
News of the World, 144–47

Ouspensky, P.D., 187–88
Out-of-body experiences (OBE), 14, 15, 26, 30, 124, 178, 182–84, 218, 225

Palmer, John, 183
Population reduction, 191–92
Psychology, and extraterrestrials on Earth
and fear of rejection, 72–74
and hallucinations, 56, 57
and incest, 57–58, 88
and loss, 58–59, 62–63
positive psychological effects, 64–66, 67–69, 96–99
psychological theories, 4–5, 16, 54–59, 61–64, 218–19
and religion, 63–64
and sleep paralysis, 56, 128
and UFOs, 55, 56–59, 127–28, 150

RA material, 2, 3, 16, 17–18, 125, 143, 156, 176, 202, 228, 233–37
Religion
and psychology, 63–64
religious conversion, 59–60
Ring, Ken, 179
Rueckert, Carla, 233–34

Sagan, Carl, 56
Samadhi, 185–86
Saturn, 125
Sexuality, and extraterrestrials on Earth, 99–103
Simpson, O.J., murder trial, 145
Sleep paralysis, 56, 128
Soul transfer. See Walk-ins.
Spielberg, Steven, 58–59, 138, 144
Spiral, 120
Spiritual evolution, of Earth, 192–94, 197–202
Star, 144–47
Star Born, 138–39, 153
Star People, The, 183
Star Wars, 129
Steiger, Brad, 138–39, 153, 183
Steiger, Francie, 183
Steiger, Sherry Hansen, 153
Strangers Among Us, 19
Subjective knowing, 35–47, 51–53
Sullivan, Walter, 127–28, 150
Suzuki, D. T., 38

Tabloids, and extraterrestrials on Earth, 144–47
Tart, Charles, 183
Telepathic communications, and extraterrestrials on Earth, 20, 25–26, 29–30, 31–32
Television, and extraterrestrials on Earth, 129–30, 141–42
Tertium Organum, 187
Thompson, Keith, 136
Tibetan Book of the Dead, 184
Twilight Zone series, 151–52

UFO-nauts, The, 63, 189–90
UFOs
and Earth's future, 191, 199, 204
and extraterrestrials on Earth, 6, 21–24, 55, 56–59, 68–70, 132, 141–42, 156, 160–61, 163
and the government, 138–39, 191
and the media, 127–28, 136, 145
psychology and, 55, 56–59, 127–28, 150
and religious conversion, 59–60
Uncommon Wisdom, 42–43

Venus, 124, 125
Visions, and extraterrestrials on Earth, 22, 74–76, 108–11, 123, 132, 161

Walk-ins, 8, 18–19, 115
and alienation, 65–66
and death, 182
and relationships, 66, 78–79, 85–88, 89–90, 96–103
and self-awareness, 33–34, 53, 80–85
soul-transfer experiences, 20–21, 25–26, 27–32, 79–85, 115–17, 159–66
Walter, Travis, 147, 154
Wanderers, 2–3, 17–18, 108
and alienation, 17, 65–66
and "amnesia," 18, 185
and death, 182
and relationships, 78–79, 89, 101
and self-awareness, 17, 33, 34, 52–53, 67–70, 73–76, 107–13, 130–33, 211–12, 228
Watts, Alan, 36